THE CROSSBOW CANNIBAL

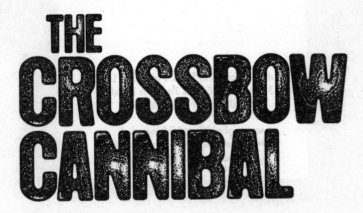

THE CROSSBOW CANNIBAL

THE DEFINITIVE STORY OF STEPHEN GRIFFITHS –
THE SELF-MADE SERIAL KILLER

CYRIL DIXON

JOHN BLAKE

First published in paperback in 2011

ISBN: 978 1 84358 359 2

British Library Cataloguing-in-Publication Data:

A catalogue record for this book is available from the British Library.

Design by www.envydesign.co.uk

Printed in Great Britain by Printed in Great Britain by
CPI Bookmarque, Croydon, CR0 4TD

1 3 5 7 9 10 8 6 4 2

Papers used by John Blake Publishing are natural, recyclable
products made from wood grown in sustainable forests.
The manufacturing processes conform to the environmental
regulations of the country of origin.

Every attempt has been made to contact the relevant copyright-holders,
but some were unobtainable. We would be grateful if the appropriate
people could contact us.

Acknowledgments

Exposing the wickedness of people like Stephen Griffiths, the self-proclaimed Crossbow Cannibal, does not glorify or celebrate them. Rather, it allows us to understand what makes them a danger and how their threat can be nullified. It also tells the victims' stories, highlights their vulnerability, and reminds us that issues like drugs and prostitution cannot be ignored.

I owe many thanks to a small posse of experts for helping me follow and understand Griffiths' case. Among them are: Jerry Lawton, chief crime correspondent, *Daily Star*; Paul Jeeves, northern correspondent, *Daily Express*; Chris Gregg, Detective Chief Superintendent (retired); Felicity Gerry, criminal barrister and author, *Sexual Offences Handbook: Law, Practice and Procedure*; David Wilson, Professor of Criminology, Birmingham City University; Andrew Cook, historian and author, *Jack the Ripper: Case Closed*; Joolz Denby, poet and author; Belinda Brooks-Gordon, author, *The Price of Sex: Prostitution, Policy and Society*; Leopard Films.

Prologue

Holmfield Court is situated just a few hundred yards from Bradford city centre. It stands on the edge of the red light area, among a raffish collection of pubs, clubs, low-rent businesses and derelict warehouses. It is a part of town where people have welcomed the protection of security cameras.

Monday mornings always brought a touch of *Big Brother* to Holmfield Court. An inner city housing block's little dramas were seen and scrutinised through the unblinking eyes of the CCTV system. In total, 16 cameras kept every doorway, corridor and stairwell monitored, and the results were recorded and stored on hard drive for Peter Gee, the caretaker. As a norm, the footage revealed nothing more than tenants going about their everyday business: taking rubbish out, bringing shopping in, or staggering home after a Saturday night session. Even so, the weekly review had to be done, no matter how uneventful.

The Monday morning playback was Peter Gee's first duty of the working week. He would turn up at 7.30am and begin the review an hour later. It was usually a stress-free start to the week: the only incidents likely to make work for him were acts of petty vandalism. To begin with, Monday 24 May 2010 was no exception.

Mr Gee ploughed through the footage from the first 13 cameras without witnessing anything untoward. He began flicking through the scene monitored by camera 14, overlooking the third-floor corridor. He had barely started watching it when he did a double take: he saw what looked like a man dragging the motionless figure of a woman along the floor of the corridor.

He rewound and watched the footage again. The same two figures were captured on camera walking into a flat at 2.31 in the early hours of the previous Saturday. He recognised the man: it was Steve, the loner who lived in Flat 33. It was 33 they had gone into. Mr Gee did not know the woman, but other tenants said Steve regularly brought prostitutes home. She was small with dark hair. Minutes later, she reappeared, running towards the stairs, frightened for her life. Steve came out of the flat, snarling and hot on her tail. He caught and attacked her, leaving her unconscious on the floor.

Now, Mr Gee found himself at the point in the footage where his attention had first been grabbed. The man he knew simply as 'Steve' dragged his victim back towards his flat. He disappeared for a second, then came back, carrying something. The caretaker, horrified but transfixed, strained to make out what it was. A cross-shaped contraption of some sort? A crossbow!

The tenant's next move confirmed it. After reaching the woman out cold on the floor, he pointed the weapon at her and fired.

All the tenants knew about the CCTV system. Steve must surely have realised that his every murderous move would be televised? After dragging his victim into Flat 33, he reappeared, bow in hand. Looking directly at the camera's lens, he gave a defiant one-fingered gesture, and then held the weapon up to the lens in a salute. A few minutes later, the cold-blooded killer held up a bottled drink to the device in a mock toast, before disappearing.

Peter Gee, his mind scrambled and his body moving on autopilot, ran to see his manager.

At teatime that day, a West Yorkshire Police armed response team smashed in the door of Flat 33 Holmfield Court. About 60 officers had come prepared for a fight, machine guns and pistols at the ready and thick body armour protecting their torsos. Residents watched with a mixture of fear and excitement as they stormed up three flights of stairs to the third floor and to the door of Flat 33. As it turned out, they were offered no resistance. The male occupant came willingly. The man known to Peter Gee as 'Steve' was Stephen Griffiths. Soon, he would give himself another name: the Crossbow Cannibal.

The armed officers had broken their way into a macabre fantasy world. They had also cracked a missing persons riddle that had troubled the police for almost a year. But the breakthrough, while a relief of sorts, would lead to a harrowing few days in their lives. It would also cause devastation for the families of Suzanne Blamires, Shelley Armitage and Susan Rushworth. All three women had been sex workers who were addicted to hard drugs. All three had gone missing while walking the streets looking for clients. All three had loving families who were at their wits' end with worry.

Nearly 30 years earlier, in 1981, Peter Sutcliffe, a married lorry driver, had been unmasked as the Yorkshire Ripper. From his home – also in the city of Bradford – he would venture out on murderous forays across the red light districts of northern England. Sutcliffe was a Bradford man and, out of at least 13 women he hammered and stabbed to death, three met their end just a few miles from his home. One was murdered less than half a mile away from Holmfield Court.

Bradford's second serial killing case in a generation would bring a sense of déjà vu. Bradford's 'New Ripper' inquiry team would pound the same territory Sutcliffe had prowled all those years before. The same backstreets and alleyways would be pored over, and the same feelings of fear, shock and outrage would grip the public.

Bradford would have to look again at the issue of prostitution and how to deal with it. After Sutcliffe was jailed, many influential people – including policemen – had called for the legalisation of vice as a way of keeping streetwalkers safe. Three decades on, the same debate would rage again. Although the world had changed, the authorities had failed to find a solution.

In 2010, Bradford was a city on the up. It had a fast-growing economy, a vibrant multicultural community and, courtesy of its industrial heritage, some of the most beautiful buildings in Britain. But just a stone's throw from multi-million pound development projects, the oldest profession went on in the murkiest of alleyways and backstreets.

Sutcliffe's shadow was cast all over the case of Stephen Griffiths. A mature student at the University of Bradford, Griffiths was studying homicide, and knew all there was to know about the Yorkshire Ripper. That Monday evening in late May 2010, detectives had the unlikely task of interviewing a student of multiple homicide as a *suspect* for multiple homicide. In crime fiction, he would traditionally be the first suspect ruled out.

What was Stephen Griffiths' story? That question led into the darkest recesses of a warped and egotistic mind. Detectives would piece together events which were grisly beyond belief. Some of Britain's most experienced police investigators were flabbergasted by what they uncovered.

THE CROSSBOW CANNIBAL

Psychologists would often talk about an aberration of the fame-obsessed society. The new millennium is the age of Myspace, YouTube and *Big Brother*: they all offer ordinary people endless possibilities for self-promotion and cheap and easy fame. But did it create a serial killer for the 'wannabe' generation?

CHAPTER 1
Lizard Man

Everybody knew Stephen Griffiths. Not necessarily by that name, but by sight or by one of several unflattering nicknames. They referred to him variously as 'The Oddball', 'The Goth', 'The Weirdo', 'Peanut' or 'Penfold', after a bespectacled cartoon mole. None seemed more appropriate, though, than 'The Lizard Man'. At Holmfield Court, the converted Victorian mill where Griffiths was a tenant, the pet reptiles he kept were a regular talking point. Despite having just one bedroom, a bathroom and a small living room with a kitchenette, the occupant of Flat 33 was happy to share his space with up to four Nile monitor lizards or boa constrictors.

The monitors were a favourite of his. They grow up to seven feet long, are native across central Africa, and are lethal predators. Zoologists advise against keeping them as pets because there are few lizards less suited to life in captivity. They can kill a cat and, when threatened, they are – pound for pound – more dangerous than a crocodile. Griffiths liked them nonetheless, and it did not bother him that his landlords – Accent Housing Association – discouraged tenants from keeping unsuitable pets. He kept his reptiles in the flat's tiny living room, in large glass tanks that were fitted with a powerful heat lamp to maintain a tropical temperature. In keeping with their diet in the wild, he fed them live rats and mice, which he either bought in bulk from the nearest pet shop, or bred himself in a separate tank in the same room.

Most of the neighbours knew about the lizards because Griffiths would walk them along the corridor outside his flat. Each specimen was about two to three feet long and he reined them in with a dog lead fastened to a leather harness. The experience of taking his exotic and mean-looking companions for a walk in public gave Griffiths a thrill. It lent him an air of mystery, and his neighbours could not help being drawn into conversation with him. One said: 'He loved those lizards and to be truthful he was someone who didn't seem to have quite grown up, despite his age. He was friendly enough but he was very introverted when it came to speaking to people within this block of flats.' Another, Rachel Farrington-Naylor, recalled: 'He used to let the lizards walk up and down the corridor. My grandson told me one day: "Look, there's a crocodile."' It was the effect Griffiths wanted, and, although proud of his creatures, he had a strange idea of animal welfare. He liked to toy with them and use them as a prop to show off his eccentricity. The monitors, for example, were sometimes taken to nightclubs in a sack and brandished about before his human companions.

Rachel Farrington-Naylor struck up a rapport with him when she told him she had a pet gecko in her flat. She accepted his offer to watch the monitors' feeding time, but was left feeling uncomfortable by the experience. 'He once asked me if I wanted to watch a rat being fed to one of his lizards,' she said. 'He came up and stood right behind my back, almost touching me. The rat was cowering in the corner. The lizard grabbed it and ripped it in half. I thought it was cruel. When he saw my face and that I was horrified, he laughed and said:

"It's all part of life.'" He showed her his rodent larder, a six-by-two-foot coffin-shaped box that he had made himself out of chipboard. He kept it towards the back of the flat in case the housing association staff visited. It was out of sight and they were less likely to smell the sawdust and rat excrement. But some time later, she met him in the corridor carrying a sack. There was a nauseating smell, so she asked what it was. 'He said one of the lizards had died and he had got it in his rucksack and was going to bury it. He said one lizard had bit the other's head, crushed its skull and killed it.' He relayed the gory details with relish.

Billy Parkin, one of Griffiths' old drinking pals, was treated to an even more twisted example of his humour. During one visit to the flat, the host was larking about with his rats, picking them up and playing with them. 'Steve decided to show off by lifting a baby rat out of its cage and popping it into his mouth,' Mr Parkin said. 'He then swallowed it whole. I've never seen anything like it, someone eating a rat. Steve thought it was quite funny, but it turned my stomach.' Another of Griffiths' friends, meanwhile, remembered: 'He used to tease them with live mice, keeping them dangling over the tanks with the lizards and snakes snapping at them. It would really amuse him.' Some of his friends were also astonished to hear him boast that he had once skinned a rat while it was still alive. They were not sure whether to believe him or not, he was such a maverick.

Griffiths' most overt statement of nonconformity was his sartorial taste. He liked to dress from head to toe in black: jeans, T-shirts and heavy, calf-length boots. Over it all, he wore a long black leather raincoat. He grew his dark brown hair long, dressed it with baby oil, pulled it back tight over his crown and twisted it into ringlets. He would get annoyed if anyone, even girlfriends, tried to touch it. He wore sunglasses with small round lenses, often in overcast weather or when he was indoors. This particular touch earned him the nickname 'Penfold', after the shortsighted hamster in the 1980s television cartoon *Dangermouse*. In addition, Griffiths wore a gold chain around his neck, and had his left ear pierced repeatedly, wearing simple, silver band earrings. Lastly, he had a flamboyant tattoo on his left shoulder bearing the enigmatic slogan 'Diane Lost War'.

His image in general was based on goth subculture, a youth trend that grew out of punk rock in the 1970s. Inspired by bands such as The Damned, Siouxsie and the Banshees, The Cure and The Mission, its followers contrasted black clothes, black eye make-up and dyed black hair with ghostly white face paint. The look outlasted punk by upwards of 30 years and was almost uniform in universities and colleges by the early 21st century.

Ironically, then, Stephen Griffiths' individual look was not so different after all. But this never bothered him, and the passing years did little to diminish his vanity or change his look. He put on weight, and the hair thinned and was cut shorter. But he was still captivated by his mysterious 'man in black' persona and loved having his picture taken. He was quite keen on photography and took many pictures of himself, with a digital camera or mobile phone. He would pout at the camera or push his dimpled chin forward and pull his thin lips into an enigmatic smile. One especially imposing portrait of him, a three-foot-square black and white photograph, was taken at a professional studio, then framed and hung on his bedroom wall. His style was reminiscent of a publicity shot for a pop band, but in Griffiths' case, there was no product to promote.

With no job to go to, Griffiths simply drifted through the days with – bar his reptiles – few real companions. One neighbour later commented: 'He was friendly enough but he was very introverted when it came to speaking to people within this block of flats. People thought he was the resident weirdo in the block and would steer away from him, but others thought he was simply a harmless bachelor, a single man who didn't have much of a social life.' An assistant at the pet shop where he bought his mice said: 'I tried to strike up a rapport with him. It's usually an easy thing to do because all the people who come here have something in common – animals. But with this one you got nothing back.'

Those friends he did keep were a bit like him: single, unemployed and on benefits or working in the black economy. In fact they were all somewhat lost souls. They would hang around one of their homes, talking, smoking and drinking cans of Carlsberg Export. They would get up late in the morning and stay up late at night, while the time in between had little significance for them.

Griffiths was a cut above the others. He was a bit brighter, articulate and knowledgeable. Although he had a West Yorkshire accent, it was slightly more refined. He used big words and, if the truth be known, seemed slightly effeminate. One of this circle of drinking friends said:

'He seemed a good bloke. He were just normal like. We'd just have a beer or a fag as we talked. We wouldn't go out but we'd sit and talk about telly or music or whatever. Before I knew him, he seemed a bit toffee-nosed. He was an educated man and read a lot of books, but we just got talking and he seemed alright.'

Another friend said he nicknamed Griffiths 'Peanut', and would get a regular trouncing from him at chess in one of their local pubs. 'He would tell you where you had gone wrong and still beat you. He had an answer for every argument you had.'

Griffiths mentioned girlfriends vaguely, but never had what could be called a steady relationship with a woman. Nor did he see much of his family, leading his friends to assume that there had been some sort of rift. He had a driving licence and, for a few years, neighbours regularly saw him out and about in a green Rover 416, but they were perplexed as to how he could have afforded it without working. The car was useful for the infrequent visits he made to see his family and to bring back shopping supplies for his feckless lifestyle. 'Once we'd been drinking and we ran out of beer,' his drinking pal said. 'He wanted to drive over to the petrol station on Brewery Lane to get some more, but I said: "You've had too much to drink – you'll get arrested." He took some persuading, but he agreed to take a taxi.'

Stephen Griffiths was not much of a communicator. However, he did engage with his fellow man if the subject of music or films arose.

His favourite bands were selected from a wide range of musical genres: reggae, punk, ragga, pop, new wave. His music collection included titles by grunge rockers Nirvana and rap pioneers Public Enemy. Prominent goth rockers The Sisters of Mercy (who hailed from Leeds) were a particular favourite: his dress sense – the long hair, black leather and shades – was reminiscent of that sported by the band's lead singer Andrew Eldritch. But he would surprise his friends by revealing that he was almost equally keen on Phil Collins and Hot Chocolate, both famous for commercial pop and schmaltzy ballads. Such choices jarred with his mean and moody image.

He was a member of several alternative music nightspots in Bradford city centre, and was regularly spotted at Rio's, a club about 20 minutes' walk from his flat. Although he enjoyed being around the crowd, he did not drink much and never mingled. Instead, he would stand on the stage looking down imperiously at the dance-floor revellers below.

Griffiths' favourite films included crime classics *Scarface*, the 1980s gangster movie starring Al Pacino, and *Reservoir Dogs*, Quentin Tarantino's quirky, violent blockbuster from the early 1990s. He also rated *A Clockwork Orange*, the dark satire, made in 1971, which was withdrawn by its director Stanley Kubrick, amid controversy over its violent content. The film was effectively banned for three decades. Griffiths was obsessed with its psychotic antihero Alex, and planned to have his image tattooed on his body. He liked horror films too. *The Blair Witch Project* and *The Evil Dead* and *Evil Dead II* were among those he recommended to his friends.

Holmfield Court stands just outside Bradford city centre. It is at the city end of Thornton Road, one of the main arterial routes leading west towards the Pennines. The building's changing fortunes have mirrored those of the city itself: industrial heyday, decline and redevelopment. It was built in 1855, in the days when Bradford, though still a relatively small town, was the wool capital of the world. The Industrial Revolution fired up a cottage trade of spinning and weaving into a major commercial force, and mills popped up all over the municipality.

Originally, the four-storey building was called Soho Mills and had been constructed from local, yellow-coloured sandstone in the ornate Italianate school of architecture. The style was popular with Victorians and many of Bradford's stunning old edifices share the same look. Soho Mills had a big, beautiful arched door and windows, with hipped eaves overhanging the side walls. Surrounding it was a labyrinth of cobbled side streets allowing the horse-drawn carts access to its different entrances. Soho Street was one, Holmfield Street another and Tetley Street another; Vincent Street, leading up to Sunbridge Road, was a larger thoroughfare running parallel with Thornton Road and into City Road.

But Soho Mills was nowhere near the biggest or the best woollen plant. That privilege probably fell to Lister's Mill, a massive silk production plant situated further south in the Manningham district. Or maybe to Salts Mill, just inside the borough, at Saltaire. They were built, respectively, by Sir Samuel Lister and Sir Titus Salt, philanthropic textile barons who helped grow Bradford from a small market town to an industrial powerhouse.

Bradford's other architectural showpieces include the City Hall, opened in 1873 and modelled on the Palazzo Vecchio (its functional equivalent in Florence, Italy), and St George's Hall, a stunning concert venue built in 1853. Bradford was a byword for Victorian splendour.

The 20th century brought a change in the city's fortunes. Previously, the textiles industry had forged ahead through thrusting innovation. After peaking in the early 1900s, the industry went into terminal decline. By the 1950s and 1960s, dozens of mills had closed down or were running at a fraction of their capacity. Although new industries were created, unemployment rose, and an image problem developed.

In 1958, J. B. Priestley, the 20th-century literary luminary and cherished son of Bradford, made a nostalgic trip through the city for a BBC documentary. It was entitled *Lost City*. Although the film-makers denied it, Priestley's reminiscences of good times past left the unmistakable impression that Bradford was a place of doom, gloom and decay. Locals complained to the BBC that it painted the town as a 'get-out-if-you-can' sort of place. Two years later, Bradford was chosen for location shooting for the film version of *Billy Liar*, Keith Waterhouse's comic novel about a young man who fantasises about leaving a dead-end, humdrum town in northern England.

These impressions aside, there was hard, fast evidence everywhere that the trade which had built the city was dying. Salts Mill, once the largest industrial building in the world, closed down in 1986. Lister's Mill, which had employed 11,000 workers in its heyday, did likewise in 1992, eight years after the closure of the much smaller player, Soho Mills.

Bradford rebuilt itself in the 1990s on new commerce and industry, tourism, and the regeneration of those old Victorian buildings. Financial enterprises such as the Yorkshire Building Society, the Bradford & Bingley Building Society and Provident Financial stepped up to the plate. Engineering and high-tech companies moved in, the retailer Morrison became a major employer by moving its head office to Bradford, and Thomas Cook, the travel giant, created 1,000 jobs by relocating its tour division to the city. In 1984, the National Media Museum opened in the city centre, and Salts Mill was transformed into a massive arts centre, with commerce, shopping and restaurants thrown in for good measure. Its highest-profile art gallery, the 1853 Gallery, houses the biggest collection in the world of Bradford-born artist David Hockney's work. Lister's Mill, meanwhile, was turned into a complex of luxury apartments courtesy of a £100 million redevelopment scheme. Yorkshire Forward, the region's business development agency, recorded Bradford's annual turnover as averaging £6 billion towards the end of the first decade of the new millennium. Business confidence was higher than the national average, exports were worth £700 million annually and tourism more than £400 million. Bradford also boasted a population that was growing by a third more than the national average. It was young, cosmopolitan and dynamic, due mainly to the influx of Asians who arrived in the 1950s and 1960s to work in the textile mills.

Soho Mills' rebirth was more modest, reflecting the fact that despite all the 'whizz bang' revamp projects, unemployment in parts of Bradford was as high as 25 per cent, there were plenty of people on low incomes, and there was dire need for social housing. In the late 1980s, Accent, a housing association with properties all over the country, bought and renovated it. It was given Grade II listing, and the large, open mill floors were sectioned off into one- and two-bedroom apartments. It was painted throughout, double-glazed and fitted with fire alarms. Cheap abstract paintings were hung on the corridor walls and a house plant was stuck in the foyer.

The surrounding neighbourhood, however, remained soulless and hard-done-by. Thornton Road, the B6145, the main drag into the city, swept in front of it. On one side of Soho Mills was a laser combat centre inside an old warehouse, on the other a training facility for digital media companies. Directly opposite was the start of the University of Bradford campus and further along, towards the city centre, a BP petrol station. In the other direction lay a string of businesses housed in low-rent, ramshackle properties: tyre-fitting workshops, second-hand furniture outlets, kitchen and bathroom salesrooms and a few pubs. There were derelict warehouses and offices in between, with chained-up doors and boarded-up windows, and with moss growing out of the cracks between bricks and pavements. The back alleys and some of the smaller streets were now blocked off, overgrown with tangled weeds and shrubs and piled up with windswept rubbish. Due to a rabbit warren of drains crisscrossing below the buildings, the pavements and roads were dotted with grills and manhole covers. On the walls were the rain-washed remains of old posters advertising university rock gigs.

Then there was the red light district. After the mid-1990s, the city's prostitutes moved from Manningham, where they had been since the 1960s, to the network of streets to the north of Thornton Road. Sunbridge Road, and its continuation City Road, formed the main market place, but the working girls also used any of the backstreets leading off them: Rebecca Street, Preston Street, Jowett Street, Gaynor Street and so on.

During the day, the area was a lively commercial district with staff, customers, cars and vans circulating. But at night, it became a virtual ghost town. The only lingerers were girls looking for punters and kerb crawlers looking for sex. 'Business' would take place in deserted car parks, blocked-off streets and back alleys, or the disused courtyards of the old mills. The transaction was swift, efficient and unsentimental, and within 25 minutes, the client would be gone and the working girl back on her pitch, leaving one more discarded condom among those already strewn over the ground. One such spot was near the bins behind Soho Mills. 'God, it was a horrible place to live,' said one former resident. 'There were prostitutes having sex in the bin area all night, doors were banging and there was shouting at all times.' Police carried out occasional purges, but were powerless to banish the murky goings-on completely. The best they could do was to maintain a peaceful state of equilibrium.

However, in October 1996 the peace was shattered in a brutal and prophetic episode centred on Soho Mills. One of the girls, Caroline Creevy, shared a flat in the block with her boyfriend. Caroline, 25, was a heroin addict and, like most of the girls, had drifted away from a loving family when she began working the streets. She was born in Salisbury, where her father worked for the Royal Army Ordinance Corps, but the family were originally from Huddersfield and had moved back in 1972 when Caroline was two. Described by her mother Pat as 'fun' and 'beautiful', she was badly affected by her parents' split in 1979 and the death of an uncle four years later. Caroline began mixing with an unsavoury circle of friends, and by the early 1990s was working as a prostitute in Huddersfield and Bradford. One of her neighbours at Soho Mills was Kenneth Valentine, an unemployed fairground worker with a history of violence towards women. Her boyfriend knew him and, after they were evicted from their flat, Valentine offered to put them up. He also allowed Caroline to entertain clients there, charging her £5 to use his bed. This arrangement continued after the boyfriend was sent to prison.

On 29 October 1996, Valentine, a sex-obsessed loner and drug user, made a pass at Caroline and she turned him down. He reacted by attacking her, beating her mercilessly and strangling her to death. As he killed her, another of the working girls, Michelle Routledge, called round for her, and, after getting no reply, listened at the letterbox. She could hear a woman's voice inside, screaming. In no position to help, she reported the incident to the police. Meanwhile, Valentine stripped Caroline's body naked, wrapped it in a rug, and crept out into the night to dump her in a storm drain.

When the police raided Valentine's flat three weeks later, they found a second prostitute locked in his bedroom. Officers feared that, had she not been rescued, she would have suffered the same fate as Caroline. In a chilling premonition of future events, Valentine was caught thanks to CCTV cameras, which had been fitted after the residents had complained about prostitutes using the doorways to service their clients. First, he was captured going out with a holdall containing the dead woman's clothes. Then, after he had dumped those, he was filmed at 4am, leaving with the rolled-up rug that contained Caroline's body. Police frogmen retrieved the corpse from the drain.

THE CROSSBOW CANNIBAL

In March 1998, Kenneth Valentine, by now 43 years old, was found guilty of Caroline Creevy's murder. Sitting at Leeds Crown Court, Mr Justice Ognall sentenced him to life in prison with a minimum tariff of 22 years, but just a few months before committing the murder, Valentine had been released from a seven-year prison sentence for manslaughter. In 1991, he had killed Janet Willoughby, a woman from Leeds, after tying her to a bed and sexually assaulting her. Afterwards, he stuffed her body into a cupboard and covered it with a duvet. His victim on that occasion was not a prostitute. It was after Caroline's murder that Accent Housing Association changed the block's name from Soho Mills (named after Soho Street, the alley down one side of the building) to Holmfield Court, taken from Holmfield Street, which ran down the other side.

Stephen Griffiths fitted comfortably into this troubled and sleazy twilight world. He did not move into Flat 33 Holmfield Court until 1997, the year after Caroline's murder, but lived in the area and knew both killer and victim. In the period between Caroline's death and Valentine's arrest, Griffiths began to suspect him of foul play and gave him a spectacular beating after confronting him in the street. Bridget Farrell, a sex worker who befriended Griffiths, said:

'We were coming out of the flats and he went for him in the doorway and screamed at him: "I know you killed Caroline." He set about him really badly. I had to pull him away. He was killing him. He was scary and had really lost it. He was screaming and screaming at him: "You murdering bastard."'

Griffiths had what appeared to be a paternal interest in the prostitutes. He kept strange nocturnal hours, often going out at

1am and coming back at 3am. Most of that time was spent padding aimlessly around the red light district. The girls were still working at that time and Griffiths would stop and talk to them as they waited about in the cold, damp night air. He smoked about 40 cigarettes a day and would politely offer the girls one as they waited together. Some of them, like Bridget, got to know him by name and would visit his flat every now and again. Griffiths had a taste for cannabis and would smoke joints as he sat drinking cans of beer with his friends. The sex workers were all addicted to hard drugs and had the right contacts to get hold of anything he wanted quickly. The city's dark underbelly seemed to be Griffiths' natural home. Nine-to-five was not for him; in fact, he never worked a day in his life. He simply lived the life of an eccentric outsider with a strong intellectual bent.

Accent charged Griffiths £145 per fortnight to rent Flat 33. For his money, he got a bedroom, situated to the right on entry to the flat; a bathroom, straight ahead; and the living room and kitchen area to the left. Each room had a window that overlooked the courtyard to the rear of the flats. Despite the best efforts of the housing association, it had never ceased to be a venue for night-time sexual encounters between prostitutes and clients, and Flat 33 had a grandstand view. Inside, the odour from the reptile tanks and the homemade rodent farm was ever-present.

Yet Stephen Griffiths was incongruously house-proud. Lisa Thompson, another of the prostitutes he befriended, said:

'He had a really nice flat – it was absolutely spotless. But everything was covered in plastic. He said it was because it was new furniture and he didn't want to get it damaged. Even his carpet had plastic on it. Most places in his flat were covered. He was obsessive. You had to take your shoes off. If he made a drink, you had to have it on a mat.'

One of his drinking friends added: 'Everything in the flat was clean. Even with the lizards and the mice and that, everything was tidy. If I dropped the ash off a cigarette onto the floor, he'd be there straight away with brush and pan cleaning it up.'

His electronic consumer equipment included a black Pioneer hi-fi and a matching flat-screen television. Griffiths also had both a personal computer, set on its own desk, and a Dell laptop on which he spent hours working. Neighbours with a view into his flat saw him bashing away at the keyboard at all hours of the night. 'He was always on the internet 24/7,' one said. But that was one area he refused to discuss with even the closest of his circle. It was strictly private. The drinking friend said: 'He wouldn't let me use the computer. If I wanted to go on it to check any of my accounts, he'd say "No, no, don't touch it. I've got work stuff on it." I thought that were a bit weird.'

The work he guarded so jealously was the academic study of murder. Griffiths had secured himself a place on a PhD course in local history at the University of Bradford. He could then have selected any one of countless inoffensive topics from the city's rich and diverse past. But Griffiths chose to specialise in Victorian homicide. He wanted to dredge up murder case histories from 1847, the year when Bradford became a municipal borough, to 1899. His thesis was entitled *Homicide in an Industrial City: Lethal Violence in Bradford 1847 to 1899*, and sought to examine the murders themselves, the killers, the victims, the police and their investigations, and how the Victorian detection methods differed from those used today. He would spend hours going through old newspapers in Bradford's central library. 'I'm studying people that have done killing,' he would proudly tell anyone who asked about his livelihood. It was another conversation-stopper that appealed to his warped sense of humour.

But visitors to his flat were left in no doubt that here was a serious student. He had hundreds of books, journals and documents about murder. They were in every room, including the bathroom and kitchen, and there were any number of bookcases, all crammed with his macabre reading material. All the notorious mass murderers – past and present – were covered, from Jack the Ripper to Steve Wright, the Suffolk Strangler. Many of them were easy-read true crime books, but many were weighty tomes about obscure and gruesome serial killers. He had read them all at least once and had an encyclopedic knowledge of their contents. Although he saw his friends as intellectually inferior, he liked to show off his scholarly grasp of barbarism and its practitioners. The unsettled looks on their faces amused and excited him. He felt as powerful and charismatic as he did when he walked the lizards along the corridor outside his flat.

Griffiths would then put his visitors at ease by explaining his ambition to be a psychiatrist after he had finished his course. He wanted to understand the inner workings of a killer's mind. His enthusiasm for murder was, he assured them, for purely professional reasons.

But the crown jewels in Stephen Griffiths' morbid little kingdom were less easy to explain away. On a shelf in his living room, sitting proudly on their own stands were two fearsome crossbows. He had bought them in a fishing tackle shop in Halifax. One was called the Jaguar. It had a heavy wooden rifle's handle, complete with trigger, connected to a metal bow. The bolts were fired at a speed of approximately 200 miles per hour, fast and powerful enough to shatter human bone. Another was called the Skeleton, and had similar lethal properties. He kept the bolts, black-shafted aluminium missiles with red and yellow feathered fletches, neatly lined up on a shelf below. On the living room wall, mounted with the same loving care he showed for the crossbows, were three samurai swords – small, medium and large. Neither the bows nor the swords served any purpose for his PhD studies and he never offered an alternative explanation for their being there. He was not a member of a legitimate archery club and had no interest in martial arts. He just liked them, he said.

Both crossbows and swords would be taken from their resting places and caressed with affection. He would fire crossbow bolts into his living room wall, leaving a peppered effect to the right of the door. Like his computer, though, the weapons were out of bounds to visitors. 'I tried to touch them once,' remembered his drinking friend. 'He just said: "Don't." Then he put his hand in the way to stop me. He didn't say why but he were really protective with them.'

CHAPTER 2

Monster in the Making

Christmas 1969 felt like a watershed in social history, even as it was happening. As the 1960s swung to a close, with them went the sense of austerity left over from the war. Consumerism was rising, as was social mobility, and so aspirations and expectations had never been higher. The 1970s seemed destined to offer even more. Everyone had a chance of buying a clean, modern house and a comfortable new car, and taking package holidays in exotic overseas resorts.

No metaphor captured the mood of change better than the introduction of colour television, just in time for Christmas. Although BBC2 had broadcast in colour for a couple of years, BBC1 and ITV, the more widely-watched channels, only followed suit in November 1969. Gone was the dour, black and white world of air raids and rationing. Coming soon was a psychedelic paradise where the likes of Morecambe and Wise broadcast their Christmas spectaculars in glorious colour.

One week before Christmas 1969, Britain made another significant break with the past. On 16 December, the House of Commons voted by a huge majority to abolish the death penalty. Capital punishment had been suspended for five years under the Murder (Abolition of Death Penalty) Act 1965. But before winding up for the festive season, the Commons voted 343 to 185 in favour of banishing the noose for good. All three party leaders – Labour Prime Minister Harold Wilson, the Tories' Edward Heath and Jeremy Thorpe of the Liberals – voted against the death penalty in an alliance that reflected the liberal times afoot. Even murderers could look forward to better times.

Stephen Shaun Griffiths was born into this season of the very best will, on Christmas Eve 1969. His father (also called Stephen) and mother Moira joked that their little gift was so keen to make an appearance that he could not wait until Christmas Day. Instead, he arrived a few hours earlier, on a chilly evening in Batley, West Yorkshire. Moira's younger half-brother, Joe Dewhirst, drove the couple the five miles or so from their new house in Thornhill to Batley Maternity Home, situated opposite the town's bus station. 'Everything was normal about the birth and everyone was naturally very happy,' Joe recalled. 'It was a happy time.'

Stephen and Moira had married in July at St Michael's and All Angels, the parish church of Thornhill. Stephen was working as a rep for a frozen food firm, while Moira, who was already five months pregnant, worked as a telephonist. Both were aged 20 and from local working-class families. The bridegroom was an engineer's son who grew up in Staincliffe, which had once been a hilltop hamlet near Dewsbury but was now a sprawl of council estates. Moira's father Eric was a chargehand, an old-fashioned title for a worker–cum–supervisor in a factory.

Moira had grown up in Thornhill, another urbanised village, perched on moorland to the south of the River Calder. It had the distinction of being named after the Thornhill family, friends of Henry III, and had wonderful views across the surrounding vales. But in the 18th and 19th centuries, rich coal seams were discovered beneath the countryside and mining took over. The collieries spawned plenty of employment opportunities, the population and housing expanded and, like Staincliffe, Thornhill became a heavily built-up area. St Michael's church, though, remained an unspoilt historical gem. It dated back to the 9th century and was mentioned in the Domesday Book. The tower and the chancel – its oldest surviving features – had been built in the 15th century, and its three magnificent stained glass windows – two dating from 1447, the other from 1493 – are regarded as among the finest in northern England.

For his wedding day, Stephen wore a classic 1960s thin-lapelled suit and narrow tie, with a short-collared shirt. He grinned proudly and toothily for the photographs alongside his new bride. Moira dressed in white, with a pretty veil half-covering her short brown hair. A gold crucifix hung about her neck and she kept her heavy-rimmed, Buddy Holly-style spectacles on for most of the day. With a new baby due, the couple were given a three-bedroom council house not far from where Moira grew up.

Stephen junior's first home, 151 Partridge Crescent, was very much of its time: a grey, pebble-dashed semi, built in the 1950s at the open end of a cul-de-sac. Towering above the front garden was a telegraph pole and alongside stood a row of garages. Across the road, Dewsbury county borough's gardens department had tried to brighten up the little dead-end street by planting some exotic honey locust saplings. They would have been better suited to a North American setting than one in West Yorkshire, but nevertheless it was a nice – if rather hopeful – touch.

The family stayed at Partridge Crescent long enough to have their second child, Caroline – who was born in August 1972 –

but two years later they were moving up in the world. Stephen senior had worked hard in a succession of white-collar management posts, and by autumn 1974 had saved enough to put down a deposit on a private house. He took out a mortgage to meet the rest of the £5,000 asking price and became a property owner for the first time. Number 6 Hazel Grove, Flockton, was a smart, red-brick starter terrace with three airy bedrooms. The village was much sought-after, perched high on the moors in West Yorkshire's southern reaches. It was separated from the main village, in a secluded little knot of houses on the A637. To the front, it looked over the main road onto grazing land carved up by dry stone walls. To the rear, the garden path led through a pretty arched gateway to a little parking area where the children could play safely. Their neighbours included local government officers and teachers who were, typically, the first in their respective families to own property. This was everything the new decade had promised.

In February 1976, the family was completed with the birth of the Griffiths' second son Phillip, and a period of relative bliss followed. The wider family came to notice, however, that Stephen – whom they called by his middle name, Shaun – was somewhat introverted. He never had much to say for himself and was harder to engage than his younger brother and sister. Joe Dewhirst, who used to see a lot of his sister's children in the middle and late 1970s, said:

'He was always very quiet and withdrawn. He didn't run about the place like the other kids. I remember him always being very neatly dressed. You could never read him. He wasn't the kind of lad you could talk to about football or things like that. He was very much a loner.'

He was a pretty boy, with his mother's dark brown hair and eyes, and he was intelligent. 'He had everything going for him,' Joe added. 'He was a very bright, good-looking little lad. You think: "He's going to crack it; he's got it all."'

Stephen was also very slight of build, so much so that his family nicknamed him 'The Stickman'. 'He was always a bit of a runt,' reflected Joe. 'I always thought that a strong puff of wind would blow him over.' A former neighbour said: 'Stephen was a bit odd. He had one brother and one sister but none of them ever played outside with other kids from the neighbourhood. They seemed to stay indoors all the time, though when you did meet Stephen, you got the impression he was a bit of a nerd. He seemed very clever.'

The 1970s ended with the Griffiths' marriage in trouble. All the hope and expectation of those early years in Thornhill had fizzled out, and in January 1982 Moira divorced Stephen senior. He married his second wife, Ann, the following autumn, and went back to live in Batley. Moira took the three children to live on a council estate in Wakefield, although the youngsters – and Stephen in particular – were fond of their father and went to stay with him regularly.

The split took its toll on the family, but it had an especially devastating effect on Stephen. He became even quieter and more withdrawn, and began getting into trouble with the police. On one occasion, he was caught stealing from a garage and brought back to his mother's front door by a couple of bobbies. Neighbours complained that he would kill and dismember birds in their back garden. One said:

'He didn't play out and you only saw him at night. We used to see him with an airgun, shooting birds, then we used to see him dissecting birds. It looked as if he was enjoying what he was doing. He wasn't dissecting them bit by bit – he was ripping them apart.'

Moira, meanwhile, tried to juggle the demands of being a single mother with a bid to recharge her social life. She was barely out of her teens when she fell pregnant with Stephen, and in the following decade had done little more than look after children and husband. Now in her early 30s, still slim and pretty, she seemed bent on reclaiming some of her lost youth. She hit the pubs and nightclubs of West Yorkshire with gusto, dressed to the nines in what were – for those days – very racy outfits. Her evenings out would last until the early hours and she would sometimes return with an admirer in tow.

Friends who tagged along every now and then were taken aback by how outgoing she was. At least once, she was spotted in a passionate kiss with a male friend in a public bar. 'She didn't seem to care what people thought of her. Her clothing was very sexy.' A former neighbour said: 'I wouldn't say that Moira was a bad mother because she clothed and fed the kids. […] She would wear short skirts, fancy tights and high heels. She had plenty of male friends.' Moira never settled down, however, and Stephen Griffiths spent the latter half of his childhood without a father figure under the same roof.

Moira and her now ex-husband decided that Stephen's future required urgent attention. Conscious that he was entering the critical years of his education, they pooled their savings and sent him to Queen Elizabeth Grammar School, a prestigious and expensive public school in Wakefield that ticked every box for the aspirational parent. QEGS, as it is known for short, was founded in 1591 by Thomas Saville under a royal charter from Elizabeth I. Its Latin motto, *Turpe Nescire* (which translates as 'It is a disgrace to be ignorant'), epitomises its quest for scholarly excellence. Young Stephen's notable predecessors had included John Radcliffe, the Oxford physician whose name was given to the city's famous infirmary; Richard Henry Lee, an American Congressman who championed independence from Britain; and John Potter, an 18th-century Archbishop of Canterbury.

Another 'Old Savilian' was John George Haigh, otherwise known as the Acid Bath Murderer. Haigh, a serial fraudster, murdered six people in the 1940s in order to steal their money and possessions. He disposed of their bodies in vats of concentrated sulphuric acid before tipping what was left away, hoping that this was a foolproof way of avoiding capture. Haigh misunderstood the legal principle of *corpus delicti*, which states that a person should not normally be tried for another's murder unless the body is discovered first. He mistakenly thought that he could not, under any circumstances, be tried if no body was found.

Haigh was born in Lincolnshire but moved to Outwood, a pit village to the north of Wakefield, when he was still young. He won a scholarship to QEGS in the 1920s and was then awarded a place as a choirboy at Wakefield Minster. However, after leaving to take a succession of junior clerical jobs, he was caught stealing from his employer and jailed for theft. Haigh's six victims were murdered over a five-year period in London and the south-east during the war years. When the police finally caught up with him after the war, he claimed to have murdered nine people in total. Haigh also told his interrogators that he had drunk his victims' blood, believing he might cheat the hangman if he could convince them he was insane. The tally of nine was never confirmed, and Haigh was hanged for the six murders at Wandsworth Prison in August 1949 by renowned executioner Albert Pierrepoint.

Haigh is part of QEGS' unofficial folklore, and all new pupils, Stephen Griffiths included, learned about the school's notorious ex-pupil. There remained for many years a desk, hidden away somewhere in the cellar, on which Haigh had carved his initials, or so the story went.

Griffiths attended QEGS from the age of 13 to 16. However, although he was intelligent, he did not live up to the school motto. Instead, it was his fascination with weaponry and martial arts that attracted the attention of teachers and classmates. As well as reading Dungeons and Dragons fantasy role-playing magazines, he would attend lessons with a briefcase containing a knife and kung fu magazines, and maintained an unhealthy interest in killing and cutting up dead animals.

One former classmate said: 'He was very quiet and pretty insignificant really. He brought with him on one or two occasions a rather vicious-looking dagger and some throwing stars. If you look at the boy Griffiths, he was a small, thin, below average-sized pupil. Yet in his books and in his games he was an all-powerful big macho type that was killing and slaying and winning.' Once, the police were called in to investigate a number of twisted poems written on a toilet wall, with lines containing threats to kill one of the school's few female teachers. The culprit was never found, but a number of Griffiths' classmates believed he was to blame.

Aged 17, Stephen Griffiths began to lose his grip. He had left QEGS without starting A-level courses, and was drifting away from his family. To them, he appeared to be suffering from depression and spent all of his time alone, either in his room or outside, wandering aimlessly around the town. In the spring of 1987, the manager of a small supermarket in Leeds caught him shoplifting and tried to apprehend him. Griffiths grappled with the man before pulling a knife and slashing him across the face. The store manager needed 19 stitches. At Leeds Crown Court on 23 June that year, he was convicted of wounding and sentenced to three years' youth custody.

While he was awaiting trial for the attack, doctors were so concerned about his state of mind that they commissioned a full report into his mental health. He was sent to Waddiloves hospital in Bradford, where Dr Peter Wood, the psychiatrist, found that he showed no evidence of 'formal mental illness' but appeared to be suffering from a 'personality disorder'. In lay terms, he was not mad but was given to abnormal patterns of thought and behaviour. In this case, there was an inexplicable fascination with weapons and a potential for violence.

Because personality disorders are not treatable in the same way that mental illness is, Griffiths would not benefit from hospital care. He was allowed to serve less than half his three-year sentence because he had spent many months on remand and had behaved himself in prison. By the end of 1988, he was back on the streets. He kept up his psychiatric treatment as an outpatient, but although his condition remained stable, he was effectively unemployable. While his classmates from QEGS were enjoying their first year at university, Stephen Griffiths was turning into a feckless drifter.

Griffiths did not return to his family after being released. His many deep-seated issues took hold, and he simply went off to make his own way in the world. 'Shaun just seemed to drop out of sight,' said Joe Dewhirst. 'Apparently he felt abandoned by his family and wanted nothing to do with his mother or any of the Dewhirsts. I don't know whether his father kept in touch.' Stephen senior, in fact, did see his first-born son every now and then. He had remained in Batley and had made a success of his second marriage, having two children with Ann. Stephen junior would visit occasionally, sometimes even bringing a girlfriend along. He also kept in touch with Caroline and Phillip.

Meanwhile Moira, for whom Griffiths expressed utter contempt, seemed to drift off into her own little world. She suffered from depression and was given a small council flat of her own, in Eightlands Road, Dewsbury, overlooking the town's railway station. Despite living nearby, still in the old Dewhirst family home in Thornhill, Joe saw her only once in 20 years, at their mother Dorothy's funeral. She never worked and did not go out much. When she did, it was to pursue the somewhat bizarre hobby of making gravestone rubbings on paper. Despite having a nest egg of £55,000 spread over a number of different bank accounts, Moira continued to claim housing and council tax benefit. Eventually, her local authority, Kirklees, caught up with her and she was convicted of defrauding them of £8,500.

In the late 1980s, police forces discovered a new investigative tool, the criminal profile. Senior officers turned to forensic psychologists who specialised in understanding what made offenders tick. Through assessing criminals such as murderers, rapists and paedophiles in custody, they learned enormous amounts about their motivation, thought patterns and modus operandi. That knowledge was now applied on a grand scale to catching criminals while they were still at large. Although the science behind profiling was not new, by the late 1980s it had developed to such an extent that profilers could routinely play a key part in cracking unsolved cases. Working on the basis that behaviour reflects personality, they could analyse crime scenes and determine key characteristics of the perpetrator, including their sex, age, race, class, profession and education. The 'signatures' left at the scene could provide a fairly comprehensive profile of the criminal. Potentially, they were priceless to senior detectives faced with a puzzling crime.

THE CROSSBOW CANNIBAL

The revolution began in 1986 with Britain's first criminal profile. Scotland Yard, together with other police forces across south-east England, were struggling to solve a series of sex murders and rapes carried out around railway stations at night. They involved two attackers, and began with the rape of a woman near Hampstead in 1982. The incidents continued with frightening regularity over the next three years, and the pair responsible were dubbed the Railway Rapists. In December 1985, they struck again. But this time, after dragging Alison Day, a 19-year-old office worker, off the deserted platform in Hackney Wick, north London, and raping her, they strangled her to death with a piece of string. During the next five months, the killers took two more victims, raping and murdering 15-year-old schoolgirl Maartje Tamboezer in West Horley, Surrey, and secretary Anne Locke, 29, in Brookman Park, Hertfordshire. Desperately seeking a breakthrough, senior detectives invited David Canter, a psychologist and criminologist from Surrey University, to draw up a profile based on what was known of the offences. John Duffy, a building worker and martial arts fanatic from north London, was subsequently arrested while following a woman through a park. Although he was alone – meaning that the intended rape did not match the pattern of the earlier railway attacks – he was questioned and charged with a number of them. In addition, the officers found that Duffy matched 13 out of 17 characteristics identified in David Canter's offender profile.

In February 1988, John Duffy was found guilty of two of the murders and four rapes. He was cleared of Anne Locke's murder, but jailed for life with a minimum tariff of 30 years. Nine years later, he named his accomplice as David Mulcahy, an old school friend. Mulcahy was finally convicted of all three murders and seven rapes in February 2001, and also jailed for life, with an identical tariff. Duffy, who gave evidence against

Mulcahy, could not be tried for Anne Locke's murder under the 'double jeopardy' law – later repealed – which prevented criminals being tried for the same crime twice. He did, however, receive a further 12 years' imprisonment after being convicted of another 17 rapes.

Not only was forensic psychology a valuable crime-fighting weapon in real life, but it also captured the imagination of the public. Crime fiction writers found the subject sexy, and a flurry of landmark novels, films and television series were based around it. American author Thomas Harris first created the serial killer Hannibal Lecter for his 1981 novel *Red Dragon*, although it was the follow-up seven years later, *The Silence of the Lambs*, which would eventually make the character a household name.

Harris's creation is a brilliant forensic psychiatrist who has been incarcerated for life after committing a series of cannibalistic murders. Lecter is of Lithuanian extraction, and becomes fixated with cannibalism after seeing his sister murdered and eaten in front of him by a band of Nazi deserters in 1944. He escapes and, later in life, tracks down her killers before torturing and murdering them. However, having achieved retribution, he develops a secret and insatiable bloodlust. In *The Silence of the Lambs*, his expertise is sought by a young female FBI agent, Clarice Starling, who is trying to solve a serial killing case.

In 1991, *The Silence of the Lambs* was made into an Oscar-winning movie starring Anthony Hopkins and Jodie Foster. It won the top five categories in the Academy Awards and earned almost £200 million at the box office.

Among those whose imagination was captured by the boom in forensic psychology was Stephen Griffiths. His increasingly disturbed mind saw an opportunity to explore what had become an obsession: weapons and violence. The experience of being dealt with by the criminal justice system seemed to fuel this obsession and give it some credibility. It also pointed him back towards academia. Griffiths could never contemplate getting a job because of his criminal and psychiatric record. But he was bright and more than capable of getting a place on some course or other. He was also intellectually vain and looked forward to showing off his professorial knowledge of the macabre.

After being released from youth custody, he enrolled on a psychology course at Bradford College and, although he was never forthcoming about his treatment at the hands of criminal psychiatrists, he was soon telling people of his ambition to become one.

With the help of the probation service and the local authority, Griffiths, now aged 19, was given a rented flat in Manningham, a once-elegant but rather run-down suburb in the north-west of Bradford. He lived by himself in his apartment, part of a converted Victorian mansion in Oak Villas, which is a leafy cut-through between two larger roads.

The address had a fascinating link for a young psychology student who was obsessed with violent crime. Griffiths' flat was not 200 yards from 9 Oak Avenue, the block of flats where Peter Sutcliffe, the Yorkshire Ripper, murdered his first victim in Bradford. In April 1977, Sutcliffe, a resident of Heaton (a smarter suburb just a few miles further out from Manningham), picked up prostitute Patricia Atkinson five minutes' drive away. She took him back to her bedsit on the ground floor of number 9, where she was beaten and stabbed to death.

Despite his stated ambition to work in the criminal justice system, Griffiths was incapable of keeping out of trouble. In

August 1989, he was hauled before Bradford Magistrates' Court for being caught in possession of an air pistol, in contravention of a bar imposed after his previous conviction. He was ordered to carry out 100 hours of community service, so was free to continue with his studies at the college.

Bradford College, like any other, was an exciting place for a young man to be. Its main building, on Great Horton Road, was just west of the city, and easily within walking distance of the city centre. The college was also close to Bradford's university buildings, and the combined mass of student life created a vibrant, colourful quarter. There were pubs, bars, discos, music venues, bookshops, cheap cafés and clothes shops, and society aplenty. Yet despite all these distractions, Stephen Griffiths just cut himself off and, once again, drifted into a world of his own. He also began to show signs of paranoia about his fellow students, seeing plots that did not exist.

In May 1991, his inner demons re-emerged. Imagining some slight from four young women at the college, he pulled a knife from a carrier bag, walked up to them and held it to the chin of one of them. Griffiths snarled at her: 'What are you laughing at, little girl?' He then held the blade to the throat of one of the other girls before walking away. They were physically unharmed but beside themselves with fear. One of the girls told her father, who, five days later, went to see Griffiths to seek an explanation. When confronted, Griffiths reacted by pulling a knife and threatening him.

He was charged with two counts of affray and possessing an offensive weapon in a public place. In October, as he awaited trial, he was assessed by Dr Peter Wood, the same psychiatrist who had analysed him four years earlier, who wrote in his report that Griffiths was strongly attracted to the idea of killing others. One month later, the prison authorities attempted to find out more about his condition and sent him for assessment to Rampton hospital, the high-security psychiatric hospital in Nottinghamshire. They agreed with the earlier assessments that he did not have an 'illness' that could be treated medically. Instead, they confirmed, he had a personality disorder. In January 1992, he was convicted of all three charges when he appeared before Leeds Crown Court and he was sentenced to two years in jail. The court was told: 'He saw a threat when there was not one there, and brandished a knife at innocent people.'

While serving his sentence at Leeds Prison, Griffiths' fascination with notorious criminals was beginning to resemble hero worship rather than a dispassionate, academic interest. One prison officer, Peter Salisbury, was so concerned that he sent a memo to the authorities, warning of the almost erotic thrill the new inmate got from discussing savagery. Mr Salisbury, a qualified psychiatric nurse, had worked with Reggie Kray, who ruled the 1960s East End underworld with his brother Ronnie, and Graham Young, the so-called Teacup Poisoner, who killed his stepmother and foreman and made more than 70 people ill by lacing drinks with toxic chemicals.

But Griffiths' undisputed idol was Peter Sutcliffe, the man who had killed 13 times, including once in his own road, Oak Villas. He told Mr Salisbury: 'What Sutcliffe did was nothing. I'm going to outdo him. He was a pussycat compared to me.' Mr Salisbury was also present when the 22-year-old Griffiths suggested 'exterminating' a mentally disabled man on the same wing and then discovered that he had drawn up a list of staff he wanted to kill. He sent a memo to the governor warning: 'He openly talks about the pleasures of killing and maiming people. When he speaks on these subjects, he does so with the enthusiasm and air of a person recounting an enjoyable sexual experience.'

But whatever his fantasies or boasts, Griffiths kept his nose relatively clean and was released from his sentence in spring 1993. He returned to Bradford and began, on the face of it, to move forward in life. Although he was back before the magistrates again the following October, and given probation after being convicted of possessing a knife in public, he began, as far as the courts were concerned, a long period of good behaviour.

Griffiths recommenced his studies and in autumn 1997, four years after his release from jail, he began a Bachelor of Science degree course in psychology at Leeds University. He had just moved into Flat 33 Holmfield Court and began amassing his grim library of homicide books. Six years later, he emerged with a second class honours degree, division one, and prepared for the next phase of his academic career: studies in evil.

CHAPTER 3

Shadow of the Ripper

St George's Day, 23 April 1977, found Patricia Atkinson in a familiar Saturday evening routine. She dolled herself up for a night out by putting on a blouse of the same blue denim as her bell-bottom jeans, handbag and platform shoes. Her top was tied fashionably at the waist and unbuttoned at the neck, and over it she wore a short leather jacket. The weather forecast predicted showers with night temperatures down to 4°C and, as a street prostitute, she was likely to be out late.

Patricia, or Tina, was a 'Lumb Lane girl'. She earned a living by selling her body on what was, in the 1970s, the central boulevard of Bradford's red light district. Manningham, a few miles west of the city centre, was the neighbourhood of choice for the city's Victorian merchant class. After the decline in the textiles industry, it became a seedy trading place for sex. Hard-up women would hang around 'The Lane' and its adjoining streets, picking up punters for sex at the bottom end of the market. They coupled wherever the street lights never reached, be it in cars or in the open. In the 1970s, there was even more derelict land than in post-regeneration Bradford. Back then, full sex among the rubble would cost as little as £5.

Patricia was divorced from her Pakistani immigrant husband Ray Mitra. After the marriage broke down, he had been given custody of their three daughters: Judy, Jill and Lisa. Aged 33, and an alcoholic, Patricia lived alone in a rented bedsit, Flat 3a, at 9 Oak Avenue, a tree-lined thoroughfare between two main roads on the edge of Manningham. Patricia had been convicted for soliciting two years earlier but continued to work the streets. She was slim and pretty, with long brown hair, and had a network of male admirers as well as regular punters. Their details were kept in her little address book and Flat 3a was where they went for sex.

For most of Bradford, Saturday 23 April would have meant a choice between *Kojak* on BBC1 or *Rich Man, Poor Man*, an American mini-series, on ITV's Yorkshire TV, then bed. But Patricia hit the town that night in a big way. By about 10pm, she was very drunk. She had stopped for a few shorts in the Perseverance, a pub on Lumb Lane, then moved on to the Carlisle, a few hundred yards away. At the Carlisle, she became something of a nuisance, at one point offering to perform a striptease when the dancer who had been booked failed to turn up. The landlord threw her out and she was last seen staggering along Lumb Lane near her regular working pitch. Around 6.30pm the following day, Robert Henderson, her friend-cum-boyfriend, called round. He could not get an answer and, finding the door unlocked, went inside to find a scene of bloody devastation. Patricia's battered and mutilated body lay face down on the bed, partially covered by her duvet. The blouse was pulled up, her black bra undone, and she wore only one of her denim shoes. Her jeans and knickers were pulled down and there was a large pool of blood on the floor. Henderson fled the carnage to fetch the block's caretaker.

The full story of Patricia Atkinson's murder would remain

secret for another four years. Only then would Peter Sutcliffe be revealed as the Yorkshire Ripper, the serial killer who had cruised the red light districts of northern England for five years, murdering women. Only then would it be known that the married lorry driver, with a distinctive beard and frizzy hair, was a citizen of Bradford. In the immediate aftermath of Patricia's death, detectives knew only that she had been beaten about the head with a heavy instrument and stabbed repeatedly in the lower back and stomach. In public, they were keeping an open mind about the murder weapon, and were unwilling to speculate about its links to other crimes, particularly the unsolved murders of three prostitutes in Leeds: Wilma McCann, Emily Jackson and Irene Richardson. In private, though, they were already convinced that Patricia's attacker had also killed all three women. The notorious soubriquet, Yorkshire Ripper, had not yet been coined, but it soon would be.

By the summer of 1977, Sutcliffe was prowling close to home once again, with an almost uncontrollable compulsion to kill. On 9 July, Maureen Long, a 42-year-old divorcee from Leeds, was in Manningham for a night out. She planned to stay over with her ex-husband, who had a house on the east side of the city. Maureen met him for a quick drink to sort out the sleeping arrangements, then went clubbing. She first visited Tiffany's, a converted Mecca bingo hall on Manningham Lane, before moving on to nearby Bali Hai. Both were big dancehalls where Bradford's workers could forget their worries by drinking, dancing and getting picked up.

Maureen left Bali Hai just after 2am alone, and, swaying merrily, joined the queue for taxis outside. Sutcliffe had also been out drinking. He was heading back towards the city centre along Manningham Lane when he spotted Maureen, and, after she accepted his offer of a lift, set off towards the ex-husband's house. As they pulled up, Maureen asked Sutcliffe whether he fancied her. He said yes, and she suggested they have sex in his car on a piece of nearby waste ground. By the time they got there, she needed to urinate and clambered out of the car. Sutcliffe followed, and, as she was squatting, struck a thunderous blow to the back of her head with a hammer. She collapsed on the ground and, grabbing her by the arms, Sutcliffe dragged her further into the darkness. He pulled up her maxi dress to expose her abdomen, and stabbed her repeatedly with a knife before driving off and leaving her for dead.

Fortunately, Maureen survived. She was found at 8.30 the following evening, fighting for her life. Sutcliffe had left her where he attacked her, by the side of Bowling Back Lane. Two gypsy women living in a caravan on the same plot heard her whimpering as they walked past and thought it was an abandoned baby. Sutcliffe, on hearing a radio report of the attack the next day, was terrified that he would be caught. 'I got a nasty shock and thought it was the end of the line there and then,' he told the police after his arrest. 'A few days after, I read that Long was suffering from loss of memory and this made me less worried about being caught.' In fact, she needed specialist neurosurgery and a nine-week stay in hospital to recover. Although she was able to offer a description, her damaged memory gave Sutcliffe fair hair, and she failed to mention the beard. The Ripper said later that just before his arrest, he had been shopping in Bradford's Arndale Centre when he saw Maureen right in front of him. Despite their eyes meeting, she did not recognise him.

On 21 January 1978, nine months after Patricia Atkinson's death, her friend Yvonne Pearson went out for the afternoon. Yvonne lived just off Lumb Lane with her daughters, one aged two years and the other five months. Like Patricia, she was 'on the game'. She had a number of convictions for soliciting, and was due to appear before Bradford magistrates on a fresh charge five days hence. A condition of her bail was that she observed a night-time curfew to prevent her repeating the offence, but she was worried that the magistrates would jail her this time so she had started planning for the longer-term care of her children and needed money.

Yvonne was 21 and a petite five feet five inches tall. She had a platinum blonde bob hairstyle, made fashionable at the time by Joanna Lumley, who was playing glamorous agent Purdey in ITV's *The New Avengers*. She dressed smartly, and on that chilly Saturday night in January wore a black polo-necked sweater and trousers and a striped woollen jacket. She left the children with a 16-year-old neighbour, and said she was going to see her mother in Leeds for a few days. In fact, she never strayed far from Manningham. She was last seen alive in a pub, the Flying Dutchman, at about 9.30pm, when she told one of her fellow drinkers that she was 'going to earn some money'.

She was reported missing a few days later. Neither her mother nor her lover, Roy Saunders – who was the father of her two girls – had seen her. It was not until Easter Sunday, more than two months later, that her body was found, hidden under a mouldy sofa dumped on derelict land. The scene was a short drive from Lumb Lane, alongside Arthington Street. Yvonne's body was spotted by a passing youth who noticed an arm protruding, and at first thought it belonged to a tailor's dummy. Only the ghastly smell alerted him to the truth. Yvonne had, like the others, suffered appalling head injuries and her clothing had been pulled aside to bare her breasts and stomach. Scattered around the sofa were piles of ashes from rubbish that had been burned by local companies. A used condom was lying nearby on the ground.

Sutcliffe had picked Yvonne up on Lumb Lane. He was driving through Manningham when he slowed down to allow another driver to emerge from Southfield Square, an oasis of greenery and yellow sandstone which had once been one of Bradford's swankiest addresses. She leaned into his car and asked him if he wanted 'business'. He replied 'Yes', she got in, and he drove her to Arthington Street. He hit her twice on the head with a hammer as she got out of the front passenger seat to get in the back. However, Sutcliffe was interrupted by the arrival of another car, and he was forced to hide behind the settee, with his victim still alive, until the driver left. He then renewed his attack, furiously kicking and stamping on her. He told the police: 'After that, I remember acting very strangely. I talked to her and apologised for what I had done, but she was dead. I was distraught and I was in tears when I left her.'

Initially, Yvonne Pearson's death was not counted as a Ripper killing. Professor David Gee, the pathologist, believed that her injuries were caused by blows delivered with a rock rather than a hammer. This was only corrected a year later, and, during those 12 months, fears spread of a copycat killer. Detective Chief Superintendent Trevor Lapish, who led the inquiry to find Yvonne's killer before the special Ripper squad took over, warned: 'Some unhinged person, jealous of the attention given to the Ripper, might be trying to follow in his footsteps. There is no doubt that the publicity could spark off this sort of reaction.'

Barbara Leach, Sutcliffe's fourth Bradford victim, was a 20-year-old student staying in Bradford ahead of her third and final year reading social psychology at the university. The contrast between her lifestyle and those of Patricia Atkinson and Yvonne Pearson could not have been greater. She was from a stable, loving family, living outside term-time in Kettering, Northamptonshire with her father David, a bank clerk, and her mother Beryl, a teacher. She had a dog called Trigger and had just adopted a stray kitten, which she named KC.

THE CROSSBOW CANNIBAL

On the night of 2 September 1979, Barbara went out for a drink with her friends to the Mannville Arms, a street-corner pub on Great Horton Road, which was situated near to both the city centre and the university campus. The pub was also a mere 200 yards from the bedsit Barbara – 'Babs' to her friends – shared on Grove Terrace. They were friends with the pub's landlord, and when drinking-up time came at 11pm, they stayed behind to help collect empty glasses and were invited for an after-hours 'lock-in'. By 12.45am, most of the group were ready to go home, but Barbara wanted to indulge her risky foible of taking a night-time stroll. Her friends were put off by the drizzly weather and she disappeared alone in the opposite direction.

Small and stocky, with curly brown hair, Barbara wore a beige cheesecloth shirt, red high-heeled boots and blue jeans, with a circular embroidered badge sewn on her bottom, bearing the slogan 'Best Rump'. Sutcliffe could never have confused her with a streetwalker. Nevertheless, after watching her part from the group, he followed her in his latest vehicle, a Rover 3.5 saloon, at a snail's pace. He told the police later that he parked up alongside the pavement so that she was walking towards him. After she passed, he swung his hammer at her head, knocking her to the ground, and dragged her by the wrists or ankles into a backyard behind some flats. Once again, he ripped open her clothes and stabbed her with a large screwdriver. Sutcliffe then dumped Barbara's body among the tenants' dustbins and covered it with a rotting piece of discarded carpet. The police found her body the next afternoon after her flatmates reported her missing.

Barbara's death emphasised the fact that not only women who worked as prostitutes were in danger from the Yorkshire Ripper. Sutcliffe murdered at least five women who simply had the dreadful misfortune of being alone in a quiet street or open space after dark. Such victims included 16-year-old shop girl Jayne MacDonald, building society clerk Jo Whitaker and civil servant Marguerite Walls. None were killed in red light areas and the Ripper could never have believed they were 'doing business'. He did not need to pretend he was picking them up: he would simply slam a hammer into their head while they looked the other way.

After Barbara's death, Bradford's student union leaders warned the 1,500 women studying in the city to avoid walking alone through the streets at night and many began taking self-defence lessons. Tricia Iddon, 20, a managerial science undergraduate from Preston, told the local newspaper, the *Bradford Telegraph & Argus*: 'Some students have also felt that the Ripper would never attack them. But now they realise that the Ripper could kill anyone at any moment. Now women students will have been frightened by the killing and be much more cautious.' In truth, during Sutcliffe's killing spree, which lasted from 1975 to 1980, *every* woman was at risk.

Sutcliffe was arrested in January 1981, 15 months after Barbara's death. It was an extraordinary stroke of luck. Two police constables patrolling the red light area in Sheffield found him in a Rover saloon with one of the local girls. Initially, they took him in because his car had false number plates. But he confessed to being the Ripper after they pressed him about a number of holes in his story and discovered that he had secretly dumped a hammer and knife near the alley where they arrested him. He told them quite candidly how he had roamed the West Riding of Yorkshire looking for victims. He would vary his hunting ground depending on the presence of police in the red light areas he frequented, and occasionally would stray as far afield as Manchester. He described in extraordinary detail why he had chosen each woman, how he had attacked her, what weapons he had used and how he had escaped. In May 1981 at the Old Bailey, he was convicted of murdering 13 women and attempting to murder seven others. Mr Justice Boreham sentenced him to life with a recommendation that he serve 30 years before being considered for parole.

After Sutcliffe's arrest, the police found a curious and perhaps telling insight into his state of mind. Written on a scrap of paper, and kept in the cab of his lorry among a stack of road atlases, was a poem he had penned himself. It read:

'IN THIS TRUCK IS A
MAN WHOSE LATENT GENIUS IF
UNLEASHED WOULD ROCK THE NATION
WHOSE DYNAMIC ENERGY
WOULD OVERPOWER THOSE
AROUND HIM
BETTER LET HIM SLEEP'

The verse seemed to be an in-joke aimed at himself, alluding to the terrible force within, while simultaneously flattering his own vanity and hinting at dire retribution if the world failed him. Sutcliffe's state of mind had been the crucial issue in the trial, as he admitted virtually everything that was put to him but tried to mislead the court about his motives. He tried to claim that he was on a divine mission to rid the streets of prostitutes, triggered by voices in his head. His argument fell down partly because, while awaiting trial, he had insisted to a number of people that he was as sane as the next man. The 'voices' story was a lie to convince the jury that he was mad. It failed.

The prosecution tried to establish whether there was a sexual motive to his crimes. Of all his victims, he had had sex with only one, Helen Rytka, a pretty 18-year-old prostitute he had killed in Huddersfield in 1978. It was suggested, but denied, that the stabbing to his victim's stomach represented a violent simulation of the sexual act. Only 20 years after his conviction did extraordinary new evidence about Sutcliffe's sexual motives finally emerge. In his book *Wicked Beyond Belief*, journalist Michael Bilton revealed that, when arrested, Sutcliffe was wearing a bizarre pair of homemade, crotchless long johns underneath his trousers. Consisting of a V-necked jumper with padding sewn into the elbows, Sutcliffe wore it with each leg in an arm, the padding aligned with the knees and the V-shaped hole between his legs. The strange apparel would allow him to kneel down alongside his victims without scraping his legs on the waste ground, while performing a sex act on himself. Despite the jury's rejection of his madness claim, he was subsequently diagnosed with schizophrenia and incarcerated at Broadmoor secure hospital in Berkshire.

CHAPTER 4

Psycho Steve

Rio's was one of Stephen Griffiths' favourite pulling grounds in Bradford. It was an underground music venue near the university, with blacked-out windows, sticky floors and grim toilets. The clientele were students, punks, metalheads and goths who paid £10 to watch up-and-coming cult bands play loud music. By and large, the Rio's crowd were young people getting drunk and having a laugh. But not Griffiths. He remained aloof, never drinking or dancing. He simply drifted through the merry-making in his trademark black outfit, sometimes carrying one of the lizards in a bag, looking for women to chat up. Often, his vantage point would be the stage, from which he could look down – literally and metaphorically – on the other nightclubbers.

Leigh Miller, a pretty blonde, was hanging around Rio's dance floor when Griffiths moved in on her:

'He sidled up to me, asked for my phone number and said: "You'll make a sad man very happy." Stephen was quite a pretty boy as well. He used to be slim and always dressed

45

in black with the big coat, the boots and the turtleneck jumpers. And he always smelt of baby lotion. His hair was tied back in long ringlets and he used to put baby lotion on it to keep it tight and shiny.'

Then in his late 20s, Griffiths was slightly older than Leigh. But she was turned off almost instantly by his self-obsession and lack of emotion. When she visited his flat, the first thing she noticed was the three-foot-square framed photograph of himself that he had hung on the bedroom wall. 'That was a bit strange,' she said. 'The first time he came to my house he asked if he could check the bed. He said: "You're not one of those people who uses the same sheets are you?" Then he sniffed them. When we were in bed I'd wake up in the night and he'd be there, propped up on his elbow staring at me. We were going out for about eight months but he didn't really show emotion. He rarely laughed or joked. We didn't argue but there was just no love. We didn't kiss, cuddle or even hold hands.'

When Leigh broke off the relationship, Griffiths sent her a menacing goodbye present. Turning to his murder library, he selected a true crime book about a mass killer and shoved it anonymously through her letterbox. *Confessions of Son of Sam*, written by David Abrahamsen in 1985, tells how David Berkowitz, a mentally-unbalanced Satanic cult devotee, shot dead six people in New York in the mid-1970s. Berkowitz claimed his killings were ordered by a demon that had possessed his neighbour's dog. Leigh said of the book:

'It was pretty spooky and I didn't read it. I'd seen inside his flat where he kept hundreds and hundreds of books on serial killers. But I called Stephen and asked why he'd done it. He said I'd hurt him. The next time I saw him I was with my dad and a friend, who's a bouncer. They took him to one side and told him he'd gone too far. Nothing like that ever happened again.'

In the early stages of his relationships, Griffiths appeared quite a catch. He was slim, quite good looking, intelligent and charming. He could carry off the mature student act very well, and the younger girls, in particular, found him urbane, but with a cool non-conformity. He could talk about psychology, criminology, music and films. But generally he did not talk about his own two custodial sentences for unprovoked violence or his damning psychiatric assessments. Instead, he turned on the patter at clubs, sometimes in pubs, and on dating websites and in lonely hearts columns. So vigorous was his pursuit of women that the girlfriends he had, from the time he moved into Holmfield Court, would frequently overlap, and he pursued any number of ambiguous relationships with female friends and some of the working girls. But he was cold and narcissistic. What they discovered through their own nasty experiences was that Griffiths was a powder keg, and women were sparks that could ignite him at any minute.

Zeta Pinder was captivated by him when they met through a newspaper lonely hearts advert in 1998. He brought a photograph of himself to their first date, in a pub, and gave it to her to keep. She found him 'a little odd but quite a sweet person'. Griffiths told her he lived with his parents and was training as a counsellor for 'people with problems'. In fact, by the time they met, he was living alone and had been diagnosed with the most acute psychiatric problems imaginable. She thought Griffiths seemed 'very camp' and asked him outright if he were gay, but he denied it. Although they had sex three or four times a week, Griffiths could never reach a climax. 'Sex would last for two, three, sometimes four hours,' she said. 'He could get aroused but could not reach a sexual peak. I was worried that he didn't find me attractive but he said that was not the case. He used to get very upset about it.' His myriad foibles included stuffing his ears with cotton wool because he had a phobia about insects crawling into them while he slept, and refusing to let her touch his hair. 'He would stroke mine, but once early on I stroked his and he pushed me away quite violently telling me: "Don't ever do that again." He was really upset and quite angry. It was scary.'

Griffiths had turned his flat into an Aladdin's cave of murder paraphernalia, with books, DVDs and magazines, plus weapons (including the crossbows and swords) everywhere. Incredibly, Zeta did not find out about the flat until two years into their relationship, when, in conversation, it emerged that he had lied about living with his parents. When he finally took her round, she was mortified.

'There were never any alarm bells until I found out about his flat. When I went in, it was just jaw-dropping. You walked in and on the left-hand side there was just a huge bookcase and it was just full of horror books on, like, the Moors Murderers and Jack the Ripper, the Yorkshire Ripper. Suddenly I was seeing a side of him I never had, with books and films about killing. He started picking up magazines and showed me pictures of the Moors Murderers.'

Zeta decided there and then that she wanted nothing more to do with him, and pretended to be sick so that he would take her home. The next day, she ended their relationship by telephone. Griffiths accepted her decision and they parted on good terms. She was one of the lucky ones.

THE CROSSBOW CANNIBAL

Amanda Judson dated Griffiths after meeting him at a club in 1999, when she was 34 and he was 30. She had no idea he was seeing other women, and, initially, like Zeta, thought he was her perfect man. Griffiths would take her out on day trips into the countryside and to restaurants and cinemas. 'He was very attractive,' she said. 'The best-looking man in the area. I could have looked at 300 men and still only fancied this one. We chatted for ages. At the end of the night we parted but agreed to meet the next day.' He introduced her to his father Stephen, stepmother Ann, sister Caroline and brother Phillip. But he told her he had no time at all for his mother Moira. 'He told me he hated his real mother Moira with a vengeance,' said Amanda. 'He never cried about his mum. He didn't have emotions or expressions. He had a stone-cold face.'

Amanda said that, even though they had a normal sex life, she nicknamed him 'gay boy' because his mannerisms were so effeminate. One of his kinks, she said, was photographing women's bottoms. 'He used to show me his collection of photos of his exes' bottoms, which he kept in a case,' she said. 'Stephen treasured them. He had taken each picture himself, carefully developed them by hand and then kept them as a memento. I told him not to expect me to pose for one. Stephen was obsessed by bums – he certainly had a thing about them. But despite his oddness, I was so in love with him.'

Her feelings were to change when, completely out of the blue, he told her he had to go to court. She asked why, and he calmly replied that he had been accused of pouring boiling water over the stomach of an ex-girlfriend called Diane as she slept. Of course, he denied doing it, and claimed Diane was unbalanced and prone to making stories up about him. Amanda went to court with him and watched him defend himself. Diane claimed he had attacked her because she wanted to leave him. The jury believed his version of events, but her story was to have a familiar ring. He later went to a tattoo parlour and had the crowing slogan 'Diane Lost War' inscribed on his upper left arm. Amanda added: 'As we left court holding hands, Stephen knocked me for six again and admitted he had been to Rampton for slashing a security guard.' He told her about his psychiatric assessments but protested that there was no law to prevent people with psychiatric problems studying full time. Griffiths revealed the depths of his obsession with Sutcliffe to her. 'Stephen always told me he would be infamous – not famous,' she said. 'He even got a dictionary out to explain the difference to me. He was addicted to serial killers and said one day he would go down in history. Stephen said he wanted to be bigger than the Yorkshire Ripper and planned this since he was a teenager.' Amanda finished with him in 2001 because she was so disturbed by his behaviour. 'My instincts were telling me something was dangerously wrong with this man. It took six months to finally get away; each time he would persuade me to stay.'

Griffiths' refusal to let go escalated in his next relationship. Before Amanda had ditched him, he had started seeing Kathy Hancock, a ginger-haired prison officer. In February 2000, one of his neighbours at Holmfield Court introduced him to her. Kathy was 27 and lived with her parents in a village near York. She worked nearby at HMP Full Sutton, a maximum security prison. 'He was a lot slimmer then, and he came across as very shy,' she said. 'I got suckered in. We started dating straight away.' He said he fancied her because she was a 'figure of authority', although he admitted that a female police officer would have been better. Although barely a year passed before she ended the relationship, Kathy battled for the best part of a decade to shake off 'psychotic Steve'. Both as girlfriend and as ex, she was subjected to a horrifying campaign of mental torture and physical abuse. Griffiths devised the most ingenious ruses to torment her and, in the end, she was forced to take out a series of restraining orders.

One of the first things Kathy noticed about Griffiths was his clinginess. He needed to touch her, embrace her and hold her hand: especially in public – the more visibly the better. But it was never done with any warmth. Rather, it was an act of possession, and if there were any chance of him being dispossessed, then trouble would follow. The couple were out in town one day when they bumped into a male friend of Kathy's, who gave her a platonic peck on the cheek. Although he showed no emotion at that point, later that night Griffiths took her to see Amanda and made her watch as he kissed her. 'He called it "balancing it out",' she said.

Initially, Griffiths manipulated and dominated Kathy with subtlety. He tried to make her feel insecure by suggesting that her behaviour was inappropriate. 'It was very slow control,' she said. 'He wants control of everything but he does it in such a passive way. He would make me think how I came across to other people. He would make you doubt the way you are.'

Kathy had her own apartment, 20 miles away in Wakefield, where she kept two dogs: Yoshi, a Rhodesian Ridgeback cross; and Taz, a cross ginger collie. Both flat and pets annoyed Griffiths: the flat gave her greater autonomy from him, while the pets were rivals for his attention. So he concocted a scheme to deal with both problems at once. Kathy had been taking prescribed medication for depression when, while she was staying over at Holmfield Court, he offered her dothiepin, another antidepressant. Soon after taking the pills, she began feeling nauseous. To her consternation, Griffiths seemed to know that would happen and started cackling. 'As I started to feel ill, he just sat there laughing at me, saying: "You're dying." He said: "You can't mix those tablets," and just kept laughing.' He refused to let her ring an ambulance, so, despite feeling delirious, she drove herself to Bradford Royal Infirmary's casualty department. She was treated overnight and, next day, went back to her own flat in Wakefield. Griffiths was there, claiming she had been burgled by raiders who had, implausibly, touched absolutely nothing in the apartment but the dogs. They were gone.

Kathy was devastated and, at a low ebb, agreed to move in with Griffiths. A few weeks later, she returned to Wakefield to collect some of her possessions and bumped into a neighbour whom she had not seen since the dogs were stolen. 'My neighbour told me that at 3.30am, Stephen had arrived and taken them. He later admitted he had. He said Yoshi had taken a dislike to him and growled when he pushed him. Taz had reacted too.' Griffiths had taken the pets to a travellers' camp near Sheffield and had given them away, knowing full well that Kathy could not bear to stay in the house without them. 'It meant from then on I was stuck in Bradford with him in his flat. Any independence I had was gone. I was crushed.'

After Kathy moved in with him, Griffiths tightened his grip on her into a stranglehold. 'His flat was like a prison,' she said. 'I couldn't go out without him. We would only go to certain shops together and he was always with me holding my hand with a tight grip.' In another ploy, he bought her a new puppy, a Staffordshire bull terrier, to replace the dogs he had taken from her.

Despite living in the same block as the friend who originally introduced them, Kathy never saw her. Her unofficial jailer refused to let her go out without him and tried to stop her visiting her family. Both her parents and the friend were so worried they called the police. 'But when the police came round to ask if I was okay, Stephen was there, holding my hand.'

It was only a matter of weeks before the abuse turned physical. The trigger was always jealousy or some other perceived slight to his fragile ego. Kathy had taken self-defence classes up to and including riot training, so she was no pushover. But Griffiths was bigger and would always come off better. Once, they were visiting his family when Caroline, his younger sister, asked if she would like to go out dancing. She was cautious, knowing that it would light her boyfriend's fuse. But he grudgingly said she could go, as long as she kept it to an hour. 'I love dancing and I was out for longer than I said I would be,' she said. 'When I got back he didn't react or show any anger in front of his family. But in the car home, he punched me on the nose.' Kathy then lost her temper and fought back, utilising her self-defence training. But Griffiths headbutted her. On another occasion, they were sitting in his flat when he lost his temper over some minor exchange between them. He punched her hard in the face and split her lip, but she came back at him. 'One of the reasons he liked me, he said, was I fought back and he loved that thrill.'

The attacks on Kathy were usually in private, several hours after she had, in his mind, showed him disrespect. He would spend the intervening period working himself up into a secret fury. This happened once when they visited his brother Phillip's house in Wakefield. In Griffiths' twisted imagination she had been flirting with another man who was visiting her brother. 'Everything seemed to be okay, but later I was in trouble because I had walked up the stairs when his brother's friend was walking down. Stephen said: "You must have said something to him." I couldn't look at anyone.'

By spring 2001, Kathy had had enough. The relationship had survived, just about, but she wanted out for good. On the very day she was planning to leave Flat 33 Holmfield Court, Kathy found out – in a roundabout way – that she was pregnant. The discovery was made when she fell and banged her head as she was clearing the flat. She had to go to hospital, and the foetus showed up on the CT scan.

Griffiths was delighted. He had always talked about having children and the prospect of becoming a father brought out what passed for his caring streak. He even accompanied Kathy to the Anglia TV studios in Norwich when she was invited to appear on television. Years earlier, Kathy had lost almost 10 stone in weight, and so had been asked to guest on *Trisha*, a morning chat show fronted by Trisha Goddard. Entitled 'Big is not beautiful', the episode allowed overweight people, slimmers and health experts to debate the issues surrounding obesity. It also gave Stephen Griffiths a first taste of public exposure.

In that period of relative harmony, Kathy tried to make a go of the relationship and the couple was given a council house in Bradford's southerly Low Moor district. But a few months later, complications developed in Kathy's pregnancy. Griffiths refused to accompany Kathy to the hospital appointment where she was told that the pregnancy was ectopic and that she would lose the baby. 'I wasn't too upset,' she said. 'It was very early in the pregnancy and to me it was not yet a baby. But Stephen's reaction was very strange. He took the positive pregnancy test stick which we had kept and he made a coffin for it.'

Escape finally came for Kathy when Griffiths took her away for the weekend to Belgium. Unbeknownst to him, Kathy had arranged for Amanda, with whom she had become great friends, to clear her possessions from the flat while they were away. On their return, all she had to do was fetch Kaiser, the pet Staffordshire bull terrier he had bought for her, from his father's house in Batley. Once that was done, she fled across north-west England, staying in friends' houses in Morecambe,

Wakefield and Manchester, before eventually moving back in with her parents. 'I was in hiding,' she said. 'But he kept finding me. On one occasion, he drove all the way from Bradford to my parents' house and stabbed all four tyres on my car. On the way back from that, he smashed his car into a tree and had the cheek to ring me for help. He asked me to take him back to Bradford, saying: "By the way, you can't use your car. I've slashed the tyres."'

She tried to cut him off completely when she had her own place in Wakefield but Griffiths began a nine-year stalking campaign. He would turn up at her house, telephone her and send menacing text messages. When she refused to get back with him, he would try to win her sympathy with a lie; if that failed, the threats would follow soon after. His most effective ploy was to acquire a pet of some sort and hint to her that he was making it suffer through neglect. This was the time, in late 2001, when he began keeping exotic snakes and lizards. One day, he rang Kathy and told her he had bought a puppy and had tried to dock its tail himself, but had made a mess of it. She recalled:

'He said he got a puppy from a pet shop and got off his head on Valium, then chopped its tail off. I begged him to let me take the puppy and he did. That was one of the reasons I stayed in touch with him. I thought if he started abusing any more animals at least I could help them. He knows my weakest point is animals.'

Griffiths even used his exotic reptiles as an emotional weapon.

'He boasted how he'd fed live rats to the snakes. I was appalled. When the snakes died, he moved onto the lizards. They were three feet long and he walked them on a lead around town. He even took them into a nightclub in his backpack. He used the animals to get people to talk to him.'

It took seven years for Kathy to summon the will to cut all ties with Griffiths. Even then, it was difficult. She made the decision to break away while on holiday in Turkey in August 2008, telling him not to get in touch, then ignoring his calls and messages. His response was to send her a string of abusive and threatening texts. One warned, in abbreviated text language: 'u have 2 months 2 leave wakefield u fat ugly slapper x'. She had left her two pet cats with a friend while she was abroad, but she had also befriended two feral cats, Flash and Smudge, that lived near her flat. 'When I stopped responding to Stephen's texts I got one saying: "Your cats are dead." I got my dad to phone the friend who was looking after my cats who said they were fine. But then he texted again saying: "Not your inside cats, your outside cats."'

Kathy never saw Flash or Smudge again. When she got back to her flat in Wakefield, all her window panes had been coloured in with yellow spray paint. He had also sprayed the word 'slag' on her outside wall. She took out a number of restraining orders, but Griffiths simply waited until the order had expired and renewed his harassment. One such injunction expired in June 2009. Three-and-a-half hours after the expiry, he was on the telephone, cackling maniacally. 'It was evil laughter,' Kathy said. 'He was taking the mickey that the injunction had run out.'

Griffiths was becoming increasingly unstable in his relationships with Kathy and with other women. He always sought to control and dominate them and, if they resisted, he would make their lives hell. 'I was completely brainwashed by him,' reflected Kathy. 'My personality had gone and I no longer knew who I was. It was 10 years of mental torture and abuse. I just couldn't get away from him.'

Several of Griffiths' girlfriends had become aware of his obsession with bottoms and his inability to climax during sex, but Kathy Hancock also noticed that he had a foot fetish. 'He would see girls going up the escalator in the shopping centre in open toes and get sexually excited,' she said. 'I didn't mind because it meant he left me alone.' However, as he entered his mid-30s, his sexual and personal conduct became more and more debauched. He began drinking heavily, taking cocaine and amphetamines, and downloading violent pornography from the internet.

Bridget Farrell had befriended Griffiths in the mid-1990s, when she suffered a breakdown after her sister was murdered. She remembered that he took her in and provided a shoulder to cry on:

'I went on the streets as a working girl and was homeless. But he took me in. He let me use his bath, fed me, and I even wore his dressing gown. He would cook for me, normally mashed potatoes, sausages and beans. He really cared for me. He would even wash my clothes for me and never demanded sex in exchange. I had feelings for him. He was like a brother to me.'

On the other hand, Bridget also said that Griffiths would go out wearing women's tights underneath his black jeans and leather overcoat. He also told her he was gay, despite the fact that he often gave her heroin in return for sex.

Another working girl who knew Griffiths was Lisa Thompson. She charged Griffiths £40 for sex, once a week at his flat for nearly four years. She said he had been good humoured and handsome when she first met him. But his demeanour changed, together with his physical appearance, as he became more thickset and cut his long hair short. He began drinking more and more heavily, downing whisky, rum and lager, and increasing his drug intake. She also discovered that he was viewing violent internet porn, and he began complaining angrily that he had been ripped off by prostitutes:

> 'He was a nice guy but then he shaved all his hair off and his attitude changed. He said a prostitute had stolen from him. When he got drunk or had a bit of smoke he got a bit teary-eyed or emotional, like something had happened in his past. He would try to say something, but just started crying and shut up. He'd get annoyed and kick you out of his flat.'

Griffiths tried out dating websites as an alternative way of meeting women. He liked the anonymity it gave him and allowed him to pitch for someone he thought was at his level. In December 2008, he joined the *Guardian* newspaper's relationship site, Soulmates. He described himself as 'serious and disciplined' and said he sought a companion who was 'not afraid to let her hair down'. The notice led to him swapping emails with one woman and trying to make contact with another. They led nowhere.

He used another site to contact women who were interested in Bradford's art scene, boasting that he had arty friends and lived near a studio. In one exchange, he told a correspondent: 'Glad you could see past the scary image I generally project to the world in general.' One of his correspondents, a yoga teacher, complained that he sent her a message on the networking site Myspace suggesting that he had watched her leaving a class. She ignored it, so he sent her another, which, this time, had a more irritated tone. 'I think he was trying to be friendly,' a colleague said. 'But she found it unnerving.'

Tori Crowther, a student at the University of Bradford, also had a strange experience after agreeing to meet Griffiths at a gig:

> 'He turned up in full goth style with all his make-up and eyeliner on and his hair spiked. But he obviously thought I was going by myself, because when he arrived and saw me with two other girls he turned around again and left without saying anything. That was the last I heard of him until last year when he emailed me out of the blue again. He said the reason he'd left was that: "I was in a dark place at the time, and when I walked in and saw you with two beautiful women I couldn't cope." I didn't reply; I thought it was a bit odd. It's terrifying to think what could have happened if I'd spent more time with him.'

In the spring of 2009, Griffiths' troubled relationships with women seemed to have reached the point of boiling over. He had amassed a history of harassing and abusing ex-partners and female acquaintances. In the previous 10 years he had been arrested no fewer than six times in total by the police responding to their complaints. That June, Pauline Bond, who was a friend rather than a lover, became the latest complainant. When she refused to see him again, Griffiths became unbalanced and bombarded her with abusive telephone calls and text messages, much as he had done with Kathy. In one, he warned: 'People have no idea what I am capable of.' Pauline had no idea how great an understatement it was, but nevertheless felt it necessary to move out of her home for three months after reporting his harassment to the police. She also accused him of stealing some DVDs from her. Pauline made a statement to the police about him on 15 June 2009. Officers called at Griffiths' flat on around 4 July and conducted a search. It was a three-week spell of significant activity at 33 Holmfield Court, but afterwards there was nothing unusual to see: at least, not with the naked eye.

CHAPTER 5
Studies in Evil

A serial killer is defined by most modern criminologists as someone who murders three or more people over a period of more than 30 days. They do not wipe out a large number of victims in one act by, say, detonating a bomb. That would be a 'mass killer'. Nor do they embark on an orgy of shooting or stabbing concentrated in a short period of time or in a confined territory. That would be a 'spree killer'. Instead, serial killers select victims at intervals with a dormant period in between. Their crimes are separate incidents motivated by desire, be it to fulfil a sexual yearning, bloodlust, or a craving for things such as power, attention or money. Having killed, their compulsion cools for a time and they are fulfilled, but in due course that too wears off and they need to kill again. It is that cycle – murder, cooling off, then murder again – that identifies a serial killer. Experts study such monsters because understanding their murderous behaviour goes part of the way towards preventing it. That is why universities offer hundreds of places each year on criminology courses. Graduates go on to work for the police, probation and prison services, in hospitals and in academia.

Stephen Griffiths enrolled as a student at the University of Bradford in autumn 2004. He was admitted through its School of Lifelong Learning and Development, set up for mature students and those from unconventional academic backgrounds. Nearly 60 per cent of its students are over the age of 21, and anyone up to the age of 80 can be accepted. At the time of Griffiths' arrival, the university did not ask applicants whether they had criminal convictions or mental health issues. He had only to demonstrate proof of his undergraduate qualifications before signing up for a £1,700-a-year PhD in local history. Courses offered by the department include 'The historical landscape of the Yorkshire Dales' and 'J. B. Priestley's Bradford'. Griffiths chose murder. His thesis was entitled *Homicide in an Industrial City: Lethal Violence in Bradford 1847 to 1899*, and, as the course was research-based, he was expected to work very much on his own.

So Griffiths simply disappeared into his own isolated world. He would shut himself up for hours with his grisly book collection. He would have long sessions in the city library, poring over back issues of newspapers and periodicals. He would, very occasionally, attend lectures and tutorials at the university, but on the rare occasions when he encountered staff or other students, he was awkward and aggressive. If a debate or discussion went against him, he would lose his temper and threaten his opponent. At one point, he had to be warned about his conduct in seminars by the university staff. Griffiths would sometimes take himself off on 'field trips' to locations connected with his gruesome studies. He told friends, for instance, that he made a number of trips to a canal where a body had been dumped. Griffiths also spent hours pacing around the perimeter wall of Wakefield Prison, nicknamed 'Monster Mansion' because of the notorious killers incarcerated there. His idea of discussing coursework outside lectures amounted to debating the pros and cons of dismemberment, acid or burning to dispose of corpses.

Ironically, Griffiths shared the few lectures he did attend with bona fide criminology students. The university runs two highly-rated undergraduate courses in psychology and crime and in applied criminal justice studies. The former gives a general grounding in the subject areas but makes much of its second-year course in psychological profiling, which examines how 'psychologists can help track down criminals'. The latter is more vocational and students have to complete a final year placement working with the police, law courts or victim support. Lecturers include international experts in their field and alumni go on to work in all parts of the criminal justice system. Their practical and regimented study of serial killers was in stark contrast to the ghoulish obsession of Stephen Griffiths.

The expression 'serial killer' is attributed to Robert K. Ressler, who, as an FBI agent in the 1970s, played a major part in developing psychological profiling as a discipline. Ressler coined the phrase while working on an FBI unit that examined violent criminals who had been jailed. The similarity between the offences committed — at intervals — reminded him of the television serials he watched as a child. Ressler's ideas have subsequently been developed to identify a 'classic' serial killer. Firstly, they are not mad but bad. That is, they do not suffer from psychosis, but have a psychopathic disorder that leaves them in a self-centred world of their own. Whether or not they go on to kill, psychopaths are extreme egotists who live by their own rules, and other people are merely their fodder. They understand the values of the outside world and can appear to fit in perfectly. However, they are simply wearing what psychiatrists call the 'mask of sanity', which allows them to hide their murderous intent. Criminologists say such maniacs begin by acting out fantasies of inflicting pain, mutilation, rape, torture and murder. They construct a world where the feelings of the victim do not matter: they are merely there to help satisfy the psychopathic compulsion. If such dangerous people are not apprehended at an early stage, they will eventually create or chance upon the circumstances in which they can act out their fantasies in the real world.

According to David Wilson, Professor of Criminology and Criminal Justice at Birmingham City University, serial killers usually become active in their late teens and early 20s and remain active until they reach their 50s or 60s. 'You have got a long time span over which they can be active. They will stay active as long as they possibly can, because they gain so much psychological benefit from the act of killing.' Professor Wilson has also explained how the young killer will not be as competent as the experienced, and their murderous technique will develop over time:

'When they commit that first murder, they are not very good at it. The urge has been building up and building up as part of a fantasy life, then they are suddenly faced with the circumstances in which they can make it real. They can actually kill instead of fantasising about killing. Then, they will have enough psychologically in the bank, through committing the first murder, to incorporate into their fantasy life for a while. They will not need to do it again until several months later.'

When the excitement from the first murder wears off, said Professor Wilson, they kill again, and again. But as time goes on, the buzz from each kill diminishes. 'This is why the gap between the first and second murder is wide, the gap between the second and third is narrower, and between the third and fourth narrower still. The gap gets narrower and narrower and narrower.'

Stephen Griffiths created an A–Z of such killers on his Myspace web page. Despite being ensconced in a private world, he was an enthusiastic self-publicist and the web offered him an outlet for his narcissism. He joined networking sites, dating sites and chatrooms, wrote blogs and did a sizeable proportion of his shopping on the web. He seldom saw much of the real world beyond the environs of Holmfield Court. But from the confines of his flat, he roamed all over cyberspace. The centre of this virtual world was Myspace, which in the early days of social networking outranked Facebook.

Its slogan – 'a place for friends' – captured the spirit of modern internet socialising, but Griffiths was no social animal. He chose, as his user identity, the peculiar-sounding Ven Pariah. 'Pariah', of course, means outcast, while 'Ven' could have been a shortened version of either 'Stephen' or 'Venerable'.

Did Griffiths see himself as the venerable outcast or a noble savage? Either way, he made his Myspace page a noticeboard for the macabre. He posted potted biographies and pictures of 120 serial killers, mass murderers and spree killers, including the most notorious in history. Naturally, the Yorkshire Ripper was there, along with Jack the Ripper, the Victorian bogeyman. But they also included Fred and Rose West, the married couple who raped, tortured and murdered at least 12 young women at their home in Gloucester between the 1970s and 1990s. Ian Brady and Myra Hindley, the Moors Murderers, were profiled, with an account of their slaughter of five children in 1960s Manchester. In addition, there was room for Ted Bundy, the American college campus rapist and killer who took at least 35 female lives in the 1970s. Plus, Griffiths paid tribute to Dennis Nilsen, the civil servant from north London who picked up 15 destitute young men, murdered them and deposited their remains down his drain.

Griffiths' Myspace page also mentioned less well-known killers such as the Sunday Morning Slasher, Carl Eugene Watts, who murdered an estimated 100 women in the United States over an eight-year period in the 1970s and 1980s. Albert Fish, nicknamed the Brooklyn Vampire for a campaign of rape, torture and murder in 19th-century New York, was also given a few lines. One of the most gruesome monsters profiled was Jeffrey Dahmer, the Milwaukee Cannibal, who raped, tortured, murdered and dismembered 17 young men between 1978 and 1991. His appalling record included necrophilia and, as his nickname suggests, cannibalism.

Also cited were references to the Columbine High School massacre in Colorado, USA in 1999, when two pupils killed 12 classmates and a teacher in a shooting spree. Griffiths also posted photographs of Michael Ryan, the gunman who shot 16 people dead in Hungerford, Berkshire in 1987. A caption read: 'Mass Murder: All in 1 Go-Go.' The hellish web gallery was accompanied by 'Order of Death', a track by the post-punk band Public Image Limited, the theme of which was a fatal stabbing. Griffiths had written next to the gallery: 'Most of my heroes don't appear on no stamps.'

Another feature of Griffiths' Myspace page was an appraisal of his preferred reading material. He described it as 'professional-academic literature' on 'aggregate homicide', 'multiple homicide, capital punishment and targeted political homicide'. They were all quasi-academic tomes about crime and criminology, all relevant to his university course. Many of these books had been bought on the shopping website Amazon, where, as well as buying, he wrote reviews of books he had read and messaged other users. He had compiled a 25-book 'wish list' featuring the titles he most wanted to read. They included *Goodbye Lizzie Borden: The Story of the Trial of America's Most Famous Murderess*. Borden was famously suspected, but acquitted, of her parents' axe murder in 19th-century America. A mind-bogglingly obscure study in crime, *Patterns of Vengeance: Crosscultural Homicide in the North American Fur Trade*, was another of Griffiths' purchases. He also wanted to read the *International Murderer's Who's Who*. In his critiques, he gave five stars to a history of female criminals, *Women and the Noose*, and rubbished a previous reviewer as a 'complete imbecile'.

Under the category of 'My films', he listed mainstream horrors such as *Psycho* and cult classics including *A Clockwork Orange*, *The Texas Chainsaw Massacre* and *Reservoir Dogs*, but also advertised his taste for slasher movies. He liked *Ravenous*, a black comedy about cannibalism in the Wild West, and *The Evil Dead* and *Evil Dead II*, which feature the familiar format of teenagers being picked off in the woods. There was *The Killer Next Door*, which tells the story of a female criminology student who suspects the eccentric artist next door is a serial killer, and the crime drama *Before the Devil Knows You're Dead*. Other cinematic choice cuts favoured by Griffiths included *Scarface*, *The Blair Witch Project* and *The Killers*.

A page detailing Griffiths' DVD collection, meanwhile, included an eight-disc set entitled *Notorious Killers* and a single disc of *Britain's Bloodiest Serial Killers*. Also on show were pen portraits of a hotchpotch of historical villains including Wild West outlaw Billy the Kid and bank robbers Bonnie and Clyde, together with Reinhard Heydrich, the Nazi SS 'Butcher of Prague' and a picture of Osama Bin Laden.

Elsewhere, he detailed the punk and indie nightclubs and bars he frequented, and highlighted his favourite bands: The Sisters of Mercy, Nirvana, Pearl Jam, Stone Temple Pilots, Queen and Duran Duran. Finally, his group memberships included a number of eccentric societies calling for Yorkshire's independence from the rest of Britain.

As 'Ven Pariah', he classed himself as a postgraduate 'university researcher' who was six feet tall, 'single' and 'straight'. He was 'athletic' and born under the star sign of Capricorn and he recorded his religion as 'agnostic'. He added:

> 'Physically, I take care of my body and face, especially the latter, which refuses to look any older than a 25-year-old's (maybe I have a "Dorian Gray" portrait hidden away). My occupation involves homicide research which demands a lot of discipline and emotional detachment. Hardly laugh a minute work either. Hence it's important for me to relax/unwind at other times... Although I'm an extremely tough, assertive individual, I'm not the overbearing type.'

Griffiths hoped to meet a woman aged between 28 and 39 who was 'serious and disciplined' but 'not afraid to let her hair down'.

Griffiths posted on Myspace pictures of two bows, together with the caption 'Crossbow is Family'. There were two pictures of himself: one the old black and white studio shot of him in pretty-boy days with slicked back hair. The other was a much more recent one, showing him bare-chested. His heavy drinking and drug abuse had taken their toll. He was overweight, pot-bellied and with sagging pectoral muscles that resembled a woman's breasts. The picture was a low-resolution shot, taken in dim light inside his flat. The glare of a weak bulb reflected off his sweaty upper body. His hair was short and thinning on top, and the skin underneath his chin hung loose like a turkey neck. His eyes were small and piggy, and his mouth was tight and straight. He had taken this picture himself. In it, he oozed menace. He captioned the shot 'Twisted Adonis'.

Next to the snaps of him was what looked like a biblical excerpt: 'The path of the righteous man is beset on all sides.' In fact it was a truncated version of a quote from Quentin Tarantino's cult movie of 1994 *Pulp Fiction*. The film features Samuel L. Jackson as an eccentric underworld enforcer named Jules Winnfield, who delivers a sermon each time he puts to death a cornered rival.

The text was in fact based on a Biblical passage from the Book of Ezekiel, Chapter 25, Verse 17, which describes the Lord inflicting his terrible wrath on the Philistines: 'And I will execute great vengeance on them with furious rebukes; and they shall know that I am the LORD, when I shall lay my vengeance on them.' Did Griffiths believe he was on some divine mission?

All in all, the website was a dramatic statement about the occupant of Flat 33 Holmfield Court. He certainly looked like Stephen Griffiths, the eccentric, lizard-loving loner who could be quite nice but failed in everything he did. But, in fact, it was 'Ven Pariah', strong, charismatic, successful. And dangerous. What it really meant was that by early 2009, Griffiths' personality disorder was deteriorating. The 'sadistic schizoid psychopath' in him, diagnosed two decades earlier, was taking over. A diet of books, magazines and films dedicated to gore had fed the monster within him until it was all-powerful. In his typically narcissistic way, Griffiths was telegraphing the change through his social networking site, but there were more worrying signs too in his everyday behaviour. At Holmfield Court, staff now regarded him as 'unstable' and 'potentially violent'. One of the previous duty managers had demanded his office be fitted with a panic button because of his threats, and the current caretaker, Peter Gee, had been warned never to take issue with him whatever he did, and never to visit his flat alone.

On 20 January 2009, Griffiths was given a conditional discharge by Wakefield magistrates for harassing Kathy Hancock. The bench imposed a restraining order, but over the following months, he breached it repeatedly. His final infringement was the menacing, cackling message he left on her voicemail in June. At about the same time, he left similar threats in messages for Pauline Bond. 'People have no idea what I am capable of,' he said.

One of his web ramblings at the time announced that, as Ven Pariah, he was the 'misanthrope who brought hate into heaven' and 'pseudo human at best – a demon at worst'. His expressions mirrored those in the handwritten poem found nearly three decades earlier in Peter Sutcliffe's lorry.

CHAPTER 6
Susan

The colour had started to return to Susan Rushworth's cheeks. She was still thin-faced, but her family noticed that the grey pallor from eight years of heroin abuse was giving way to a healthy flush. Susan's mother Christine Thompson had given her £3,000 to fund a course of treatment at the Bridge, a rehabilitation clinic in Bradford city centre. She had also taken Susan, 43, a mother of three and a grandmother, back to live at her semidetached house in Thornton, the Pennine village that was the birthplace of the Brontë sisters. For six weeks she was clean of drugs and had given up her other dangerous habit: prostitution.

Susan helped her 72-year-old mother to care for her sick father Barrie. Christine and Barrie had been devastated by her descent into drugs and vice, and were delighted to see her fighting back at last. Susan was getting along famously with her two older children, James and Kirsty, and she was even well enough to see her youngest child, nine-year-old Aaron, regularly for the first time in months. Next year, they had decided, they would take a holiday together and Susan had been

71

busy buying clothes for herself and for the children. 'She was beginning to get the flesh back on her face,' Mrs Thompson said. 'She was a lovely girl. She hated what she had done to us by getting into the drugs but she still cared for us.'

On Monday 22 June 2009, however, Susan vanished. There was to be no holiday in the sun and her fight back would come to an abrupt end. Baffled and heartbroken, her family called the police and a search was launched, but nothing was heard from Susan again. She spent the Sunday night before her disappearance with her parents in Thornton, which lies on Bradford's western fringes. It had been Father's Day and the family rallied round for Barrie, who was suffering from dementia. But on the Monday at about 11.30am, she took a single-decker bus from the nearest stop, on Thornton Road opposite the New Tyke pub, towards Bradford. She was supposed to go to a chemist in City Road to pick up her methadone prescription. Instead, she got off the bus early, just three miles away, and about 30 minutes later she visited her rented bedsit at 10 Oak Villas, a converted Edwardian mansion in a quiet side road in Manningham. She spoke to some friends who thought she appeared fine. Then, dressed in a green zip-up fleece, blue jeans and white trainers, she walked out of the house, turned right, right again, and headed for a cut-through between some flats to the main road. Her final rendezvous, with a friend, was to be at the gates of Lister Park, one of the beautiful open spaces from Bradford's Victorian heyday. She never turned up.

Her family never heard from her again. Her mobile telephone was never used again and her bank account remained untouched. Alarm bells rang immediately because she had never gone missing before. Some working girls were in the habit of moving around, looking for different patches. But not Susan. She had slipped into the lifestyle through a series of personal disasters and could never be described as a hardened professional. She never lost touch with her family for long, and the new hope she had found gave her all the more reason to stay. Susan was also an epileptic and had no medication with her when she left. It was another thing Susan would not have done. By Tuesday 23 June, it was clear that something was seriously wrong.

Just over a week after Susan's disappearance, the police issued a media appeal for information about her. It included her description and some detail about her last movements but very little about her lifestyle, perhaps because it was feared that the mention of drugs and prostitution might dampen public sympathy. Officers blitzed Oak Villas and the surrounding area, questioning neighbours and passers-by in a trawl for new clues. At this stage, the level of concern was expressed in fairly muted terms. Two weeks later, though, detectives were speaking much more gravely of her prospects. By this time, the case had been assigned to West Yorkshire Police's Homicide and Major Enquiry Team. Detective Superintendent Dave Pervin revealed that Susan was a heroin addict and a 'street sex worker' who had spent the previous Saturday with a regular male 'friend' at a hotel in Ilkley. The man was not a suspect, and officers were working on the theory that her drug addiction was behind her disappearance. One theory was that she had fallen foul of a rogue batch of heroin that had killed a number of other addicts. In the week following Susan's vanishing, four men died within as many days after taking the drug. The police arrested three men on suspicion of supplying the contaminated drug and warned users to take greater care than usual over what they bought. Detective Superintendent Pervin commented: 'I fear she has come to some harm. I fear the worst because of the lifestyle she has led and the time since she was last seen, and because it is out of character for her not to be in contact with her family.'

One month on, the police offered a more optimistic assessment. Officers had four unconfirmed sightings to check out and were beginning new searches, including of the railways around Canal Road, not far from Oak Villas, and Bradford Beck, the stream over which the city had been founded. They had already dredged Lister Park's lake. They were willing to discuss the possibility, however remote, that Susan had 'gone underground' or had collapsed in an epileptic fit and was being cared for by an unknown friend. Detective Chief Inspector Jon Hoyle said: 'We have got to be hopeful that she is still alive.' An old friend of Susan's captured the fearful mood in a heartfelt message on the *Bradford Telegraph & Argus* newspaper website:

'I PRAY TO GOD THAT YOUR FOUND SAFE AND WELL SUE I HAVE KNOWN YOU SINCE YOU WERE SMALL AND SUCH A LOVELY GIRL. SUCH A SHAME YOU CHOSE THE LIFE YOU DID SUE AND CHANGED YOUR LIFE FOR THE WORST.'

But September 2009 arrived without a significant lead. Three months to the day after Susan went missing, Detective Superintendent Pervin renewed the appeal, pointing out ominously: 'We are obviously concerned about her and with every day that there is no news, we become increasingly so.' As Christmas loomed, so did her 44th birthday on New Year's Eve. This time, the police went even further in a bid to wring information out of the public. They arranged for her two eldest children, James (24) and Kirsty (21), to address a press conference. Typically, the pleas of a distraught relative, accompanied by photographs and film, will generate the most sympathy and jog the most memories. This was the big one. Kirsty, who had serious problems of her own, gathered herself together to describe how the family could not bear to be without Susan for Christmas and her birthday. Without heroin, she said, her mother was 'just a normal person and a lovely, caring mother who left us wanting for nothing'. James begged: 'We ask anyone who can put an end to our misery to come forward.' Yet no one did.

Susan Rushworth was born Susan Carol Thompson on the last day of 1965. Her parents, Barrie – a French polisher at a furniture warehouse – and Christine, already had two children: Jane, four, and Paul, one. The couple had been married a little over four years and Susan was to be their last child. The family lived first in Manningham but were aspirational, and, with Barrie's trade and Christine helping out by taking cleaning jobs, they were able to move to 5 Thorpe Avenue, in the village of Thornton.

Thornton is not only part of Bradford for administrative purposes, it is also the gateway to Brontë country. The literary sisters Charlotte, Emily and Anne, together with their artist brother Branwell, were born in the village in the early 1800s, when their father Patrick was parson of the village church. Although the Thompsons lived on the Bradford side of the village, their little cul-de-sac was a stone's throw from some breathtaking views across the surrounding countryside. Behind the little knot of houses where they lived was a valley that ran down to a little beck. There was a pleasant walk down the side of the valley, then a stunning view to where the beck ran under Thornton viaduct. In the cold months, the mists gave the high ground an eerie beauty, and in the spring and summer it was alive with birdsong. Susan's brother Paul Thompson said: 'She always kept close to me as a child. The age difference was only 16 months between us. We had a nice childhood – brought up in open air really. We played out more than we stayed in. We were both at the same school together from growing up, from being children.' Susan thrived in the village environment and got a place at Thornton Grammar School. She did well, but not well enough to go on to further education, and she left, aged 16, in 1982.

At the age of 17, Susan suffered a brain haemorrhage which came close to killing her. In the event, she lost her power of speech and the use of her right arm. She had to learn both abilities all over again. She was also left with epilepsy and was doomed to spend the rest of her life on medication. As well as the fits, she suffered a raft of minor but nagging health worries. But she was a battler and, to the delight of her family, adapted quickly and never moaned.

Barely a year after the haemorrhage, in October 1984, she found happiness, marrying David Rushworth, a 24-year-old Thornton postman. They married in St James's, the village's Victorian church. It is very much part of the Brontë story, since Patrick Brontë, the head of the family, had been parson in the chapel that the Victorian building replaced. Susan and David bought a grey stone terraced cottage on Thornton Road and Susan gave birth to James a year later, followed by Kirsty in November 1988. 'Susan married quite young and she had her children in her early 20s,' Paul said. 'She loved the home life. She loved looking after her children. She was a really, really good mother. She really looked after them well.'

However, in the early 1990s the Rushworths' marriage began to flounder. The couple's split in 1994 left Susan lonely and vulnerable, and she became an easy target for unsavoury people. Sibling Paul said:

> 'When she divorced, she fell in with like the wrong crowd. She were taken in by people easily. She were quite easily led. She were too trusting with some people and I

think that's how she got tied up in the old drugs scene. Somebody told her to try something, it would be good for her, maybe take her mind off the way she felt with her epilepsy and the other problems she had, but that was her downfall.'

In 1998, Susan moved into 2 Lapwing Close on the Bell Dean estate with a new boyfriend, Christopher Watson. The sprawling warren of streets is less than a mile from her mother's safe, comfortable semi in Thornton, but the social geography is a world away. The jobless and their families live on housing benefit and income support. Many of the young mothers are unmarried and, according to locals, the estate is riddled with drugs. During the five years when she lived on Lapwing Close, Susan had a third child, Aaron, to Watson, but split from him shortly afterwards. More significantly, by the time she moved out, she had become a regular heroin user. Friends and family blamed her descent on one of her boyfriends, and before long she was working the streets to pay for her habit. Aaron was sent to live with his father. Tragedy followed tragedy, and Kirsty, still in her teens, was sucked in as well, becoming first a heroin addict, then a prostitute. Mother and daughter worked the streets together, selling their bodies for £30 a time, to fund cravings for heroin and crack cocaine. A neighbour at Lapwing Close said: 'We used to find needles in our back garden. At the time we had young children and so it wasn't something you could put up with. She was nice enough but there was another side to her that we saw which wasn't very nice.' Another added:

'They were a nice enough family when they first came. There was Susan, a boyfriend, Kirsty and the baby. I think the older lad used to go over to Thornton where his grandmother lived. Susan was alright, nice like. But you get a lot of druggies round here and you get to recognise the signs. Susan was very thin and the colour had gone from her face. There were needles being left round the gardens and on the close, and there were people coming round to the house all the time. I mean, if someone turns up at the house, stays for a few minutes then disappears, what other reason would they be coming for? First it was Susan, then Kirsty got into it too, and it all went downhill. It was a shame really. It was very sad. Kirsty used to be like any other teenager. Always trying to do her own thing. She didn't want to go to school, shall we say. Then we would see Susan standing round on City Road and at the bottom of Preston Street. Kirsty were there as well, both of them working together.'

There were mixed feelings among the working girls about Susan and Kirsty. Some accused the mother of encouraging her daughter, while others thought she should have done more to stop her. However, she was supported by friends of Kirsty, who describe her as wilful and rebellious. One said:

'Sue was always talking about the kids and the family and about how she wanted to get clean and pack the drugs in. She hated Kirsty doing it, but Kirsty was always really stubborn and wouldn't stop. She wouldn't listen to her. She would try to stop Kirsty doing it. Sue just wanted to have a home to go to. She was flitting between this place and that place, and there was no security. She didn't have a bloke that I know of.'

In the 1980s, the use of hard drugs soared, bringing a new and more dangerous dimension to street prostitution. Surveys regularly show that the vast majority of girls who work the lower end of the market are on drugs such as heroin and crack cocaine. Although the price of drugs has come down, the cost of a habit is still high, and many girls can only hope to fund it through work that provides a steady stream of cash in hand. Bradford street prostitutes can earn up to £300 on a good night. Chronic addicts become locked in a cycle of getting a fix, having a high, coming down, needing another fix, selling their body to get the money, then going out to meet their dealer. They go on the streets to pay for the addiction, but that same addiction stops them from leaving the streets behind.

Susan Rushworth was caught in that spiral. Her mother Christine said: 'She used to say: "Mum, it is an evil drug." But she just couldn't get off it. She was beautiful, happy and very caring. She would talk to anyone. Her problem is that she was too kind and too trusting.'

By 2008, Susan was living in a rented bedsit that put her within easy reach of the pushers and punters. Number 10 Oak Villas was in a quiet, leafy road that had once been the home of Bradford's wealthy middle classes. Many of the Edwardian sandstone villas had been bought by private owners and restored to create dream properties. Prices for a six-bedroom detached house on the road could reach £750,000. But number 10 was something of a halfway house; its residents were generally jobless and penniless. Coincidentally, Oak Villas runs into Oak Avenue, and from Susan's top-floor flat it was just possible to see, 200 yards away, the ground-floor flat where, three decades ago, Patricia Atkinson had been beaten and gored to death by her murderous punter Peter Sutcliffe. The same road was also a previous address for Stephen Griffiths.

The Lumb Lane that Patricia and Yvonne Pearson knew was no more. Residents gradually got fed up of seeing the girls and their punters hanging around on 'The Lane' and feeders like Bertram Road, Church Street and St Paul's Road. As recently as 1990, there were 1,361 arrests for soliciting in Manningham and a hardcore of 30 street women touted for custom around The Lane. But change had to come, and the unlikely impetus was an ITV drama series, *Band of Gold*. Screened from 1995, the programme told the story of a group of girls working around The Lane and the trials and tribulations they endured. It was gritty and widely acclaimed, pulling in up to 14 million viewers. But it also gave The Lane a fame of its own. Within months of the first episode, both the police and Manningham's residents were blaming the series for a rise in prostitution. They claimed that more girls – many of them very young – were being lured in, together with punters from as far afield as Edinburgh, Cornwall and Germany. In one unsavoury episode, a little girl found a used condom on the pavement and, thinking it was a balloon, tried to blow it up. Whether or not *Band of Gold* could be blamed, the locals set up a pressure group, Manningham Residents Against Prostitution, to push for a crackdown.

Vigilantes and troublemakers infiltrated the movement and violence flared on a number of occasions. Once, a 14-year-old prostitute suffered a fractured skull when she was run over. A few days later a café used by the girls was fire-bombed. Luckily, nobody was injured. Legal measures had also been taken to tackle Manningham vice. In 1993, the authorities had pumped £143,000 into the Urban Crime Fund Ace Project, a counselling service for sex workers. Shortly after the 1995 disturbances, they followed it up with the £700,000 Streets and Lanes Project, aimed at steering teenage runaways away from prostitution. All these factors, together with strict policing by the vice squad, meant that by the time Susan Rushworth found herself on the streets, the red light areas of the city had shifted south, away from Manningham's residential areas. As the first decade of the new millennium drew to a close, the red light zone was centred on the commercial areas of City Road, Sunbridge Road, Rebecca Street and Thornton Road. At night, the streets were pretty much deserted and there were plenty of places for girls to turn a trick: entrances to derelict buildings, gateways, loading bays, back alleys and scrubby waste ground were there in abundance. But, by moving further away from the community, the girls had left behind the eyes and ears that gave them some protection.

Susan's family had not given up hope, despite the passing of time since her disappearance in June 2009. In the opening months of 2010, her father Barrie was becoming increasingly ill and, because of his dementia, did not always grasp what had happened to his youngest daughter. He would sometimes ask Christine, now having to care for him without Susan's help, why she was crying. 'I had to try and tell him that Sue wasn't coming back,' she recalled. Kirsty, who had tried to stay clean since her mother's disappearance, told how she had stayed strong for her brother James and half-brother Aaron. 'I was just being there for the rest of my family and my little brother especially, because he was only nine at the time. I just had to be strong for everyone else.' But they were confronting the reality that their daughter, mother and sister would not come back. They suspected that, after suffering an epileptic fit two weeks before she disappeared, Susan had become depressed and had sought out heroin to take her mind off it.

March brought another major initiative. Susan's case was featured on BBC One's appeal show *Missing Live*, broadcast every morning to millions of viewers. Previous series had managed to reunite up to 17 missing people with their families, so highlighting Susan's disappearance on the show was a major coup for the family. Paul and James sat in the studio with presenter Louise Minchin while Susan's life, good times and bad, were reconstructed for the viewers. It was the biggest platform for the appeal so far, and it revealed in dramatic terms how the mother of three really had suffered so badly. It showed photographs of her and Paul as children, side by side, with pink gleaming faces and matching school ties. It showed her with a trendy 'big hairdo' from the 1980s, and at her wedding, looking full-faced and pretty in a white veil. Susan was seen lying in a maternity bed with James in her arms, and, later, holding him as a bright-eyed toddler with Postman Pat pyjamas. It showed her elegant in white on holiday with her mother Christine, and with James and Kirsty on a day out. The show also pictured her ashen-faced and haggard in the police mugshot that was circulated when she vanished. Minchin pointed out the stark deterioration in her health. It spelled out how untypical her story was. She was not a partying teenager who did drugs for fun and got hooked. This was a housewife and mother who led a sheltered and family-orientated life.

James was filmed in his grandmother's house and outside the pretty little cottage in Thornton where he spent the first 12 years of his life. 'We had a nice family home,' he said. 'It were a nice village. She were very popular round here, was my mum.' He added: 'My mum were brilliant. I could talk to her about anything. She were a good mum. We always had everything. We never went without. She were fun – outgoing. She were brilliant.' Attempting to fight back tears, he continued: 'Her drugs problem came in her older life. She only started taking them when she were 35. She had money in the bank... everything... and it all just went. We had a lovely house and it all went. By this stage I'd moved out so I didn't really know about the drugs until she got too far into it.'

Susan's brother Paul, who last saw her on the Thursday before she vanished, was filmed in City Road, as he told of his heartache at her descent into prostitution. 'It is an area where my sister used to – I suppose – look for business. It were just so embarrassing to see her and upsetting to see her and see how she'd fallen.' The programme also featured a reconstruction with a painfully thin, hunched actress walking around the red light zone, in clothes matching Susan's green hoodie and jeans. 'All the family wanted to help and did what they could for her,' Paul said. 'But the help she wanted was just more money for more drugs. She just didn't care about anybody apart from herself and the drugs. That's all she wanted – money for drugs.' But he described how, after taking the rehabilitation course, she cut her drug intake and took methadone instead. 'I think she was trying to put her life back together,' he said. 'She realised she had come to the end and she needed to do something to get her life back on track. It seemed like she had a bit more purpose in life. I felt for her. I felt: "I hope she can do it. I hope she can do it."' James also welcomed the changes: 'It were like having me normal mum back.'

Nonetheless, *Missing Live* also emphasised that the nine-month hunt for Susan had so far thrown up no real leads at all. 'I've walked through the city centre,' said Paul, 'and even thought I've seen her from the back myself, and when you get up close it's not her. It's just an awful sinking feeling in your stomach.'

Detective Superintendent Dave Pervin was shown describing the searches that his team had made. He stood with James in an incident room and pointed at a map on the wall that had two large sections of cross-hatching. The shading represented the areas where door-to-door inquiries had been made, but, despite every house being searched, it yielded no results. He also told Susan's son that, despite scrutinising every piece of footage available from CCTV cameras operated by Bradford Council, bus companies and private firms, they had found nothing: 'We have had detectives sifting hours and hours and hours of CCTV and we don't get a single image of your mum on any of those. It really is a mystery as to where she might have gone.'

Pervin addressed the cameras anxiously and with carefully-chosen words:

'My experience in these sorts of cases is that normally by this time, someone would have turned up. Not the case here, which gives [the] family hope and there's always a chance that she is out there somewhere. And that maybe she doesn't want her family to know that. But if that is the case, then somebody knows that, and somebody will have been in contact with her, and someone will have seen the photos of her that we've put out.'

One person who seemed interested in the riddle was Stephen Griffiths. Griffiths had lived in Oak Villas, Susan's last address, during his early years in Bradford, and had spent the small hours padding around the black maze of streets and alleys where Susan worked. When James and Kirsty made their appeal at Christmas in a local newspaper, one of Griffiths' friends pointed it out to him, and remarked that it was odd that a body had not been found. A smirking Griffiths began to enthuse about the many ways in which it was possible to get rid of a body. On another occasion, he asked one of the working girls, Lisa Thompson, who had gone to school with Susan, if her family were 'upset' about her disappearance. Yet there would be no further news about what had become of Susan until the end of May 2010.

CHAPTER 7
Shelley

At 10.09pm on Monday 26 April 2010, Shelley Armitage strolled into view of a CCTV camera in Sunbridge Road. With her back to the lens, she took nine paces forward. Then she stopped, turned, cocked her head to get a better view down the street around a line of parked cars, hesitated for a second, then walked back towards the camera. She swayed a little to the left, then playfully grabbed an end of her cardigan belt in each hand and, pulling it taut behind her, sashayed along the pavement and disappeared from view. After her 15-second cameo, captured in the surveillance camera's eerie monochrome, Shelley, just like Susan Rushworth 10 months previously, vanished into the bleak emptiness of Bradford's red light area.

Shelley had been her usual high-spirited self. She was dressed smartly, in tight-fitting dark blue jeans and a white vest top visible beneath her long, grey, waist-tied cardigan. She had also kept her looks, wearing her dark brown hair long at the back and parted at the side so the fringe hung diagonally across her forehead. Her skin was clear, and her pretty eyes and nose were framed by fine cheekbones. But nevertheless, aged 31, Shelley's life was in a mess. She was a drug addict and alcoholic, and she was funding her addictions by charging men for sex.

Sunbridge Road lies at the centre of Bradford's modern-day red light district, and late on that Monday night in April, Shelley was there, eyeballing the oncoming motorists, to look for business. Two days later, when she failed to appear at home in Bentcliffe Walk, Allerton, her boyfriend, Craig Preston, became worried and called the police.

In the week she disappeared, she was due before the city magistrates charged with using threatening words and behaviour. She was also awaiting sentence at the Crown court for the more serious charges of assaulting a police officer and possessing a knife. Shelley's fortunes echoed those of Yvonne Pearson, the Ripper victim who vanished back in January 1978 while facing a tough sentence for soliciting. They were both facing the stern judgment of the courts and there was perhaps good reason to leave Bradford behind for a while. Indeed, a few years earlier, Shelley had done just that, taking off to live in Huddersfield for a few months, and working its red light district instead. But this time it was different. She wanted to be at home with Craig, her childhood sweetheart, and she had just bought a puppy, which she doted on. Shelley had many friends and had told some that she planned to try for a baby.

With those relatively bright prospects, she left home on 26 April at about 7pm. She met up with a friend and went for a bite to eat at a café on City Road. Afterwards, Shelley Armitage headed for the kerbs and corners of Sunbridge Road, but, barring that one CCTV appearance, she was never seen by her friends again.

The first public appeal for Shelley's whereabouts was issued a week later. Officers were mindful of the ominous similarity between Susan's disappearance and Shelley's: both were prostitutes working the same streets and had vanished in quick succession. But they kept the inquiries separate and Shelley's case was treated as a stand-alone missing persons investigation.

Hundreds of posters bearing her photograph were dotted around the city. Detectives also interviewed her family, friends, potential witnesses and the other street girls. They searched derelict buildings, yards, storage containers and lock-ups. They also made inquiries over in Huddersfield, chasing up associates from Shelley's brief stay there.

Officers circulated a description of Shelley and, a few days later, released the haunting CCTV footage of her. The publicity generated more leads, but none led anywhere. Shelley's mobile remained unused, she failed to claim her benefits and she did not turn up for the Crown court sentencing date. Detective Superintendent Sukhbir Singh, of the Homicide and Major Enquiry Team, said:

'We have been continuing investigations in the Bradford area and have uncovered useful lines of inquiry regarding what may have happened to Shelley, which we are now actively investigating. She is still missing and we still remain very concerned about her. It is very out of character for Shelley to disappear like this, and her friends, partner and family are extremely worried.'

By 18 May, as many as 30 officers were directly involved in the search for Shelley Armitage and many others were employed on the fringes. The police had received reported sightings of her, but admitted that they could not 'firm them up'. Sukhbir Singh stood in the spot on Sunbridge Road, close to a mosque, where Shelley's image was captured on camera. Once again, he urged those with information to come forward. 'I would emphasise,' he said, 'this is still a missing from home inquiry. There's no information that has come into the inquiry three weeks into it to suggest she has come to any harm as a result of being a sex worker, or in any way linked to her being a sex worker.'

Shelley Marie Armitage was born on 22 September 1978 in the maternity unit of Bradford Royal Infirmary. She was the oldest child of Daryl Armitage, a machine operator, and Gill, his wife of a few months. Younger siblings Gemma and Carl would follow later, but initially it was just the three of them living in a council flat in Owlet Road, in the Windhill area of Shipley. Owlet Road was a long sloping rat-run used by drivers trying to escape the traffic on the major roads out of Shipley. At the bottom of the hill was a cemetery, the haunt of vandals, drug-takers and underage drinkers, and the road cut through a sprawl of 1960s pebble-dashed council properties.

As the family grew, the Armitages moved to a bigger house in Rowantree Avenue, a three-bedroom semi further east. They were strict Roman Catholics and the young Shelley attended St Joseph's Catholic College, a traditional all-girls' school in Cunliffe Road, Manningham, the next parallel road along from Oak Avenue off the main Keighley Road. The school boasts an impressive academic record, and one of its alumni is Kathryn Apanowicz, a soap actress (notably in *EastEnders*) and partner of the late television presenter Richard Whiteley.

Shelley is remembered more for her looks and personality than for her scholarly prowess. Friends speak fondly of a big-hearted, gregarious girl who was 'always at the centre of things'. She loved music and make-up and nice clothes, and her ambition to become a model was not at all far-fetched.

One classmate who remembered Shelley, Sharon Osoba, said: 'I just know that she was drop-dead gorgeous. She was the one who caught everybody's eye. She was dressed just right and everything. She had a load of mates and if anything was going on, then Shelley would always be at the centre of it.' Lynsey Barron, one of Shelley's closest school friends, used to have stopovers with her, when, in the privacy of their bedrooms, they would talk excitedly about music, fashion and boys. They both wanted to be models and would occasionally catch a train to Huddersfield together, to investigate ways of getting a foot in the door. 'There was potential there and Shelley could have been a beautiful model,' Lynsey said. 'She was caring, friendly and compassionate.'

Another from Shelley's wide circle of friends added: 'She was a lovely-looking young woman with a personality to match. She could have done anything with her life.' Even when Shelley began going out with Craig Preston at the age of 16, she would still find time for her girlfriends. Anna Kennedy, who knew her later on, said: 'Shelley had a heart of gold and a beautiful smile. She would do anything for anyone.'

After leaving school, Shelley worked briefly in a bank and a hairdressing salon. It was about that time that she began experimenting with drugs. Her parents discovered some of the paraphernalia at their house and confronted her about it, but, despite the evidence, she flatly denied being a user. They spent their savings on rehabilitation courses for her, but she never completed them. Daryl Armitage said: 'When she was young, she was never a problem, but when she left school at 16 she got in with the wrong crowd at the wrong time. By the time we realised something was wrong, she was already hooked on drugs.'

Lynsey Barron said she began taking drugs at the same time as Shelley but managed to escape by moving from Bradford to Leeds. Shelley's habit got worse and she was unable to fund it in any way other than prostitution. 'We both started drugs but Shelley never managed to get out of that spiral. We used to see Shelley on the beat now and again. She is not that sort of girl and we had plans to travel. She didn't have a bad upbringing.' Daryl Armitage added: 'Everybody said they never imagined Shelley doing what she was doing. No one could understand why she worked on the street, but it was all down to drugs.'

Sheila Wilson, who runs a meal club for the girls and the homeless at a Christian mission in Sunbridge Road, commented:

'These girls just drift in and out, and Shelley had been coming in and out for about three years. She was lovely and would always come and give us a hug. She used to ask after my husband if he wasn't here. She had lovely long hair. She was just a really nice girl. But, like a lot of the girls, although she had up times, she had down times as well.'

On the streets, Shelley's big heart was combined with a toughness that worked to everyone's advantage. She could hold her own with any of the sharks out there, and she used her strength of character to protect her friends. One said:

'Shelley was very outgoing, a very chatty, bubbly sort of person. Anything she could do to help you, she would. She was quite tough and if you were having problems with one of the other girls, she would stick up for you. Say, like if you were having problems with a punter or someone had taken your money or something, she would speak up for you.'

After Bradford's prostitutes were forced out of Lumb Lane in the mid-1990s, they touted for business around a network of streets to the north-west of the city centre. The main arteries – City Road, Sunbridge Road, Rebecca Street and Thornton Road – and some of the intersecting streets such as Preston Street and Wigan Street are purposely broad enough to accommodate heavy goods vehicles. The pavements are also wide, and the overall effect is a landscape which is bleak and empty.

At the time Susan and Shelley went missing, the legitimate traders were businesses using low-rent, high-availability commercial land. Hence, kitchen and bathroom showrooms, second-hand furniture stores, storage depots and tyre and exhaust workshops had found homes among the Victorian sandstone mills and newer concrete sheds. There were plenty of medium-sized offices, some apartment blocks, a few pubs, a snooker hall, a corporate gym and a laser combat centre. But what was striking in a property-obsessed age was the amount of derelict land and the number of ramshackle buildings so close to a city centre.

In neighbouring Leeds or Manchester, developers had reclaimed virtually every scrap of spare land and period property within a few miles of the central area. In Bradford, many of the edifices from its industrial heyday were now boarded-up shells. The cobbled entrances to their courtyards had become paths to a gloomy, isolated prison, enclosed on four sides. Litter and stone rubble piled up in corners, and weeds and shrubs reached out from cracks between the paving and the brickwork. There were scrubby patches of waste ground and any number of unkempt side roads, back alleys and gateways. Some had been closed off for years by iron gates held together with rusty chains and padlocks. And, of course, soiled condoms and used hypodermic syringes, the tell-tale signs of drugs and prostitution, were dotted over the ground.

During the hours of daylight, the red light area was drab but unthreatening. Cars and vans trundled between business meetings and deliveries, and staff and customers wandered about on foot. But after nightfall, it became a dark, brooding netherworld. The alleys and gateways turned into black holes, hiding who-knows-what kind of menace, and the derelict courtyards – bad enough in daylight – became the stuff of gothic horror.

All was pitch black and silent. Only the navy blue sky, set against the darker walls, served as a reminder that the yards were closed in on all sides. The main arteries were badly lit and deserted. The only people out and about would be sex workers, standing in ones and twos on the street corners, or the odd bobby on patrol. The only vehicles would be on their way elsewhere, pimps dropping off girls, or kerb crawlers looking for sex. Few people lingered after dark for lawful reasons.

Poet and author Joolz Denby, who acts as a cultural ambassador for Bradford, said:

'When night-time comes on Sunbridge Road it is strangely empty of anything, given it is so close to the centre of town. It has this strangely empty, echoey, dark quality. There doesn't seem to be enough street lights, or seem to be anybody about. I'm sure there are, but it doesn't seem that way. There are a lot of small businesses there, so during the day there are a lot of vans and customers going in and out. But in the evening you are left with this long, straight stretch which isquite dark and there are all these alleys which you wouldn't know about. The girls come down through there. It is a lonely place.'

Some of the boarded-up premises were said to house cannabis

factories and crack dens, but Try Mills, located off Thornton Road, witnessed something worse. Waheed Akhtar, a drugs baron dubbed 'The Colonel' discovered that heroin worth £250,000 had been stolen from a car parked outside his home in east Bradford. Suspicion fell immediately on three of his associates. Akhtar kidnapped all three and held them captive in one of the disused mill's storerooms. There, they were beaten, whipped and tortured while Akhtar and a specially-recruited team of thugs interrogated them. One victim, Naveed Younis, was suspended with a noose around his neck as he was battered. He suffered more than 20 injuries, including a stab wound to his chest. Another, Daniel Francis, had a gun pointed to his head by one of the inquisitors. Akhtar's man pulled the trigger, leaving the terrified Francis thinking he was about to die. The weapon was empty and just clicked harmlessly. Francis still had all four limbs and both hands smashed, though, and his jaw was broken and he suffered kidney failure. He survived, but was in a coma for two weeks and in hospital for four. Akhtar, who had masterminded a heroin distribution network linking Bradford, London, Manchester and parts of Lancashire, was jailed for 25 years in 2003.

Bradford's vice squad, part of the city's south division, had tried with some success to clean up the area. As well as the regular blitzes on kerb crawlers, the police have used some quite innovative methods to tackle street prostitution. In 2008, officers set up automatic number plate recognition camera checks to monitor vehicles around Sunbridge Road and Rebecca Street. The system uses high-tech cameras to read and photograph the number plate of every car and van driving past. It boasts pinpoint accuracy, and is able to trace the vehicle owners quickly. All suspects were sent written warnings or 'acceptable behaviour contracts' (ABCs) through the post, and in the first 10 months of the year, 188 ABCs were sent out.

Offenders came from as far afield as Derbyshire and Lancashire, and all faced fines if they failed to heed the warning.

Bradford's vice team emphasised their 'always prosecute' policy against kerb crawlers. At the same time, they referred the women to programmes aimed at encouraging them to leave the streets. The Bridge Project, which tried to help Susan Rushworth, was one. Others included the Together Women's Project and Ripple. Detective Superintendent Geoff Dodd, head of the vice squad, said at the time:

'We have made significant progress, but I feel there will always be men prepared to abuse women. We can arrest prostitutes day in and day out, but the more mature and sensible approach is to help them get out of that lifestyle and to stop them getting into it in the first place. We are utterly determined to resolve this problem although there is a huge amount for us to do.'

Once in the grip of drugs and prostitution, few girls break free. Lynsey Barron managed it by moving to another place. Julie Hird, who also knew Shelley, escaped 12 years in Bradford's red light area by going into rehab. Julie had gone off the rails in her late teens, feuding with her family, running away from home, and hanging around, smoking cigarettes and cannabis. She was introduced to heroin at the age of 18 and became addicted. By the age of 19, she was pregnant, but her son and two subsequent children were taken into care. Prostitution became a way of earning money after she split with her boyfriend:

'When we broke up I had no way of support, so I started selling myself on the streets of Bradford. When you come to that point in your life, you don't feel like you're worth anything. People didn't treat me with respect. They used to abuse me. I used them to get what I wanted, but you get treated like dirt.'

Julie went on to say that the heroin was her master and controller. 'You are not living. You are existing. I couldn't get out of bed without a bag of heroin. I couldn't brush my hair without heroin. There was no way I could get a job.'

Shelley had been trying to get off the streets too. In November 2009, she signed up for a residential rehabilitation course in South Wales. The project, run by a Christian charity, Teen Challenge UK, was based in Brynamman, a beautiful spot in the Black Mountains, in the Brecon Beacons Park.

She was certainly in need of help after recent events. After setting up home with Craig Preston, first in Lime Vale Way, south of Clayton, then in Bentcliffe Walk, she found herself in more trouble with the law. In April 2009, Craig, who was five years her senior, had been driving her round Bradford in his Audi saloon. He was nearly three times over the drink drive limit, and his erratic steering caught the attention of a beat bobby. The officer approached the car when it stopped, but the couple began arguing with him and a scuffle broke out, after which they were arrested. The officer suffered scratches to his face and neck.

It was while waiting for her case to be heard that the rehab place came up. She declined because, according to friends, she did not want to be separated from Craig. In March 2010, she pleaded guilty to assault and two counts of possessing a knife and was due to be sentenced on 17 May.

After Shelley failed to show up, her parents, boyfriend and friends scoured the streets looking for clues as to what had become of her. Daryl Armitage said: 'The remarkable thing is that Shelley was so well liked we had half of Bradford looking for her.' Sheila Wilson, meanwhile, remembered her final encounter with Shelley:

'The last time I talked to her was on the Wednesday before she went missing. She came in and we had a long chat, but she was upset. She said she was not well. The last thing I said to her was: "You take care." Not meaning "watch out" but just "watch your health". Little did I know that it would be the last time I would see her.'

The last of Shelley's friends to see her alive was almost certainly Bridget Farrell, who had been looking for business with her on the evening of 26 April. Three days later, Bridget was passing Holmfield Court when she bumped into her old friend Stephen Griffiths. She told him that her friend was missing and asked if he had seen her. He replied: 'Don't worry babe. She'll be okay.'

CHAPTER 8

Suzanne

L ate May 2010, and Sunbridge Road was its usual desolate self. Susan Rushworth had been missing for 11 months; Shelley Armitage for four weeks. The police had no idea what had happened to them, and they warned the working girls it was not safe on the streets. Most of the girls believed that their two friends were dead, but the craving for heroin and crack spoke louder than the police officers' advice. If they did not work, they did not score. It was as simple as that.

In the small hours of Saturday 22 May, just a few girls were out, dotted along the strip of Sunbridge Road and City Road like phantoms in the night. Suzanne Blamires was one. She was an alcoholic as well as a drug addict, and often carried a plastic bottle full of booze as a makeshift hip flask. Her friends said it gave her a bit of Dutch courage against the air of danger surrounding their work. But it meant she was often unsteady on her feet, and occasionally, notwithstanding the cold, she would fall asleep in a factory doorway.

Suzanne used the alias Amber when she worked. It was useful for putting a distance between herself and the hazards of the job. Awkward punters and pimps were less likely to trace her if she was using a 'street name'. It also allowed the girls to form a mental barrier between the work they did and what remained of their family life: a street name was like a new identity you took on when looking for business. Suzanne came from a middle-class home and grew up with ponies and luxury holidays. But by May 2010, aged 36, she was in a bad way. She had been a prostitute for more than 10 years, beaten up by a violent boyfriend who used her to fund both of their drug habits, and named and shamed in the local newspaper for propositioning an undercover police officer. She had been an elfin beauty in her late teens, her black hair cut short, with sparkling eyes and a big smile. Two decades later, she had skinny legs and a bloated face. Her eyes were glassy with dark rings around them, and the hair was bedraggled and pulled back into a pony tail. Her designer outfits had been replaced by leggings and a grubby Nike anorak.

The previous evening, Friday 21 May, Suzanne left home at 7.15pm. She lived at 9 Barkston Walk, just three streets away from Shelley's flat on a council estate in Allerton, out towards Thornton. At 11pm, an old friend, who had returned to Bradford for the weekend after moving away, saw her near the junction of City Road and Sunbridge Road. She reminded her that Shelley and Susan were still missing and begged her to be careful. They hugged and the friend left. Sometime after 2am a young woman named Rosalyn Edmondson saw Suzanne on Sunbridge Road. It was the last sighting of Suzanne Blamires.

The next morning, Suzanne's boyfriend Ifty Hussein became worried when she failed to call him. He checked her flat, but her bed had not been slept in. He went to her mother Nicky's house, a few miles away, but she had not been there. His search went on until late on Saturday evening, when Nicky called him to say that Suzanne had not been in touch. Ifty called the police, and shortly before midnight officers arrived at Mrs Blamires' house in Claremont Avenue, in the Idle district of the city, to gather full details of her movements. Unlike the Rushworth and Armitage families, they would find out all too soon what had become of her.

Norman Blamires was already a successful businessman when his eldest daughter, Suzanne Marguerite, was born on 26 February 1974. He was only 22, but had worked his passage at a van dealership, then gone into business for himself as a scrap metal merchant. Suzanne's mother Maria was born in Burnley, Lancashire, but when still young moved to Bradford with her family. She preferred to be called Nicky, and was soon known by no other name. At the time of Suzanne's birth, Norman and Nicky were not married and lived with their respective families. However, they were committed to each other, and Nicky used her husband's surname rather than her maiden name of Firth. Like Shelley Armitage, who would become her friend and neighbour in later life, Suzanne was born at Bradford Royal Infirmary's maternity unit. She was followed by a sister, also called Marguerite, two years later, and after more than a decade's gap, their younger brother Luke.

After his daughters were born, Norman moved back into car sales. He set up his own successful string of dealerships in Tong, the district in south-east Bradford where he grew up and where he took his own family to live. The girls were raised as strict Roman Catholics, attending St Columba's, a modern red-brick church round the corner from their house, and Suzanne and Marguerite attended the primary school attached to it. The Blamires moved house regularly during the girls' childhood, each house better than the last, as Norman's commercial interests prospered. At one point, he had four different properties. Norman was doing so well, he was able to indulge his passion for racehorses; he bought several, including one he named SueMag after his two daughters. Suzanne and Marguerite were complete 'daddy's girls' according to their family, and both were treated like goddesses by their doting father. Each had ponies, and he would take them out each weekend to stables up on the moors.

Michael Brankin, who married Marguerite in the 1990s, said:

'Norman idolised them and gave them everything they wanted – jewellery, fur coats, lovely homes, and basically spoilt them rotten. He was fairly straight-laced so they were brought up in a very cosseted and protected environment. But both girls had him wrapped round their little finger.'

Suzanne did well at school, once impressing the St Columba's priest so much that he read out an essay she wrote, aged 14, about the dangers of drugs. She argued with passion that people who meddled with drugs were throwing their lives away. The congregation were overwhelmed by the teenager's wisdom. She seemed to have a maturity that belied her youth.

Suzanne loved reading generally, and philosophy in particular. One of her favourite books was Salman Rushdie's *The Satanic Verses*. She excelled in literature at school and, after getting good GCSE grades, she took and passed A-levels in psychology, sociology and English literature. She wanted eventually to be a nurse and worked part time in a care home to get experience. After leaving school, she got a place on a three-year course at a nursing college in Bradford. Pretty, funny, focused and always immaculately dressed, she seemed to be on her way to great things.

But while studying for her nursing qualifications, Suzanne's social life took off and she began going out clubbing, regularly travelling to Leeds for its lively rave scene. In due course she began experimenting with drugs. Her best friend at the time, Rachel McGuiness, said Suzanne was bright, lively and funny, but could not stop herself trying to live life on the edge. 'There were no half measures with Suzanne. So when she started drinking, that was it – she'd go for it. She always wanted to do more, to experiment more, go that little bit further.'

Rachel believed that the drugs were Suzanne's way of breaking free from a very sheltered childhood.

'She started experimenting with pills and cocaine. It was the early 1990s so lots of people were doing it in a social way, but she had quite an addictive personality and I think it gradually took her over. She had a wild streak in her that perhaps was rebelling against her upbringing. Her childhood was very protected, and I think this was her way of breaking free.'

Suzanne began dating Rachel's brother Simon, a trained weaver who had given up the mills to start his own window-cleaning round. Simon was six years older than Suzanne, but still deeply embroiled in the drug-fuelled rave scene. When they married, at Bradford Register Office, in July 1994, Norman – who did not like Simon – refused to attend. He did pay for the reception though, and gave them a house to live in, rent-free, not far away from the family home. Michael Brankin, Suzanne's brother-in-law, commented:

'[Norman] didn't like him [Simon] and although Marguerite and I begged him to go to the wedding he wouldn't go. Simon introduced Suzanne to party drugs such as cocaine and ecstasy and they would party every weekend. It was Suzanne's first serious relationship and maybe she thought it was all new and exciting, or perhaps it was a way to rebel against her dad.'

The couple's hedonistic weekend lifestyle began to encroach on their weekly work routine. Suzanne's college attendance became erratic. She had become addicted to heroin, and eventually the college authorities lost patience and dropped her from the course. To compound matters, her marriage to Simon crumbled because of their addictions and they went their separate ways. It was a sad turn of events for a woman who, as a teenager, had been so opposed to drugs.

Suzanne was so beyond control now that even her doting father would not risk having her around the family. 'Her drug addiction caused quite a rift,' Michael Brankin said. 'Norman was horrified and wouldn't have her in the house. Nicky would try and help Suzanne by giving her money, but this only supported her habit. She would manage to get herself off the drugs, and then would relapse.'

At the end of the 1990s, she began going out with Ifty Hussein, a small-time drug dealer. He introduced her to crack, and it was not long before she took up prostitution to pay for both her habit and his. In September 2001, she was caught in a vice squad purge near the university. She was one of a number of sex workers who had ventured away from Sunbridge, City and Thornton Roads in an attempt to target students. However, the man she propositioned, in Richmond Road, between the university and Bradford College, turned out to be a plain clothes police officer. At the time, Suzanne was aged 27 and living in a council flat near Cleckheaton, in the neighbouring borough of Kirklees, which was miles away from her family. The story made the *Bradford Telegraph & Argus* newspaper. Shortly after the story broke, in December 2001, Norman Blamires died, and Suzanne's life went into freefall. 'I think his death affected both girls very much,' said Michael Brankin.

Life with Ifty Hussein descended into a nasty haze of drugs, prostitution and violence. She would be seen regularly with cuts and bruises, and more than once had to be taken to hospital. 'He got her hooked on crack,' Brankin said, and went on:

'Before then it had only been heroin, and she moved in with him to some grotty council flat. He stopped dealing and started to pimp her out. She was a good-looking, beautiful lass so she was popular and made lots of money to start with but the drugs and the drink ravaged her. They would do drugs together and she was alcoholic too. She would drink 14 cans of super brew a day. The family felt terrible – I don't know how Nicky coped. She was close to both her daughters and she would try and look after them in whatever way she could. She begged Suzanne to leave Ifty, as he beat her up, but she wouldn't leave him. Once, Ifty was jailed for assaulting Nicky, and while he was inside, Suzanne went back to live with the family. As soon as he was released though, she returned to him within a few days.'

Nothing could be done to prise her away from the boyfriend and the seedy lifestyle he dragged her into. Michael Brankin continued:

'Nicky knew her daughter was a prostitute but she even got a job, after Norman died, to give money to Suzanne in an attempt to keep her off the streets. But she could only give her so much and nothing was ever enough as Suzanne's appetite was too great. The only saving grace is that her father died before all this happened and didn't see the hell hole into which she descended.'

Bradford's vice scene is at the roughest end of rough trade. Academic research into prostitution suggests that it is more downmarket than in other cities. While 'street' sex workers account for no more than 15 per cent of prostitutes in the average urban area, in Bradford they make up two-thirds. The street end of the market is more visible than other forms of vice. It is also where the problems of violence, drug dependency and poor health are concentrated. In consequence, the city's red light area is more of a headache for the authorities.

Dr Belinda Brooks-Gordon, author of *The Price of Sex: Prostitution, Policy and Society*, said national studies show that the 'street sector' accounts for between 10 and 15 per cent of a town's sex trade. A streetwalker is no more typical of a prostitute than 'Belle de Jour', the high-class escort whose anonymous internet blog became a runaway success in the early years of the 21st century. Belle de Jour was later identified as American-born research scientist Brooke Magnanti, and her musings inspired *The Secret Diary of a Call Girl*, a successful television drama, which began in 2007 with Billie Piper in the starring role.

Dr Brooks-Gordon said:

'The vast majority of sex work goes on indoors, in women's own homes, at shared flats or walk-up flats, and it's a lot more normal than people think. These women have nothing to gain from raising their head above the parapet and everything to lose. They can lose their families, their premises, their children – everything. We know from some very good studies that this off-street sex work is the most common. That has always been the case. We tend to think that the number of street workers is much higher than it is, because they are in the front line. They are the visible ones and the ones in danger. It's a bit like the Army. The vast majority of people serving are medics, chefs, engineers, or in admin or whatever. They are not in danger. It is only the front-line soldiers who are visible and at risk. But the street sector of sex work is the most vulnerable sector, and that deserving the higher proportion of public sector resources.'

Shortly after Stephen Griffiths' arrest, a survey conducted for West Yorkshire Police Authority revealed that, out of 180 sex workers in Bradford, 107 of them – a mighty 59 per cent – were 'street' and 73 were 'off-street'. All but three of the 180 prostitutes located were women. Of those on the 'front line', 91 per cent were from the white British ethnic group. Of those who worked in massage parlours and houses, only 61 per cent were white British. Eastern Europeans made up 21 per cent of the remaining 39 per cent, with six per cent Asian.

Another discovery was that the street women were older. Only 12 per cent of them were under the age of 24, compared with 33 per cent of those working indoors. The research team concluded: 'Street workers… are generally older, with many working to support drug addictions. Off-street workers are more likely to come from outside the UK, be trafficked and be moved around the country at short intervals.'

The survey suggested that Bradford's red light district was full of girls like Susan, Shelley and Suzanne: local girls who became hopelessly trapped by local drug dealers. Joolz Denby, the city's cultural ambassador, said:

'These girls are desperate. They are not out on the street because they like shagging and blokes. *Pretty Woman* was only a film. They don't like what they are doing. Why is there not more money invested in refuges for street workers, where they can be encouraged to train and get other jobs and get a detox? Because nobody wants to be on their knees in a filthy alley in the pissing rain giving somebody a blow job for a tenner. That's the bottom line. It's gross, it's harsh and it's the truth.'

One of Suzanne's friends, a former working girl who uses the street name Stacy, said they followed parallel paths into prostitution:

'I started about two months before her, but we both got into it through the fellers we were with. We both got into crack through them. The boyfriend used to supply it at first, then they'd get you to go on the streets to pay for it. Each night it varied, obviously, but you could have a good night and make £200. But other times it could only be £50–£60. My habit used to be £100 a day but I started cutting down and ended up on £20 a day after that. I've been on it and off it.'

Stacy, who gave up prostitution a month before Suzanne disappeared and moved to the West Midlands, also said that she had tried to persuade her friend to leave Ifty:

'He used to beat her up if she didn't go home with £100 or more every night. He used to batter her black and blue. If she'd have left him, she would have got off the drugs. She didn't like being on them – she hated them. She only did it to stop her getting a beating every day. I know that she would have got off it because she wanted to be with her family again. He used to bruise her face, her body, everything. She went into hospital twice in the 10 years. He broke her leg once and he knocked her unconscious. She had a bad head injury. He was really nasty. I once dragged him off her in the street. A couple of times I got her away from him but she always went back. Sometimes she'd be crying her eyes out, saying: "He's beaten me up again over money." I had my own flat at one point, and I said to her: "Come and stop with me for a little while." She stayed with me for about two or three weeks and obviously he found out she was living with me and knew where I was living. He come up and said how sorry he was and he'd never do it again and she went back to him. I still stuck by her though, no matter what.'

Suzanne and Stacy hung about the same stretch of Sunbridge Road, waiting for punters. Incredibly, they managed to salvage pleasure from the hopeless treadmill they were on. They shopped together, watched films together, talked about music together and visited each other's homes.

'We just started talking, stood near each other, and from there a friendship developed. We used to watch out for each other, we took note of who got into what car and made a note of the registration. If neither of us were back within half an hour, then we'd start getting worried and started looking for each other. Just to make sure that we were both alright. Suzanne loved films and music. She liked romantic comedies, *East is East* or *Hitch*, and things like that. Music-wise, she used to listen to a band called N-Dubz. We would have a good laugh together. We used to meet up at my place, doing each other's make-up and girly things like that. She did use to drink a lot – really strong cider and lager, at home and on the street. She would put it in an empty pop bottle. I think it made her more confident when she was out there on the street. But she wasn't one of those who would be nasty or violent when they had a drink. She was actually more chilled out. She were a lovely girl. All my memories are happy, brilliant of her.'

On Friday 21 May 2010, Stacy was back in Bradford for the weekend. She met up with Suzanne on Sunbridge Road some time before midnight. She was wearing her black anorak and leggings, and her black hair was pulled back and tied with a pink bobble. Over her shoulder was slung a pink plastic handbag. All the girls were scared, but none were in a position to give up working. Some talked about carrying weapons for protection. Suzanne was a bit tipsy but just glad to see her friend Stacy again. 'We was just having our usual girly chat, having a cuddle and that. I had to go and meet somebody, and I said: "Please be careful, because nobody knows what happened to Shelley." I just gave her a hug and then left her.'

Stacy never saw Suzanne again.

A few minutes' walk from where the friends were saying goodbye, a nightmare was unfolding. Inside Flat 33 Holmfield Court, Stephen Griffiths was psyching himself up to inflict unimaginable pain and humiliation on whichever victim fell easiest within his grasp. Just over 24 hours earlier, at 9.30pm on 20 May, he had written:

'Ven Pariah has finally emerged into the world.
What will this pseudo-human do, one wonders.

Poor Stephen. Pretended to be me, but he was only the wrapping.

He knew, towards the end, that I supplied the inner core of iron.

Hatred bound tightly in flesh.

At very long last, the time has come to act out.

Think about the number four. Maybe add a couple more.

All of this before the war. Ven Pariah embraces destiny and he still smiles.'

On Saturday morning, Bridget Farrell – who used Tessa as her street name – called round to see Griffiths for a chat. She had fallen out with her boyfriend and her 'head was in bits'. But instead of the kind, sympathetic Stephen, who had taken her in and looked after her all those years back, she found him distracted and volatile. His flat, which he had once kept spotless, was in turmoil.

'There were clothes all over the place. It was like a bomb had hit it. It was normally so tidy. I asked: "What's happened here?" He just shrugged. He said he'd been overdoing his uni stuff and hadn't been feeling too good. He said he couldn't handle it any more. He thought he was cracking up. He started banging on his temple, and saying: "All this work is cracking me up. It's doing my head in."'

On the coffee table, there were some macabre drawings. One showed a head clamp, another depicted a guillotine, and the third a set of fearsome-looking medical forceps. Griffiths started rambling about how the Yorkshire Ripper got a disease from prostitutes and cut their intestines out in revenge. 'He was laughing about it,' said Bridget. Still believing that he might be gay, she said to Griffiths: 'You've got no worries: you don't do women.'

Griffiths replied: 'You're right Tessa – I don't do women.'

Bridget added: 'It was the first time I'd felt uneasy with him. He'd always been there for me before then. I would have trusted him with my life. But that day something had changed. I can't say what. I just wanted to get out.'

And so she did.

In the early hours of Monday morning, Griffiths went on Myspace for the last time. He listed his mood as 'evil' and spoke of achieving 'four of my more important accomplishments'. He went on:

'I am Ven Pariah and I am many, many things with various labels attaching themselves to me in consequence of each.'

'Admittedly the order broke down after this, but the fact that it existed at all has been exceptionally convenient.'

'I don't know who to thank sometimes, maybe God.'

CHAPTER 9

Operation Pinstripe

Peter Gee was only half concentrating on the screen. There was no need to. He had reviewed the CCTV footage at Holmfield Court every Monday morning for more than three years, and there was seldom anything to report. Why should Monday 24 May 2010 be any different?

Peter was 53 and enjoyed being the flats' caretaker. He got along well with most of the tenants and had made some good friends during his time there. His inspection of the surveillance footage was the first task of the working week, and allowed him to ease in gently before the more arduous work later on. Residents had asked for the system a few years previously after complaining about prostitutes and drug dealers hanging round the doorways. There were 16 cameras in total, covering the front entrance and pavement stretching along Thornton Road, the stairways, the lifts, the landings and the corridors. Somewhere in the region of 1,000 hours of footage had to be checked.

That Monday, Peter had fast-forwarded through about 800 hours of eventless footage. Aside from capturing tenants coming and going and minding their own business, the first 13 cameras had shown little but white corridor walls, grey lift interiors, brownish carpet, cheap reproduction paintings and a withered house plant in the front foyer.

Camera 14, positioned in the third-floor passageway at the far end of the corridor from Flat 33, told a different story. Peter Gee's screen now showed a man dragging a motionless human form along the corridor floor. The caretaker recognised the standing figure. It was Stephen from Flat 33. Peter did not know his second name but had been told enough about him to know he was dangerous. His boss had warned him never to go to the flat alone. Now deep in breathless concentration, Peter wound the footage back for a more considered look.

At 02.29 on the morning of Saturday 22 May, the front entrance camera catches Stephen coming through the door with a woman. They get into the lift. Although, the CCTV system is mute, it appears that the resident of Flat 33 is holding court, his left arm gesturing as he tells a story. He is clutching two bottles of lemonade to his chest with his right arm. His guest is a little unsteady on her feet and draws heavily on a cigarette as she listens to him. She is shorter than him, with a chubby face and jet black hair pulled back tight and tied up with a pink bobble. She is wearing a black anorak and leggings and a pink plastic bag is slung over her shoulder.

At 02.31, camera 14, fixed high on a wall, captures Stephen leading the woman away from the camera towards his flat. He is looking back and talking to her. She seems perfectly relaxed as she disappears with him into his flat.

At 02.34, the third-floor camera catches her fleeing out of his doorway and back down the corridor in mortal terror. She runs towards the lens, but is looking over her shoulder. Stephen pursues her at speed, wearing black leather fingerless gloves, and with an indistinguishable wiry contraption in one hand, as well as a primeval snarl on his face. He catches up with her and attacks, knocking her to the ground. She goes limp. The assailant now grabs his victim's motionless form, and, walking backwards, drags her towards his flat. Leaving her in the doorway, he steps over her body and wanders back down the passage to retrieve the contraption. It is now clearly visible as a crossbow. He walks to his own doorway, where he points the bow at his victim and fires from close range. Then he grabs a leg and continues the process of dragging her inside.

At 02.55, Stephen comes out of the flat, with the crossbow in his right hand, and swaggers down the passage towards the camera, leering and looking straight into the lens. As he nears it, he raises his left hand and gives a one-fingered gesture of abuse to the camera. He edges nearer and, just as he is almost underneath the camera, raises the butt of the weapon to the lens with his right hand. Supporting the weapon between his thumb and adjacent finger, he opens his fingers into a wave.

After returning to the flat, he comes back out at 03.01, drinking from a bottle of Sprite lemonade. As he passes underneath the camera again, he raises the bottle to it in a mock toast.

Ashen-faced and numb with shock, Peter Gee had seen enough. There was no doubt about what he had just witnessed. It was cold-blooded murder committed brazenly for the camera. He called his manager, and together they called the police.

At 4.50 that Monday afternoon, a fleet of police cars and vans arrived outside Holmfield Court. Thornton Road was brought to a rush-hour standstill as 60 or so officers poured out onto the pavement. A substantial number of them were clad in body armour and armed to the teeth with machine guns and pistols. They were mobilised after Bradford South's vice team had viewed the surveillance footage discovered by Peter Gee. The vice squad was charged with policing the red light area and its officers knew most of the girls by name. Sergeant Helen Metcalfe, one of the most experienced team members, recognised the crossbow victim as Suzanne Blamires. Suzanne had been reported missing 48 hours earlier. With Susan Rushworth and Shelley Armitage also both missing for some time, senior detectives had had a contingency plan in place in the event of a third working girl disappearing. It was called Operation Pinstripe. Now, the answer to the riddle seemed to have arrived on their doorstep. But they could assume nothing. As far as they knew, all three girls could still be alive somewhere.

Some armed officers who streamed into Holmfield Court set about ensuring that the other tenants stayed inside their flats. Others remained outside, keeping the entrance clear. Briefed on the contents of the CCTV footage, they knew Griffiths had weapons and was unstable, so they had to be prepared for a dangerous confrontation. At the same time, it was possible that he had hostages in the flat, so they were forced to proceed with great caution. One resident said:

'The whole place was surrounded. I tried to walk out of my flat and police shouted: "Get inside and stay inside." You could see dozens of officers with guns. Some had machine guns. We thought they had found a terrorist. It was incredible. We were held for two hours while the police moved in.'

Moving stealthily up the three flights of stairs, the officers stopped outside Flat 33, paused, then broke down the door. But instead of meeting the defiant, crossbow-wielding maniac from the footage, there was merely a weak voice from inside, calling 'I'm in here'. As they entered, they met Griffiths, dressed in a thin dark grey jumper and black combat trousers. One of the team cautioned him and told him he was being arrested on suspicion of assaulting Suzanne Blamires. His characteristically surreal reply was: 'I'm Osama Bin Laden.'

They handcuffed him and led him out of the flat, back down the stairs, and outside into a police van. As they ushered him towards the vehicle, he told them to make sure they closed the door before they left. Glyn Tucker, a security guard who lives on the second floor of the complex, said:

'The armed response came through the main door, up the stairs to the third floor where he lives. About 10 minutes after that the armed response came back downstairs and then a few ordinary police officers went up and brought him down in cuffs. I was really shocked. I've lived here for three years and to think there's never been something like this here.'

As a matter of urgency, the police team now needed to find out whether Suzanne was alive, and, if she was, where she was. They looked around Griffiths' flat. They could see the two crossbows – the Jaguar and the Skeleton – propped up against a chair, together with some feathered bolts, now lying on the kitchen work surface. They saw his mammoth collection of homicide books, and they saw lots of bags and holdalls lying around on the floor. But there was no sign of Suzanne, Shelley or Susan and, to the naked eye at least, there was no sign of them having been there. The flat was designated a crime scene and sealed off for the forensic teams to pull apart.

Outside the block, a small crowd of residents and passers-by had gathered to watch the drama. Very few of them were aware of Griffiths' past convictions, his psychiatric record or his history of violence to women. To them, he was just the Lizard

Man: the oddball student who dressed in strange clothes and kept himself to himself. Now, they had seen him arrested in the fashion of Public Enemy No. 1. Glyn Tucker, the neighbour, was one of the few who sensed something untoward. Griffiths had told him he had been in Armley, a notorious Victorian prison in Leeds, for 'something serious'. He added:

'When he was saying he'd actually been in prison he had a look in his eyes. They looked dangerous, in a sense. When he started talking to me about that you could tell he was sort of dangerous. He had an air of dangerousness about him. It was just the way he was. He wasn't that large but he was near six foot. He said: "I'm studying people that have done killing," which I found a bit disturbing. I was really shocked. When he was actually put into the police van I did come out of the main door and there were quite a few residents outside and they were really shocked by what was happening.'

At 6.41 that evening, Stephen Griffiths was booked into the custody suite at Halifax police station, nine miles from Bradford. Its reception area was a long, brightly-lit room with a front desk running along its length. The custody officers sat behind the counter, and CCTV screens showing images from the cells were mounted on the walls. He was led in, handcuffed and flanked by a group of uniformed officers wearing yellow, high-visibility waistcoats. They stood behind him as he was addressed at the counter by a female custody officer. She told him he was being admitted and asked if he was okay. He nodded, but asked if he could have a drink of water. They removed his cuffs.

The opening formalities completed, a detective stepped forward from the end of the desk and formally arrested him on suspicion of murdering Suzanne Blamires. In reply, Griffiths blurted out: 'This is the end of the line for me.' After more than two decades, the secret world of Stephen Griffiths was about to be opened up.

During the next 24 hours, the unremarkable-looking suspect with the thinning brown hair and a slightly camp voice revealed the mysteries of his 'other self' to officers. He confessed to crimes that could have been rejected by Hollywood for being too far-fetched. He offered up admissions voluntarily, and regardless of whether or not he had a solicitor present. His police interviewers were granted a florid and gloating account of how he had turned his rented flat into a charnel house. But he was not being helpful or unburdening himself. There was not a shred of remorse in his voice. At best, he was matter-of-fact in his description of appalling savagery, at worst he boasted to the officers about what he had done. Crucially, he refused to give them any information which would help them find all of his victims' remains. To cap it all, he blamed everything on his alter ego: Ven Pariah, the pseudo-human.

In one of his outbursts, Griffiths told them: 'I've killed a lot more than Suzanne Blamires; I've killed loads. Peter Sutcliffe came a cropper in Sheffield. So did I, but at least I got out of the city.' He said he had once put a poisonous substance into a shop. Asked how many women he had killed, Griffiths held up six fingers.

By mid-evening, the police had not managed to get a solicitor for him, but were still hoping that Suzanne could be found alive. They interviewed him under emergency regulations to find out if she could still be rescued. Griffiths, by this time changed into jogging top and bottoms (issued by the police), told them that if they meant Amber, she was 'gone'. As they took that bombshell on board, he admitted calmly that he had eaten part of her flesh. But she was not the first; she was the third victim he had cannibalised. 'That's part of the magic,' he said. Relishing every word, he revealed not only that Suzanne was beyond any medical help, but that in fact there was nothing left of any of the three.

Griffiths had said he would only be prepared to talk to the officers about 'five Bradford cases'. He told them he knew how to get rid of a body and repeated his boast that they would not find the remains of his victims. Just as the interviewers were winding up, he blurted out: 'Suzanne Blamires: I knew I was giving myself up on that one.'

Nearly 24 hours later, detectives were able to interview Griffiths formally. He was led into a tiny room with laminate walls and a small wooden table pushed against one wall. The suspect sat at a bench next to his solicitor with the two officers facing them. On a third side of the table sat an 'appropriate adult': an independent volunteer appointed to keep an extra eye on the suspect's needs. These volunteers are brought in for juveniles and 'vulnerable' adults, for example those with a mental illness. In Griffiths' case, she was appointed after he told the police psychiatrist on Monday night about his history of mental health assessments. Slumped over the table, with his head down and eyes closed, Griffiths began by confirming his informal admissions of the day before. Then he was asked about a number of cuts that appeared on his hands. He told them, flippantly, that they were caused by 'slicing and dicing'.

Griffiths added: 'I, or a part of me, is responsible for the murders of Susan Rushworth, Shelley Armitage and this Suzanne Blamires, whose name I thought was Amber.' He continued:

'The murders, they were horrific; butchered, dismemberments, eating parts of all three of them. In the first case with Susan Rushworth, in the aftermath, I got the cooker, was taken apart, and gotten rid of. So it's six months without a cooker or something before somebody moving out of the flat gave me the present one, which you will find traces of Shelley Armitage in. But with the third one, I actually went for it, just tried eating bits of her raw. All three killed and dismembered.'

Susan, he announced, had been killed in the bedroom. He hit her with a hammer. There was a lot of blood. Forensics would find DNA traces on the walls. He had set fire to parts of her body in his flat and on a sofa outside the building. The fire brigade was called, but nobody suspected anything. He told them he 'remembered' shooting Suzanne in the flat, then cutting her up by hand. His earlier victims had been dismembered using power tools. He added: 'The creature that I was, it was just meat in the bath that was chopped and churned, some of it eaten raw and I don't know after that. I don't know where she is.' Griffiths went on to tell them: 'It was just a slaughterhouse in the bath tub, just like the other two.'

Griffiths admitted cutting Suzanne into tiny pieces, in order to help him move her body. He explained about his crossbows and said he had killed Shelley and Suzanne with them.

In a series of exchanges with Griffiths, the officers tried to test his story and find out more about where he had disposed of the women's remains.

Detective: What were you setting things on fire for?

Griffiths: Well, to destroy DNA, but like I say in such a reckless crazy manner, I can't believe, mind you, I don't know, I think... the caretaker perhaps had other things on his mind, but otherwise I cannot believe... the smoke that must have been billowing out of the windows, although I did keep them shut for a while as well, so that is why I got a lot of soot all over me and eventually I got a breathing mask on.

Detective: How do you know that fire destroys DNA?

Griffiths: To be perfectly honest, that is something I always kept meaning to check up on the internet. Certainly, I think the principle I operated on was: Well, it certainly isn't going to enhance the quality of the evidence.

Detective: ... If you can't tell us where, what sort of location have you put them into?

Griffiths: Can't know, where a robot, where a computer would put them, you know a rational, emotionless aberration would put it.

He explained about his PhD studies in homicide, and told them he had severed all ties with society. All his friends had gone, one by one, and over the last few years a 'civil war' had raged inside him between Stephen Griffiths and Ven Pariah. He did not have a problem with prostitutes and he was not 'street cleaning like Peter Sutcliffe'.

Next, he was asked about Suzanne and his motives for murder.

Detective: Why did you feel the need to kill her?

Griffiths: I don't know, like I say, sometimes you kill someone to kill yourself, or kill part of yourself. I don't know, I don't know, it is like deep issues inside me.

THE CROSSBOW CANNIBAL

Detective: Why did you feel the need to kill any of the girls?

Griffiths: I don't know, I don't know. Well, I'm misanthropic, I don't have much time for the human race.

Hardened detectives were left drained by the Griffiths interviews. He sat for hours, detailing the goriest acts of barbarism imaginable, carried out on other human beings for no apparent reason. There was no motive, there was no anger, no hate; there was no real emotion at all. Just ritualistic slaughter and a chilling nonchalance few if any of them had encountered before. If anything, he seemed simply to be enjoying the limelight. It was as if this was his big moment. His destiny. His 15 minutes of fame.

The officers were certain he had murdered the three girls, but they were not sure about his claims of killing six. One officer said: 'Griffiths is a wannabe celebrity – and a particularly evil one. He realised he couldn't achieve stardom using any kind of talent because he didn't possess any. So he set out to achieve it through notoriety. We believe his crimes were motivated by a twisted desire for fame.'

Griffiths claimed to have killed six women. He provided corroborating detail in the deaths of three of them. But not only had he murdered and dismembered them; he had, he said, eaten them. Why would anyone do that? Whatever the motive, the practical problem was verifying which parts of his story were true. Were there the bodies of other missing women out there that they did not know about? And what was that curious little reference to Sheffield and Peter Sutcliffe about? Although Griffiths had a touch of arrogant blarney about him, they could not write off his claims. Critically, the police had to provide answers for the relatives of Suzanne Blamires, Shelley Armitage and Susan Rushworth. All three families were aware of the developments and naturally distressed. The investigation team, from West Yorkshire's elite Homicide and Major Enquiry Team, had enormous amounts of ground to cover, and it was clear that Griffiths was not going to give them any more help. 'We just don't know what we are dealing with at the moment,' one officer sighed. 'It is absolutely horrific, the stuff of hell. There are three missing women being looked at regarding him at present. But there is the obvious fear there could be more.'

Operation Pinstripe's first objective was to gather enough evidence to charge Griffiths or, if his claims did not stand up, release him. Since the 1980s, deciding whether or not to charge has been taken by the Crown Prosecution Service. The decision depends entirely on whether the evidence provided by the police is strong enough. Massive cases are handed to its regional complex casework unit, staffed by the cream of prosecution officials and lawyers. From an early stage, they liaise with the police to ensure that both know the strength of the evidence and the course the prosecution might take.

In Griffiths' case, the investigation team had to find out whether evidence existed elsewhere to corroborate his claims of being a serial killer. Felicity Gerry, a criminal barrister, author and commentator on legal issues, said:

'Your first thought would be to ask what other evidence is there apart from what he says. You have got to work out whether you have enough evidence to prove it independently from what the suspect says. That's the most important thing, because you do get people who say they have killed people when they haven't. Your second thought would be to ask if the offences all fit together. Do they all support each other? In this case, they obviously would, because you have got three murders of three women in what seems to be a similar brutal way.'

Felicity Gerry said that if there was a confession to three murders, but weak forensic evidence on one, that charge could still stick. It would be corroborated by the other two being perpetrated in a similar way.

'You start from the premise of looking at them individually. Can you prove each of them individually and then if one is a bit weak, can you prove it globally? Is it supported by the other evidence?'

At the very least, the surveillance footage was damning in relation to Suzanne's murder. But what had happened to her body remained a mystery. And, as far as the murders of Shelley and Susan were concerned, investigations were only just beginning.

CHAPTER 10

Dragnet

During the early afternoon of Tuesday 25 May, a foreign object was floating in the shallows of the River Aire. An abandoned black rucksack had been caught in the current of Shipley Bridge weir pool and stranded near the bank. It was only a matter of time before someone spotted the bag, as many people wandered down to the pool to watch the resident mute swans glide by. Visitors were also in and out of the print workshop, the car showroom and the fascia sign shop on the bank near Otley Road, part of the A6038.

It was one of the shop's customers who reported the rucksack to a member of staff, and he clambered down the bank to investigate. The bag seemed heavy, 25 kilos maybe. He would have needed both hands to lift it clear of the water, but he did not get that far. As he tried to raise it, the bag came open and out fell a human head.

Two hours later, the car park between the showroom and the print workshop was crawling with police. It was cordoned off with trademark blue and white crime scene tape and an array of force vehicles were squeezed in alongside those of the companies' staff. The investigation team set up two large blue and white tents on the tarmac next to the river wall as a weatherproof mobile base. Divers from the underwater search unit, clad in black wetsuits, unloaded scuba equipment from the vans, kitted up, then climbed down a set of steps from the top of the 12-foot river wall to the water's edge. They sifted methodically through the weir pool's cloudy water and scoured the foliage at its edges. Each diver had a dedicated partner on the bank, with whom they could communicate via a cable radio link. Meanwhile, scene of crime officers – known colloquially as SOCOs – emerged, clad in white all-in-one forensic suits, with plastic gloves and shoe covers to prevent cross-contamination of the scene or of any evidence lying there. Their job was to search the river bank and collect items passed up by the frogmen. Periodically, they would hand down a blue plastic bag, a diver would put something inside, then they would send it back up. All of the items were photographed and numbered.

While all this was going on, staff from the business premises along the river, as well as passers-by, stopped to look at the unfolding drama. Andrea Davey, who watched the build-up from her sandwich van in Dockfield Road, which runs off Otley Road, said: 'Everyone's talking about it; no one can believe it. Lots of things go on down here, but not that.' By the evening, the underwater search team had recovered more body parts.

The grisly find at the River Aire was a key development in Operation Pinstripe. If Griffiths had told the truth about murdering at least three women before dismembering and disposing of their bodies, there was vast potential for minute traces of forensic evidence to be scattered over a wide public area. Contact traces from both him and his victims could lie within every square centimetre of ground he had trodden. The trail would have begun inside Flat 33 Holmfield Court, then extended out into the corridor, down the stairs, and outside. Now, following the latest discovery, it led to Shipley Bridge, three miles away. There could even have been other places, as Griffiths had told them very little about disposal sites, so they had to search everywhere.

Officers faced a race against time to recover what they could before it was washed away by the river or rain, or touched, trodden on or otherwise spoiled by unwitting members of the public. Inside the flat, virtually everything was of interest: the walls, floors, furniture, rugs, bedding, curtains, blinds, ceilings, windows, washbasins and sinks, along with the occupant's clothing and personal possessions – plus, of course, any items that were not his and could have belonged to a victim. They looked for specks and smears of blood, body matter and other DNA, maybe even bone fragments or fibres traceable to the missing women's clothes.

Not to mention weapons. Over the next few days, they recovered, among other things, his crossbows, bolts, 30 knives, computers, bags and holdalls, and a digital camera. In addition, they carried away sections of tile from the bathroom, carpet sections and a mattress.

Officers evacuated the other third-floor residents and applied the same crime scene analysis techniques to the corridor outside Flat 33. In the light of the dramatic surveillance footage, their hard surfaces could be a goldmine of forensic material. Outside Holmfield Court, the search continued apace. Officers cordoned off the pavement in front of the block, together with the courtyard and Soho Street, where another forensic tent was erected. Workmen who had been using a mechanical digger to replace gas pipes were brought into the search. They excavated lumps of soil and concrete, and then broke them up with the digger's claw before policemen crouched on their hands and knees to sift through the rubble. Officers extended the crime scene to the other side of Thornton Road, digging out a hole where workmen had been laying cables. Once again, the SOCOs went nose-to-the-ground to pore over the pieces. Dog handlers with brown and white spaniels ferreted around Holmfield Court's back courtyard and the overgrown alleyways that led to neighbouring buildings. The animals were also led to sniff about near the utility trenches, dug during the previous few weeks. Plain-clothes detectives moved in and out of the block, and, behind the building, the underwater search team went down a drainage culvert, which was usually covered by iron plates.

Meanwhile, community support officers stood guard at the block's entrance and at the edge of the cordon across Soho Street, while two police vans, including a scientific support team vehicle, were parked outside. The diving squad also plunged into Bradford Beck below Bradford College, about 200 yards away on the other side of Thornton Road. Furthermore, a team of SOCOs scrabbled around in skips alongside the college's hall of residence in Laisteridge Lane. Just as at the river, passers-by hung around to witness the dragnet in action, and traffic queues built up as motorists slowed down to 'rubberneck'. Overhead, a hovering helicopter's rotors whirred away incessantly.

The trawl spread into the red light area. At the bottom of Albion Street, a side road running off Sunbridge Road, officers began searching around some bins and rubbish that had spilled onto the ground outside an anarchist social club called The 1-in-12. They used poles to poke through the contents of crammed black bin liners, while the sniffer dogs scampered around their ankles. Workers had complained about a 'rotten smell' coming from somewhere nearby, and given the events of the last few days, the source had to be traced. A shop assistant at a nearby music store said at the time: 'There is a really nasty smell. It's like an abattoir.' Along Sunbridge Road, the investigators found some items of interest near a parking bay next to the Provident Financial insurance company offices. They pulled out a pair of grey and white trainers and a red coat, and sealed them both inside brown paper evidence bags.

Meanwhile, the police were still foraging for clues that might help them find all three victims. At 9 Barkston Walk, Suzanne's neighbours witnessed 'swarms' of SOCOs walking in and out of the flat, and carrying 'lots of stuff' away while a uniformed officer guarded the way in. The neighbours were also shown pictures of Suzanne and asked if they recognised her. Three streets away, officers returned to Bentcliffe Walk, having spent a month searching for Shelley. The missing persons inquiry was now a murder hunt, and so they rummaged through the bins and garden once again. Not far away, the team set up base in the car park of the New Tyke, the pub in Thornton where Susan Rushworth had caught the bus on the day she vanished. They searched the surrounding terrain once more and examined the area next to the Villa Roma Italian restaurant on the other side of the road.

At the height of the search, police were looking at about 130 different sites. No fewer than 45 detectives were assigned to the case, together with 70 other officers.

The operation was masterminded by West Yorkshire's Homicide and Major Enquiry Team, known in force circles by the acronym HMET. The elite squad comprises around 250 of the country's top police investigators. Not only does it boast some of the finest crime-solving brains, but it benefits from a dazzling array of specialists ranging from fingerprint technicians and crime scene managers to computer whizz-kids, CCTV analysts, ace interviewers and court preparation experts. As all of this would suggest, HMET's remit is to crack the most serious and complex cases, mostly of murder, but also of other less straightforward offences such as non-domestic rape, kidnappings and blackmail.

The events unfolding in Bradford during the last week of May 2010 were of the kind that had prompted HMET's launch five years earlier. Chief Constable Colin Cramphorn had asked Detective Chief Superintendent Chris Gregg to assemble a squad capable of solving the most complex and protracted cases. As one of the country's top detectives and a policeman of three decades' experience, he was the natural choice to head the squad. DCS Gregg was also a Yorkshireman, beginning his career in Huddersfield, where he worked as a constable on the inquiry into the Yorkshire Ripper. Later, after transferring to CID, he investigated some of Sutcliffe's other killings, including that of Bradford student Barbara Leach.

Chris Gregg left the force in 2008 to join a forensic science consultancy. He said of HMET's formation:

'We wanted to create an outstanding team of investigators. We wanted to make sure we had the best system in place, from crime scene management through to investigation through to the court, then to the aftermath, the ongoing victim care and support.'

Before HMET, West Yorkshire Police had no dedicated homicide squad, despite being the fourth biggest force in the country. Scotland Yard in London had such a team, but elsewhere, whenever there was a murder, an investigation team was assembled from the relevant police division's CID. The detectives involved would put aside their other investigations – assaults, robberies and so on – to concentrate on the more urgent job. Chris Gregg explained:

'That has happened historically, since Robert Peel was a lad. When a murder investigation came in, forces had to – for want of a better word – cobble together a team from around the force area to go and investigate. It would cause great disruption with day-to-day activities, and if it was a difficult investigation like a whodunit, it could go on for months and months, and draw resources away from core policing in their local area.'

Early in the new millennium, Her Majesty's Inspectorate of Constabulary recognised that there was a better way of staffing murder investigations and suggested that all metropolitan forces follow the Yard's example. West Yorkshire was the first to comply, launching HMET on 1 April 2005. Under DCS Gregg, there were eight detective superintendents, one detective inspector and six detective sergeants. There were 94 indexers, whose function was to record and file information on HOLMES, the Home Office's major crime computerised database. A further 150 staff were employed in management roles. 'The one thing I wanted to impress on the team was that we were raising the bar,' Chris Gregg said. 'This was going to be a unit which was driven hard to achieve the highest of standards. There was nothing we feared in the world of criminal investigation, but there was no room for any big-time Charlies.'

Not only did the new squad avoid disrupting routine police work, it was able to investigate crimes more efficiently because officers were specialists rather than generalists. They would do the same job repeatedly and become experts, carrying out the tasks more quickly and accurately. They were also able to be more creative and innovative with their craft to get better results.

Just three months after the squad was launched, its expertise faced a challenge of the highest level with the inquiry into

Britain's first suicide bombing. On 7 July 2005, four Islamic terrorists carried out synchronised explosions on London's public transport system, killing themselves and 52 innocent commuters. All four had strong West Yorkshire connections. Mohammad Sidique Khan, the leader, lived in Dewsbury and had spent most of his life in Leeds; Shehzad Tanweer and Hasib Hussain lived in Leeds; and Germaine Lindsay, while resident in Aylesbury at the time of the attacks, had lived in Huddersfield earlier in his life. Although the inquiry was led by Scotland Yard's anti-terrorist branch, HMET's officers were tasked with weeks of round-the-clock inquiries, gathering local intelligence and forensic evidence.

Soon afterwards, DCS Gregg was to enjoy a great personal triumph with the arrest of 'Wearside Jack', the hoaxer who had – with such disastrous consequences – fooled the squad pursuing the Yorkshire Ripper back in the late 1970s. In its opening few months, HMET had started reviewing 'cold' cases, crimes that remained unsolved despite the best efforts of generations of investigators. An obvious example of this was the man who had helped Peter Sutcliffe to remain at large by distracting the police with bogus confessions. The perpetrator had posted his hoax mail from Sunderland, and had of course left his saliva on the envelopes. In the age of DNA analysis, the deposit was dynamite. A forensic scientist tested a piece of sealant gum from the envelope's flap. The DNA matched a sample on the national DNA database, taken from John Humble, a depressive alcoholic, when he happened to be arrested for being drunk and disorderly in 2000.

Five years on, in October 2005, Humble was arrested once again, and was formally accused of perverting the course of justice. In February 2006, he admitted four charges at Leeds Crown Court and was sentenced to eight years in jail. Trial judge Norman Jones, the Recorder of London, told him that the Ripper's last three victims would have 'stood a better chance' of surviving if it were not for the hoax. They included Barbara Leach. DCS Gregg said after Humble was sentenced:

'We knew this was unresolved. If there was an opportunity to find out who was responsible we would take it. It started out as a long shot, but it was worth it. I worked on the original inquiry as a young policeman and to be at this end of it now is quite remarkable.'

November 2005, shortly after Humble's arrest, saw HMET being handed yet another mammoth investigation to tackle. PC Sharon Beshenivsky, a probationary police officer, was shot dead while attending reports of a robbery in Morley Street, the main road out of Bradford city centre to the south of Thornton Road. The gang had opened fire as they fled from a bungled raid on a travel agent's. Beshenivsky's colleague was also hit, but although she received serious chest wounds, she survived. Although detectives were quickly able to identify the gang involved, it took another four years and an astonishing display of detective work to round them all up. In particular, the CCTV specialists could ascertain that there were a total of three getaway cars: a silver Toyota Rav 4X4, a green Toyota Corolla and a black Mercedes. Only the well-trained eyes of the team's footage experts could have quickly linked all three vehicles to the robbery as they sped through the city. Even then it took weeks of scrutinising the images caught by Bradford's extensive camera network. Chris Gregg explained:

'It sounds the simplest thing to put somebody in front of a monitor and say "watch that" and find a suspect vehicle. But it is such a difficult task. To have people who know exactly how to grid off a screen, how to document things so that you are not jumping backwards and forwards, is actually quite a specialised process.'

Later in the inquiry, HMET needed to extract one of the gang – Mustafa Jama – who had escaped after the robbery to his native Somalia. The team needed to prepare a diplomatic approach to the Somali Government that was strong enough to secure co-operation at all levels, right down to the police who would arrest Jama. The suspect's father was a former MP, so every detail of the representation had to be perfect. Then, once they had located him in a remote region of Somaliland, the arresting officers had to send a photograph by laptop back to Yorkshire, so the team could match it up with file pictures.

In a series of trials, Jama and five other defendants were convicted of a range of offences including PC Beshenivsky's murder. They received sentences including life with a recommended tariff of at least 35 years. Only the robbery's planner, Piran Ditta Khan, has so far eluded them. He is believed to be hiding in Pakistan. 'These cases would distract the most capable of units anywhere in the country,' Chris Gregg said. 'We were tested to the full there, but we came through it.'

So, as HMET reached its fifth anniversary, its team members were being tested yet again, this time under Chris Gregg's replacement, Detective Chief Superintendent Max McLean. Although Griffiths was behind bars and had confessed, every detail of his story still had to be verified.

On Wednesday 26 May, the underwater search team – which had cancelled all its training exercises to concentrate on the murder inquiry – moved 200 yards further west to the other side of Shipley Bridge. The remains recovered on the previous day, together with evidence from the River Aire and Holmfield Court, had been taken away for examination at the Forensic Science Service's specialist laboratories in Wetherby,

Birmingham and London. The police were certain that the grim parcels contained what was left of Suzanne, but they would need to wait another few days for tests to confirm it. Jawaid Akhtar, the force's Assistant Chief Constable in charge of crime, gave an update from the windswept car park overlooking Shipley Bridge weir pool. 'This is a very thorough and painstaking inquiry into three missing people who were sex workers, with all the necessary resources and expertise devoted to it. The families of Suzanne, Shelley and Susan are all being supported by our family liaison officers as the inquiry progresses.'

The following day, police announced that the body parts found in the Aire had 'confirmed a positive match' to Suzanne. The grim responsibility of identifying her fell to a new unit, the specialist victim identification team. Less than a week after she was last seen, officers were forced to relay the worst possible news to her family.

On the afternoon of Thursday 27 May, detectives from Operation Pinstripe charged Griffiths with the murders of all three women. Peter Mann, the head of the CPS's West Yorkshire complex casework unit, announced:

'I have carefully considered all of the evidence provided to me arising from their investigation into the murders of Suzanne Blamires, Shelley Armitage and Susan Rushworth. I have decided that there is sufficient evidence to charge Stephen Griffiths with their murders, and that it is in the public interest to do so. Accordingly, I have authorised the police to charge him this afternoon. He will appear at Bradford Magistrates Court tomorrow morning and he will then be remanded in custody to appear at Bradford Crown Court tomorrow afternoon.

'The events of the last few days have understandably been very upsetting for the families and friends of Suzanne, Shelley and Susan as well as for the wider public in Bradford. Their families have been informed of my decision by the police and I hope soon to be able to meet them and explain the trial process to them and answer any questions they may have. Mr Griffiths now stands charged with three extremely serious criminal offences and has the right to a fair trial. It is extremely important that nothing should be published that could prejudice his trial.'

Despite charges being brought, there was still work to be done in constructing the case and in finding out what had happened to the bodies of Shelley and Susan for the sake of their respective families and friends. ACC Akhtar assured the public that 'all the necessary resources and expertise' were being put into the case.

Saturday morning – 29 May – brought yet another dramatic development. About 200 yards from where Suzanne's body parts had been found, the divers hauled out of the waters of the River Aire a black, wheeled canvas bag of the type used as hand luggage on airline flights. Inside was what can only be described as a killing kit, consisting of hacksaws, knives and razor blades, together with what appeared to be a quantity of body tissue. Nearby, the frogmen found two polythene bags with what appeared to be bones inside. The grisly hoard was sent off for laboratory analysis, but the team faced the additional drawback of having to wait for the flight bag to dry out naturally, so as to maximise their chances of extracting clear fingerprints and DNA samples from the cutting equipment.

The following Monday was a Bank Holiday, but that made little difference to the inquiry. That afternoon, West Yorkshire Police announced that the bones had been found to be animal waste used in food preparation. However, they were more circumspect on the contents of the flight bag:

'We are waiting for the black bag to dry out. We have to take our time and allow it to dry naturally. At the moment, it's not possible to say that it is automatically linked with our inquiries. We are reasonably confident we have got virtually all the parts belonging to Suzanne, and our efforts are now directed towards tracing Shelley and Susan.'

On Wednesday 2 June, the force confirmed that the tissue in the black canvas bag had indeed belonged to Shelley Armitage. It was a minute section of her spine, which, although no body had been found, signalled that its owner was no longer alive. Fully aware that similar results were likely to trickle rather than flood in, officers urged the public to be patient: 'West Yorkshire Police wish to stress that to search the locations with the level of care and thoroughness which is required will be a lengthy process.'

CHAPTER 11

Cold Cases

Stephen Griffiths' claim that he killed up to six women meant that there could be three other murders to investigate. Although the Bradford officers suspected him of being a braggart and a liar, his assertion could not be ignored lightly. While HMET concentrated on investigating the murders of Susan, Shelley and Suzanne, inquiries came in from colleagues in other police forces in the North of England: South Yorkshire, North Yorkshire and Liverpool.

The re-examination of unsolved cases is standard procedure in serious crime cases, as Chris Gregg, founder and former chief of HMET, explained:

'It is a crucial part of the research to find out what else somebody has done. If somebody has been arrested for a serial killing or serial rape, we always work from the premise that they don't just start killing or raping people in the most brutal fashion overnight. There is always a build-up. Even if they have no previous convictions or convictions for serious violence or sexual offences, we would have to look deeper into their background. We pull in all the research capability we can and expertise we can, to start understanding the type of offending this particular person may have been committing, so that we can home in on crimes that are outstanding.'

If there was no suspect, detectives would, among other things, call in a behavioural analyst and a forensic psychologist to provide a profile. But if there was a suspect, the investigation team could begin looking at what other offences he might have committed, with the help of the National Policing Improvement Agency (NPIA). A national body established to help forces operate more efficiently, the agency provides a service to all British constabularies. This includes the expert work of a Serious Crime Analysis Section (SCAS), tasked with recognising serial killers and rapists from the characteristics of their early offences. Using a computerised database known as the Violent Crime Linkage Analysis System (VCLAS), they would, for example, consider whether a particular killer or rapist tied their victim up, and, if they did, with what: rope, tape, cables, wire, a dog lead perhaps? What weapon was used? Was it a knife, scissors, a chisel, a screwdriver? Was the violence necessary to incapacitate their victim or was it gratuitous? Where did the attack take place? What locality was it in, or was it on the same kind of terrain, be it parkland, a common, or in a city centre?

Chris Gregg said:

'All the components are broken down into very fine analytical detail. Offenders of this type tend to follow the same patterns. For example, killers and rapists attack in certain places. In the case of killings, the attack site and the body disposal site will, in 90 per cent of cases, have a connection with the killer. They may live nearby, they may have used it earlier in their life, it may be somewhere they are familiar with socially, or with work. There will be some connection and it is finding what that connection is.'

To that end, Max McLean, Gregg's successor, passed the files on the Bradford murders over to SCAS, based at Bramshill, Hampshire, and asked them to sift through the detail and report back. Max McLean said:

'It can provide guidance and advice on timelines by checking the movements of suspects and missing people to see if there are any crossovers. Working with the NPIA allows us to focus our own resources on the preparation of case papers on the three women who have been killed. Our priority is to focus on the challenge in hand – ensuring the case relating to Suzanne Blamires, Susan Rushworth and Shelley Armitage is properly prepared.'

Among the cold cases linked to Griffiths were the unsolved murders of two Bradford prostitutes dating back many years.

Rebecca Hall, also known as Becky, was last seen on 13 April 2001, when she was just 19 years old and had a four-month-old son named Jordan. Her body was discovered in Thornton Street (just a few hundred yards from Holmfield Court) nearly two weeks later on 26 April, exactly nine years before Shelley Armitage was to go missing. Her killer gave her a savage beating and left her lying naked in an alleyway behind a company car park used by the working girls and their punters. She died of severe head injuries.

Max McLean, then with Bradford South CID, was in charge of the murder inquiry, and his team's inability to find Becky's killer was to be a source of lasting regret. Becky had disappeared in much the same way as Susan Rushworth, Shelley Armitage and Suzanne Blamires. She left home in Little Horton to work in City Road, never to come back. Max McLean's squad conducted the usual intensive searches of the alley and its environs, going so far as to dig two feet down into the ground. They recovered most of her clothes, the catch from one of her earrings and some 'low-level' or weak DNA samples from her body and clothes. They swamped the city with posters appealing for information and interviewed her friends, family, known punters, fellow street workers and men with a history of attacking prostitutes. A criminal psychologist told them the murderer was likely to be a client who lived quite close to the scene, and there was a theory that Becky had been kept captive before being killed. In all, Max McLean's team followed up 1,500 lines of inquiry and took nearly 300 statements, but to no avail.

The murder of Yvonne Fitt dates back even further. She went missing over eight years before Becky's murder, when Manningham was still the heart of Bradford's red light district. Yvonne, then aged 33 and with an 11-year-old daughter, seemed to bounce between Bradford and Leeds, and had lived at addresses in Manningham and Harehills. She was last seen in Bradford's Department of Social Security offices in January 1992. Eight months later, on 12 September, a man collecting wild mushrooms found her body, which was buried just beneath the soil at a beauty spot called Warren Point, near Otley on the outskirts of Leeds. Yvonne's body was so badly decomposed that it took scientists five days to establish that she had died from multiple stab wounds. Intriguingly, they also established that she had died no more than two months before her body was found, leaving a six-month window unaccounted for. It begged the question of whether she too could have been held captive.

THE CROSSBOW CANNIBAL

Detectives checked almost 140,000 missing persons records just to confirm Yvonne's identity, took more than 100 witness statements, interviewed more than 600 people and arrested three in connection with her murder. But nobody was charged.

Other cases with less obvious relevance to Bradford were brought to the murder squad's attention. North Yorkshire Police referred details of their most recent whodunit: the disappearance of pretty chef Claudia Lawrence. Claudia, a 35-year-old single woman who worked at the University of York, had spent the night of 17 March 2009 with a boyfriend, but then simply vanished. She was reported missing when she failed to turn up at work the next day, and, despite months of searching, the police had no idea what happened to her. No body was ever found, but six weeks after her disappearance the police upgraded the inquiry status from missing persons to murder. During the investigation, officers discovered that Claudia Lawrence, unbeknownst to her doting family, had what they described as 'complicated relationships'. Officers complained that a lot of her friends were 'less than candid'. But, desperate for new leads, they offered her 'acquaintances' the cloak of confidentiality for a limited time if they came up with new information. They went as far afield as Cyprus in search of an answer. Claudia had met a number of people there, was thought to have been offered a job on the island, and received her last text message from someone there.

The search for Claudia was bolstered by a £10,000 reward, offered by the Crimestoppers charity, for information leading to the arrest of anyone connected to her disappearance. They reconstructed her last known movements for a feature on the BBC's *Crimewatch* programme and took 1,200 telephone calls offering new information. Separately, Claudia Lawrence's father Peter campaigned tirelessly to keep the story in the public eye, his tactics including a video appeal on the clip-sharing website

YouTube. However, as of May 2010, her whereabouts remained a mystery.

Despite spending £600,000 and assigning up to 30 detectives at a time to the case, no firm evidence about Claudia's disappearance was found. They were also unable to trace the man with whom she spent 17 March 2009. After Griffiths' arrest, a North Yorkshire Police spokesman, said: 'Consultation will take place with our colleagues in West Yorkshire Police to ensure that any factors that are common to both cases are identified and investigated promptly.'

Merseyside Police made a similar request for help, over three unsolved killings going back 16 years. Anne Marie Foy was a veteran of Liverpool's vice trade, having worked in it for two decades. A mother of four and a grandmother, she was aged 46 and had become a prostitute to feed a long-standing heroin addiction. She was caught on CCTV walking towards a car in the red light district on 15 September 2005. Her body was found by a member of the public in a park on the University of Liverpool campus. She had been beaten and choked to death, and then dumped in undergrowth.

Another Merseyside mystery surrounded the death of Susan Kelly, a 38-year-old prostitute who was found with her throat cut in the Anfield area of Liverpool in September 2000. She suffered no fewer than 29 injuries: slashes, stab wounds, a broken nose and jaw and six broken ribs. She had also been strangled and was left half-naked by her killer. Susan was a mother of one who had been diagnosed with schizophrenia and, according to her mother Cathy, had gone into the sex trade as a result of her mental problems. Her body was found by a dog walker on the morning of Monday 4 September. Her neighbours had seen her going out the previous night.

Julie Finley, 23, was not a prostitute, but was a drug user, had many friends in the sex trade, and lived on the fringe of

THE CROSSBOW CANNIBAL

Liverpool's red light district. She was last seen behind Liverpool Royal University Teaching Hospital at 10.30pm on 5 August 1994, talking to an unknown white man. Her body was dumped naked 15 miles away, on the edge of a carrot field near the new town of Skelmersdale, Lancashire. It was found at lunchtime the next day by a cyclist. Julie had been strangled. Despite a murder investigation covering Merseyside, Lancashire and Cheshire, manned by up to 15 detectives who made 20 arrests, no one was brought to book.

The week after Griffiths' arrest, a Merseyside Police spokesman said:

> 'It will be a case of seeing what they know about their suspect and looking at the crimes here to see if there are any similarities. Then it will come down to DNA to link or eliminate him from the inquiries. Whenever something like this happens, we always look to see what links there could be on open cases.'

South Yorkshire Police, meanwhile, were keen to find out if any new information was forthcoming about the deaths of Sheffield prostitutes Dawn Shields and Michaela Hague. Dawn, 19, was last seen getting into a car in Broomhall, the city's red light district, in May 1994. Her naked body was found buried under rocks and debris by National Trust wardens at Mam Tor, a beauty spot in the Peak District. She had died from severe head injuries. Michaela, 25 years old, was also picked up in Sheffield's red light district, this time on Bonfire Night 2001, and taken to an isolated car park in Spitalfields. She was stabbed 19 times in her neck and back, and found dying by another prostitute. Before she died, however, she was able to give the police a description of her attacker. Michaela left a five-year-old son.

When the Bradford case unfolded, Detective Chief Superintendent Steve Talbot, head of specialist crime services for the South Yorkshire force, said: 'We will always review our cases in the light of such an arrest, whether it be in a neighbouring county or elsewhere in the country, and once West Yorkshire Police have addressed their initial priorities in this case, there will be liaison between the two forces.'

But could Griffiths really be responsible for all these killings? His history of mental illness and violence certainly predated the earliest of the cold cases. He had also lived within easy driving distance of crime scenes in neighbouring areas such as South Yorkshire, North Yorkshire and Merseyside. His jobless loner's lifestyle afforded him the bonus of being free to move about. There was no daily routine to tie him to Bradford and no wife, family or work colleagues to spot giveaway absences or changes in his behaviour. A total of six victims, the number Griffiths had offered to the police, would not be exceptional in the history of serial killers.

The generally accepted definition of a serial killer is one who has killed at least three people over a 30-day period with a 'cooling-off' spell in-between. The most prolific is Harold Shipman, the family doctor from Hyde, Manchester, who ended the lives of elderly patients with lethal injections of morphine. He was proven to have killed 218 people but is suspected of killing more than 250. Shipman's killing history spanned a quarter of a century.

On a list of serial killers compiled by the Wikipedia reference website, 11 people have each claimed in excess of 50 victims. Harold Shipman was one. Another was Luis Garavito, a Colombian rapist and killer of 138 street boys who tempted his victims by befriending them with offers of sweets and small gifts. He was arrested in 1999. Pedro Lopez, another Colombian, killed 110 young girls before he was caught in

1980. Chris Gregg's view is that such serial killers have an unstoppable compulsion:

> 'Some people are born evil and born to be cruel and these are the people who go on to commit these horrific crimes. They always get caught in the end thankfully, some sooner than others, but if they weren't caught, they would just continue hurting people. They are usually caught after their latest crime, there is a mistake or the police catch up with them. I can't think of one who has just stopped. The exhilaration they get will drive them on until they are in their grave.'

Street prostitutes are, of course, the classic easy target for people with such a killing compulsion. The very nature of their work takes them out into areas at night, where there are no police, no passers-by and very few lights. Of all the sex workers who become victims of violent crime, three-quarters are street prostitutes. Their attackers simply disappear into the night. In the two decades before the arrest of Stephen Griffiths, 20 prostitutes were murdered by person or persons unknown. In 1996, a special nationwide police project, Operation Enigma, identified 210 unsolved murders of women to be targeted for review. Many of the victims were sex workers.

Dr Belinda Brooks-Gordon, author of *The Price of Sex: Prostitution, Policy and Society*, said that street sex workers can become 'a magnet for violent men', and that the attacks begin when the trigger is somehow pulled:

> 'For an abuser against sex workers, it can be a case of them snapping. It can be her saying something that reminds him of a humiliation or an incident in a past life and that's what causes it. Others can go looking for an offence. That's

what happens with rapists. They are hyped up, either feeling horny, had a bit to drink or had a row with someone close in their life, and they go out looking for a victim.'

Above: CCTV footage of Shelley Armitage on Sunbridge Road in Bradford, shortly before she disappeared.

Below: Criminology student Stephen Griffiths was later arrested and charged with three murders.

©Rex Features

The victims of the self-named 'Crossbow Cannibal'.

Above left: Shelley Armitage.

Above right: Susan Rushworth.

Below: Suzanne Blamires – pictured at her wedding, aged 20, and shortly before her death.

Above: Crossbows recovered from Stephen Griffiths' flat. ©*Rex Features*

Below: Police carried out a thorough search of the streets surrounding Griffiths' home and of the River Aire, where some human remains were found.

©*Getty Images*

Above left: Peter Sutcliffe, the Yorkshire Ripper.   ©*PA Photos*

Above right and below: Three of Sutcliffe's 13 victims. *Clockwise from above*: Patricia Atkinson, Barbara Leach and Yvonne Pearson.

© *Rex Features/Getty Images*

CHAPTER 12

Deja Vu

In a sense, Bradford in 2010 had seen it all before. The swoop at Holmfield Court and search of the River Aire reminded the city of that first week in January 1981 when Sutcliffe was arrested for the Ripper murders. Nearly 30 years on, another local man was being held on suspicion of killing prostitutes. Details began to emerge on the evening of Tuesday 25 May, and by the Thursday morning the world's media were eagerly awaiting developments. That this was only ever going to be perceived as a 'second' or 'copycat' Yorkshire Ripper did nothing to undermine the story. Rather, the freakishness of one small city spawning two serial killers in a generation made it a massive front-page story.

Bradford was swamped by journalists looking for background on both suspect and victims. James Naughtie, host of BBC Radio 4's Today programme, summed it up perfectly. Interviewing Manningham councillor Qasim Khan and Niki Adams (spokeswoman for the English Collective of Prostitutes) on that Thursday morning, he suggested that Bradford must have a sense of 'déjà vu' which took the city back to the 'awful days of the Yorkshire Ripper'.

It had been on the Wednesday afternoon that a police briefing on the banks of the Aire confirmed rumours that had been circulating throughout the northern media pack. Mobbed by a crowd of journalists and with a thicket of broadcast microphones thrust into his face, Assistant Chief Constable Jawaid Akhtar read from a prepared statement fixed to a clipboard:

'As you are aware, police yesterday recovered human remains from the water at Dockfield Road, Shipley. Those appear to be the remains of one person, who has yet to be identified. Police have this morning obtained a warrant of further detention from Bradford magistrates to continue questioning, until tomorrow evening, a 40-year-old man arrested on Monday.'

ACC Akhtar, West Yorkshire's most senior officer with responsibility for serious and organised crime, went on to reveal that the suspect was being questioned about Suzanne Blamires' murder and would subsequently be quizzed about Shelley Armitage and Susan Rushworth.

Reporters got wind of events after Monday morning's drama at Holmfield Court. As with any big story, a grapevine reaches out from those closest to it. The word spread from tenants or passers-by who had witnessed the armed officers storming in through the front door, or had heard about the awful CCTV footage. They passed it on to friends and relatives, people in the post office, the bus queue, the supermarket, the pub and so on. Tuesday's gruesome discovery in the river provided more gossip. The police forensic teams and divers caught the eye of hundreds of people on the Otley Road, whether they were in cars or on foot.

By Tuesday evening, newspapers, radio and TV stations and

agencies all knew that Yorkshire was the scene of something significant and horrible. The West Yorkshire Police press office informed journalists who called that they had found 'what are thought to be human remains' in the Aire near the Otley Road.

On Wednesday morning at 7am, the *Bradford Telegraph & Argus* website reported the story beneath the headline 'Police hunting missing vice girls probe grim discovery'. Complete with a short video report, the *T&A* told of the 'discovery of chopped-up human body parts', quoting witnesses to the riverside search. The report linked everything to the missing Shelley Armitage and Suzanne Blamires. At this stage, neither Susan Rushworth, nor indeed Stephen Griffiths, was mentioned.

In the age of rolling TV news and the internet, it takes just minutes to bring a big story to a wide audience. Shortly after the Assistant Chief Constable had spoken, the *Yorkshire Post*, the county's authoritative morning newspaper, was able to turn his words into a comprehensive website report with accompanying video. It brought all three women into the story, giving background on their lifestyles and quoting people who knew or had seen them. The *YP* also reported searches being carried out at Holmfield Court and in Sunbridge Road. At the block of flats, it said, officers were 'standing guard outside'. Because words and pictures are syndicated by agencies, and cribbed by rival media, identical reports popped up all over the web. By midnight that day, BBC Radio Bradford was reporting that the police believed the body parts recovered were those of Suzanne Blamires. Earlier, the position had merely been that they were from one person, as yet unidentified. The station broadcast an interview with two distressed sex workers, describing how the dangers of their lifestyle left them 'nervous and frightened'. But they explained why they had no choice but to continue. 'If I wasn't a drug addict,' one said, 'I wouldn't be standing here now.'

It was only with Thursday's editions of the national newspapers that the story was put into its sensational context. Under the headline '3 Dead: New Ripper Terror', the *Daily Express* revealed in its front-page splash story that a criminology student was being questioned about the murder of prostitutes 'on the streets where the Yorkshire Ripper once wreaked terror'. Page seven described Griffiths' arrest in detail, while later editions also published a potted biography of the 'Loner obsessed with killers'. The potential links to Bradford's other missing prostitutes, Yvonne Fitt and Rebecca Hall, were raised. The piece was illustrated with photographs of Susan, Shelley and Suzanne, with a large picture of Sutcliffe gazing menacingly out over them. The *Express*'s Paul Jeeves wrote: 'The case has chilling echoes of Peter Sutcliffe's killing spree which left women across the north of England prisoners in their homes between 1975 and 1980.'

The *Express*'s sister paper, the *Daily Star*, ran the headline 'Terror of New Ripper' over a piece by its chief crime correspondent Jerry Lawton. Along with a colour picture of the police search on the banks of the Aire, it published a black and white shot from the 1970s, showing uniformed officers scouring a field for clues to the murders carried out by Sutcliffe.

Under the splash headline 'Uni Boffin Quizzed on Crossbow Cannibal Killings', the *Sun* revealed that the police believed Griffiths may have eaten some of Suzanne's body parts. To a world unaware of what the suspect had said in interviews, it was a startling revelation. It also seemed too bad to be true. Cannibalism cases are not unheard of, but extremely rare. The *Sun* had also found out about the CCTV footage from

Holmfield Court, and gave a chilling description of its contents. In coverage spanning five pages, the paper also published a graphic that showed the proximity of the key locations in the Griffiths and Sutcliffe cases. Alastair Taylor, the paper's northern reporter, said the disturbing events would 'once again throw a spotlight on Bradford's notorious red light district'. He added that the area 'remains run-down and grimy despite numerous operations to try to clear up problems of drugs, crime and prostitution'. Taylor also went into detail on Griffiths' sinister virtual existence, reproducing the Ven Pariah web pages under the headline 'I'm a Demon'.

In the *Today* discussion on BBC Radio 4, Niki Adams (of the English Collective of Prostitutes) argued that the police did not do enough to protect the working girls after Susan's disappearance. She said that they should have promised an amnesty for the women in return for information until the mystery was cleared up. *Daily Telegraph* columnist Harry Mount commented on the public's interest in serial killers. He wrote: 'The build-up of headlines about the Bradford case only confirms what is already clear: nothing fascinates the British more than the flesh-creeping possibilities of a serial killer on the loose.'

The story's appeal extended beyond Britain. Even if overseas media outlets did not send their own staff to cover it, they bought agency copy and devoted vast space or air time to the latest British serial killer. The *New York Times* expressed wonder at the 'voracious tabloid papers competing in a frenzy over the latest killings'. It too pointed out: 'It was the resonance of another serial murder case involving a man from the Bradford area that helped make the latest killings a newspaper sensation.' The *Australian Herald* reported that: 'New Yorkshire Ripper fears have sprung up in England with three prostitute killings in the city of Bradford.'

It seemed that everybody wanted to know about the suspect in the second Yorkshire Ripper case. What was his name? How old was he? What was his job, his family background? Why would anybody want to commit such an awful crime?

Crime has always fascinated the public and a big crime story will always dominate the news. As the most serious offence on the statute book, murder is of huge interest. Although it is not true to say the gorier the murder the better, serial killers are always guaranteed top billing. Arguably, the very foundation of the mass media owes an enormous amount to this appetite.

The Whitechapel murders in 1888 were the first series of killings to capture the imagination of the press. They also sparked a revolution in the way crime is covered and led to colossal rises in circulation. The connection is explored by historian Andrew Cook in his book *Jack the Ripper: Case Closed*. Cook claims that the infamous butcher, who a century on would lend his soubriquet to Peter Sutcliffe, never existed as such. In fact, he writes, a series of murders were attributed to one man simply to boost a newspaper sales war. Traditional theory has it that, over a two-month period, the knife-wielding maniac killed five prostitutes: Mary Nichols, Annie Chapman, Elizabeth Stride, Catherine Eddowes and Mary Kelly. Cook argues that the murders were actually the work of three men – one psychopath and two copycats. The theory of a single serial killer, padding through the fog, was, he says, contrived by T. P. O'Connor, a colourful journalist–entrepreneur who had launched *The Star* newspaper in January 1888. Pioneering a racy reporting style that would develop into modern tabloid journalism, O'Connor saw great potential in the Whitechapel murders story, and the public bought his single killer theory in a big way. Cook writes:

'*The Star*'s trail-blazing emphasis on the single killer pitch had seen its circulation rocket from an average of 143,000 copies sold per day before the murders began to an average daily sale of 232,000 by the time of the Annie Chapman murder on 8th September.'

After the emergence of a murder suspect, dubbed 'Leather Apron', *The Star* found another circulation winner, pushing sales up again to 261,000. Cook said of O'Connor:

'He thought, three prostitutes in the same area – must be the same bloke. He didn't know if it was the same bloke and he really didn't care. It was a great story and it worked. *The Times* and the *Telegraph* had reported it in a very matter of fact, clerical kind of way. There was no human interest edge to it at all. O'Connor cut out long sentences and went for a punchy delivery. He won the circulation war hands down because *The Star* went on to become the best-selling evening newspaper. As soon as he started with the serial killer line, two or three other papers adopted the same line, then within a few weeks they are all riding his coat tails because his circulation has taken off.'

O'Connor was quick to realise, suggested Cook, that a multiple killer on the loose was a bigger hook than a series of unrelated murders:

'It is because of the latent suggestion that you could be next. It could be you or someone you know. When you are talking about isolated murders, the implication is that the killer was only intending to kill that one person, whether we know the reason or not. It will be the end of the line as far as he is concerned. When you are talking about somebody who has an insatiable appetite for it, you are whipping up a climate of fear. There is very little climate of fear with a one-off.'

The Star, which evolved over the next century to become the *Evening Standard*, tapped into an enduring taste for crime, punishment and horror, which goes back further than the Whitechapel murders. Just a few years before those, crowds turned out enthusiastically to watch public hangings at London's Newgate Prison, near the current site of the Old Bailey. Cooke said:

> 'It was only a decade before that people were turning up at Newgate in the way people turn up to the Emirates these days. Thousands of people wanted to watch, and there would be people wandering round selling the Victorian equivalent of burgers. But you can take that back further or bring it up to the present. People are essentially people, with the same motivations and drive. But the difference was that there was a much higher gore threshold in those days. You could say things and describe things which you would not do now. Today we like it nice and packaged.'

Between the Whitechapel murders and the arrest of Stephen Griffiths, serial killers have surfaced regularly to absorb and horrify readers, viewers and listeners. Britain's most notorious include John Christie, who strangled to death at least six women in the 1940s and 1950s at his lair at 10 Rillington Place, Notting Hill, West London. Like the former QEGS pupil John George Haigh, Christie was hanged.

In the 1960s, Ian Brady and Myra Hindley – dubbed the Moors Murderers – appalled the public because, among other reasons, a woman was involved in committing the atrocities. Both were convicted in 1966 shortly after hanging was suspended, but were doomed to spend the rest of their lives in jail. In the 1970s there was Sutcliffe, and in the 1980s Dennis Nilsen. The 1990s brought the unmasking of Fred and Rose West, and after the turn of the millennium, Steve Wright, known as 'the Suffolk Strangler', throttled five prostitutes in a 10-week killing frenzy in Ipswich.

Such is the public's fascination with these sexual psychopaths that they make headlines long after they are locked up. Fred West, who hanged himself while on remand in 1995, and Hindley, who died of bronchial pneumonia 36 years into her sentence, remain notorious after their deaths. And barely a week goes by without Sutcliffe's name appearing in the newspapers or on radio or television. Even as the world digested and reeled from the latest Bradford arrest, the Ripper's 30-year minimum jail term was approaching its expiry date. Consequently, at the age of 64, Sutcliffe launched a legal bid to have a finite limit imposed on his sentence. He failed, Mr Justice Mitting telling the High Court that he should spend the rest of his life in prison. His offences, he said, 'make it appropriate to set a whole-life term'. Nearly three decades after he was first named as a serial killer, Peter Sutcliffe was front-page news again.

Throughout Thursday 27 May, the story of Stephen Griffiths' arrest continued to grow. More and more journalists descended on West Yorkshire as national news editors sent London-based reporters to strengthen their teams in the north. Reporters milled around Holmfield Court, grilling neighbours about the oddball at Flat 33. By plundering public records such as the electoral roll and the register of births, deaths and marriages, they found Griffiths' mother Moira and father Stephen, sister, brother and other relatives. Old friends and girlfriends were found, together with the many casual acquaintances who had noticed the suspect's peculiar behaviour. The victims' families – who had already given a number of interviews when the inquiry was still a missing persons case – were found and re-interviewed. The quest for information spread from Bradford to the surrounding towns of Dewsbury, Wakefield and Leeds.

The internet age brought a new dimension to the search. Because Griffiths was an avid user of networking sites, computer-savvy journalists were able to trace his movements on the web. They were able to access his Myspace pages and copy his bizarre ramblings. Crucially, from their point of view, they were presented with a selection of photographs of the suspect. Once upon a time this process might take reporters all day as they would scour his known associates for a priceless 'collect' picture. Today it was there for the taking.

In addition, the web provided a forum for the army of murder 'anoraks' to share their thoughts on the alleged serial killer. *Casebook: Jack the Ripper*, a specialist web magazine, generated a lively discussion on the Bradford case. One contributor, using the nickname 'Silverstealth Constable', posted photographs of police forensic teams at work. In one, two uniformed officers searched through discarded clothing on a piece of waste ground to the side of Holmfield Court, while a third, dressed in a white forensic suit, looked on. Another showed a police diver standing chest high in a canal near where the body parts were dumped in the Aire, while six of his colleagues stood on the towpath alongside a pile of scuba equipment.

Friday morning (28 May) brought news that Griffiths had been charged with the murder of the three missing women and would appear before Bradford magistrates later that day. The development put the media under even greater pressure to avoid publishing or broadcasting material that might prejudice his trial. Strictly speaking, legal proceedings against a suspect become 'active' when they are arrested, and from that point on, journalists have to be careful about what they say. In these circumstances, editors walk a tightrope between satisfying the public interest in a suspect and staying within the law, and can often lean towards their duty to publish. However, once charges are laid, the risk of prejudice becomes greater, and generally more caution is exercised. If it is not, defence lawyers can use the coverage to argue that their client could not get a fair trial. Consequently, the prosecution, magistrates and judges have to be on their guard against breaches.

That said, there was enough new detail in the run-up to Griffiths' appearance in the dock to keep the public gripped. The *Sun*, for instance, ran Billy Parkin's story about Griffiths, under the headline 'I Watched Crossbow Killer Eat Live Rat'. Between Thursday 27 May and Saturday 29 May, the Bradford murders featured on 12 tabloid front pages spread across the top five titles – the *Express*, the *Sun*, the *Star*, the *Mirror* and the *Mail*. But the broadsheets made much of the story too: it hit the front page of *The Times* and the *Daily Telegraph* three times and the *Guardian* twice. Only the *Independent* failed to use it on its front page. ITN's flagship programme *News at Ten* – broadcast by ITV – led on the story on three consecutive nights, from the Wednesday to the Friday.

The Griffiths sensation ended domination of the news agenda by the aftermath of a general election. The formation of a new government coalition of Conservatives and Liberal Democrats just a few weeks earlier had been the major talking point until Bradford. The story also put a dampener on World Cup fever.

Griffiths' court appearance came exactly two weeks before the competition was due to kick off in South Africa, and the whole country, whether interested in football or not, could not help being caught up in the mood.

For reasons of sensitivity to the victims, BBC1 was forced to re-shoot a storyline from *EastEnders* that featured a prostitute being strangled. Lucas Johnson, an unstable preacher played by Don Gilet, had picked up a girl in the red light area, driven her to a secluded area and forced her to pray for forgiveness before attacking. The BBC changed the story in recognition of 'the recent tragic events in Bradford'.

By contrast, Next Media Animation, a 3D animation studio based in Taiwan, seemed unruffled by criticism of one its cartoons, which showed the crossbow murder of a woman who bore a striking resemblance to Suzanne Blamires. Michael Logan, the company's spokesman, said the two-minute film was part of Apple Daily Taiwan news coverage and based on contemporary reports. With no sign of irony, he added: 'We're not insensitive to feelings of crime victims.' More controversy occurred when Lady Gaga, the pop star best known for her shock-factor performances, was criticised by some for a show that had cannibalistic overtones. Performing at the Manchester Evening News Arena in early June, she played dead after a male backing dancer sank his teeth into her neck, releasing fake blood.

Stephen Griffiths' relatives may have been tracked down by journalists, but they had little to offer about him. They pointed out that they had hardly seen him since his late teens. His father, grey-haired and shell-shocked on his doorstep in Batley, said they had not spoken in a decade. 'All our sympathies are with the victims and their families,' he said. 'That's all I want to say.' His mother Moira added:

'I think what they have said he has done is horrible and shocking. It makes me feel horrible just thinking about it. It's the kind of thing you never think will happen to you and then it does. I think I'm still in shock. I haven't seen him for years and years. I moved here and he began to lose touch with all the family. I've not heard from him in a very long time. I feel very confused. It's too early to say if I will be there or not.'

Joe Dewhirst, Moira's half-brother, said he barely recognised his waif-like nephew from the photograph of Ven Pariah in the newspapers. 'It made no impression on me until a relative told me who he was. I picked up the paper again and had a closer look and, of course, the face, nose, mouth were unmistakable. The only thing different about him was the physique.'

The story provoked a serious debate about prostitution, how best to deal with the social problems associated with it, and whether legalisation would work. David Cameron, the new Prime Minister, told the BBC's Leeds-based television magazine programme *Look North* that the murders merited a re-examination of the prostitution laws. 'I don't think we should jump to conclusions on this,' he said. 'There are all sorts of problems that decriminalisation would bring.' He did, however, accept that a tough stance on kerb crawling had 'worked elsewhere' and tackling drug addiction would help women caught up in vice.

Fellow politicians also contributed to the debate. Philip Davies, Tory MP for Shipley, said he had a 'lot of sympathy' for the idea of legalising brothels, pointing out that they would banish the necessity for women to work on dark, lonely streets. Bradford South Labour MP Gerry Sutcliffe called for 'control zones' where women could be allowed to sell sex freely and without fear. Marsha Singh, Labour MP for Bradford West, pointed out that legalised brothels had been successful in Europe, but warned: 'Until ways are found of properly siting legalised brothels, the problem will continue.'

Some Bradfordians began to feel that their city was cursed. They had suffered the decline of the textiles trade and the terror of the Yorkshire Ripper. Then, in 1985, there was a fatal fire at Bradford City's Valley Parade football ground, killing 56 people and injuring a further 265, on a day when fans had expected to celebrate winning the English third division. Furthermore, in 2001, the city was hit by race riots, when an estimated 1,000 Asian and white youths fought pitched battles stoked up by the far right.

Joolz Denby, poet and cultural ambassador for the city, thought morale had slumped in the wake of a bad press going back 50 years:

> 'The decline in the textile industry in the 60s and 70s, in combination with the Ripper, and then the fire and the riots, has seen the morale in Bradford plummet. What most people thought when this happened was: "Why Bradford? Why do we have to have this again?" The press have not been helpful to Bradford. They have seen a dog down and kicked it. People read the papers and read jokes about Bradford – it's riot-torn or racially unstable – and think: "Bloomin' hell, do I live there? It doesn't seem that way to me."'

Denby, who is also an award-winning crime author and manager of a Bradford rock band called New York Alcoholic Anxiety Attack, said the outsiders' image of Bradford is misguided. 'Bradford in itself is incredible. Everybody gets on in an incredible way. There is a strong sense of being a Bradfordian – of being, in a lot of ways, very straight, speaking your mind.

There is all the arts, the galleries and festivals that we have here.'

Then there are the buildings. Shortly after Griffiths was arrested, English Heritage published a tourist guide to Manningham, detailing hundreds of hidden architectural gems dotted around the former Victorian enclave. It was, the guide said, on a par with Bath. 'Bradford is exceptionally – heartbreakingly – beautiful,' Joolz Denby said, and explained further:

'I go all funny when I look at the town hall. There are little things you could walk past a million times and not see. Then you'll suddenly see some exquisite carving which you haven't noticed before. On summer evenings you can see the fading sunlight pick out the crystals in the sandstone so that they start to twinkle away. It's unbelievable. Then, 10 minutes out of the city centre and you are on the moors. Potentially, Bradford could be so huge.'

CHAPTER 13

The Crossbow Cannibal

All eyes were on Stephen Griffiths. Court number 3, a small stuffy room on the first floor of Bradford Magistrates' Court, was crammed full. Some of the latecomers were allowed to stand in a line along the back of the room. On the landing outside, another two dozen or so were too late even to stand and had to wait at the door for news. Susan Bouch, the district judge presiding over Griffiths' first court appearance, sat opposite the packed press benches. To her right, Griffiths, with several days' stubble growth and wearing black jeans and a black military-style shirt with a white T-shirt visible underneath, was flanked by two security guards and partitioned off by a 12-foot glass security screen. To her left – so they faced the defendant head-on from no more than six yards away – sat eight friends and relatives of Susan and Shelley. Standing out among them was Gemma Armitage, Shelley's pretty blonde younger sister. Suzanne's relatives stayed away, as did those of Griffiths.

The atmosphere in that sanitised, concrete-and-tile 1970s court building had never been so tense. Griffiths was brought up from the cells at 10.02am, just a shade later than the listed time of 10am and shortly after Mrs Bouch had taken her seat. He was not handcuffed, and, after being shown into the dock, swung his arms around as if they were stiff from being manacled together. A young man in the public gallery was so transfixed that he remained standing and staring at the defendant after the court was told to sit. A police officer had to gently remind him to take his seat.

The first court appearance in any high-profile case is nearly always a high-tension, low-drama affair. Lawyers, police officers, probation staff, court officials and journalists are there for professional reasons. Family and friends of the victim and defendant attend to offer moral support. Members of the public are eager to get a glimpse of the suspect everyone is talking about. The room is invariably packed to the gills. However, there is seldom much action or dialogue outside the brief, legal formalities to be completed. The hottest ticket in town frequently fails to deliver a show. But not at Bradford Magistrates' Court on Friday 28 May 2010.

Immediately after Griffiths was settled in the dock, Amarjit Soor, the court clerk, asked him: 'Can you give the court your name please?'

He scratched the top of his head before replying: 'The Crossbow Cannibal'.

There was a quiet gasp as both officials and observers struggled to take in what he had said. Journalists stopped writing and stared at each other in disbelief. Colour drained from Gemma Armitage's face and two other family members stared in horror at Griffiths before starting to weep. There was no attempt to admonish him and his performance had not yet finished.

Miss Soor asked: 'Can you give the court your address please?'

Griffiths hesitated then replied: 'Erm… Here, I guess.'

Mrs Bouch asked if it was possible to check his date of birth, and Miss Soor asked him if it was 24 December 1969. This time, there was a straight answer. 'Yes,' he said.

In what remained of the three-minute hearing, Miss Soor read the formal charges to him. He was accused, she said, of the murder of Suzanne Blamires between 21 and 25 May 2010, the murder of Susan Rushworth between 22 June 2009 and 25 May 2010, and the murder of Shelley Armitage between 25 April and 25 May 2010. As the indictment was put to him, Griffiths glanced around the room and fidgeted, playing with his fingers. He was then told he could sit, and did so, clasping his hands together in what resembled a praying gesture.

Clare Stevens, the prosecuting solicitor, told the court that it was his first appearance in connection with the offences. She asked for the case to be committed to Bradford Crown Court under Section 51 of the Criminal and Disorder Act, and said arrangements had been made for him to appear there that afternoon at 2.15pm. But Griffiths had another rabbit to pull out of the hat: he wanted to be represented by none other than the solicitors who represented the Yorkshire Ripper. He had asked for someone from the Bradford law firm Lumb & Macgill, knowing full well that Kerry Macgill, the founding partner and now a judge, represented Peter Sutcliffe after he was arrested three decades earlier. Not only did Griffiths want them to represent him, but he wanted his request made public. Phillip Ainge, the Lumb & Macgill solicitor chosen to represent him, told Mrs Bouch that his instructions were simply to acknowledge his client's transfer to the higher court. 'These are early stages of what will be a long process,' he said. Griffiths was then handcuffed and led out of the dock and down to the cells.

Almost immediately, the court adjourned. Mrs Bouch left

first, then, in a highly unusual move, the victims' family members, several openly sobbing, were taken out through the magistrates' exit to avoid the crush to leave court.

Within an hour of the hearing, news of Griffiths' grandstand performance had been broadcast all over the globe. More than 40 journalists were at court, either inside or out, and after they had checked with each other that they had heard what they thought they had heard, they began calling their news desks, filing copy and preparing broadcasts. Every British national newspaper from *The Times* to the *Daily Star* had reporters there. The BBC, ITN and Sky were present, as were Yorkshire's own rich and varied media, from the weekly papers to the *Yorkshire Post*. The Press Association, the national news agency, together with Ross Parry, the freelance outfit that covers West Yorkshire, ensured that the story went further afield, directly or indirectly supplying it to overseas newspapers, radio and television stations and websites. Foreign wires such as Reuters and Associated Press picked up the story, so that by lunchtime the theatrics of the self-proclaimed 'Crossbow Cannibal' had grabbed the attention of every country that was awake.

The big question was what Griffiths' motives were. He was certainly playing to the gallery. Few villains, if any, have delivered such an arresting line in any court appearance, let alone in the opening few seconds of their first. But had he planned this as part of a quest for notoriety? He had studied enough criminals to know that the real monsters usually acquire a chilling soubriquet: Jack the Ripper, the Yorkshire Ripper, the Moors Murderers, the Suffolk Strangler? Was the Crossbow Cannibal his own self-styled nickname?

It appeared initially that it must have been. Although the term had been coined in a headline in the *Sun* newspaper,

Griffiths had spent the last three days in custody being quizzed intensively by detectives. Only later did it emerge that he had been shown Friday morning's newspapers, including the 'Crossbow Cannibal' headline and accompanying story. Was it an ironic dig at the media for the gung-ho way in which they had covered his arrest? Griffiths' penchant for tasteless jokes was a key trait. But whether he had a point or not, his only achievement was to pile on the trauma for the grieving relatives sitting in front of him. One journalist covering the case said:

'It was crashingly insensitive. Those people had probably mustered all the courage to be in that room, out of a sense of duty to their loved ones. To have this guy making flippant remarks within a few feet of where they were sitting is unbelievable. Gemma's face just went white and so did a few of those around her.'

Four hours after appearing before Mrs Bouch, the self-proclaimed Crossbow Cannibal was shown into the dock at the city's Crown court, housed 400 yards away at the new, state-of-the-art Bradford Combined Court Centre. Under the Coroners and Justice Act 2009, there is an obligation to get murder case defendants before a judge as soon as is 'reasonably practicable'. For the early hearings, it was to be James Goss QC, a distinguished West Yorkshire lawyer who had been appointed to the circuit bench just six months before.

Educated at Charterhouse public school in Godalming, Surrey, and Durham University, James Goss had previously been head of chambers at Number 6 Chambers in Leeds. He specialised in homicide and sexual offences and, during 35 years at the bar, had prosecuted some of the north's most high-profile cases. In 2002, he secured the conviction of Gary Hart, a motorist who had caused the deaths of 10 people in the Selby rail crash. Hart, exhausted after spending the night telephoning a mistress, fell asleep at the wheel of his Land Rover and careered off the M62, straight into the path of an East Coast mainline train. He was convicted of 10 counts of causing death by reckless driving and jailed for five years. Four years later, Mr Goss successfully prosecuted predatory paedophile Peter Voisey for kidnapping a six-year-old girl who had been left in the bath of her home in North Tyneside. Voisey raped and abused the child in his car, then dumped her naked and screaming in a back alley. He was jailed for life with a minimum tariff of 10 years.

For Griffiths' first appearance before the Crown court, no prosecuting counsel had yet been appointed, so Miss Stevens presented the case again. Griffiths was represented by Ian Howard, a highly-regarded Bradford defence barrister. The court officials left Griffiths no scope for drama this time. As he stood in wood-panelled court number 2, the clerk asked him simply if he was Stephen Shaun Griffiths. Clasping his hands in front of him, he replied: 'I am.'

The second hearing lasted a little longer than the earlier one, and the number of victims' friends and relatives had swollen to 18. They sat in the public gallery, craning their necks to get a better view of the defendant behind a smoked-glass screen. Griffiths nodded in agreement when Mr Howard said there would be no bail application. Judge Goss told him he need not appear in person at his next appearance at the same court, 10 days later, on 7 June. Rather, he would follow the proceedings from prison via a video link. The defendant nodded before being led quietly down.

An extraordinary day in criminal history ended with ugly scenes outside the court, as the man who had just declared himself the Crossbow Cannibal was driven away. A small but vocal crowd shouted abuse at the large, white, box-shaped prison van as it sped away from the precincts. One protestor had to be restrained by police, as he shouted: 'Here comes the dirty rat. F***ing maniac.' Another screamed: 'F***ing murdering bastard. Die!'

Griffiths was taken to Wakefield Prison, the grim Victorian-style jail that houses some of Britain's most notorious murderers. In months gone by, he had told people his premonition that he would be inside Wakefield, a remark they took for quirky black humour. Of course, it was another sick joke that only he was in on. Griffiths knew he had killed, and they did not. He was amused by the baffled and mildly disturbed look on their faces, and the knowledge that he was offering them a vague chance of guessing his dark secret. His delusions of grandeur were fed by the certainty that they would never work it out. How could they?

After the half-hour journey to Wakefield, he was driven through the gates of the complex he had spent so many hours hanging around outside. The trip left him a few miles from his first home in Dewsbury, and 10 miles from the smart semi in Flockton where he had spent his middle childhood. Now, though, his abode was to be a single-occupancy cell, complete with kitchen and washing area, in Monster Mansions. Its 600-strong list of inmates reads like a who's who of grisly crime. At the time Griffiths arrived, they included Robert Black, a serial sex killer serving life for the murder of three young girls; Roy Whiting, a paedophile who kidnapped, raped and murdered eight-year-old Sarah Payne near her home in Sussex; and David Bieber, an American bodybuilding fanatic who shot dead a Leeds bobby on the beat. Also incarcerated there was Sidney Cooke, member of a notorious child sex ring who took part in the fatal gang rape of a 14-year-old boy, Jason Swift, and in the suspected murder of eight other children. Yet another inmate was Charles Bronson, the self-styled prison hard man whose original seven-year robbery sentence had been extended repeatedly because of his habit of beating up officers and fellow prisoners. Many of Britain's whole-lifers – prisoners who were told they would spend the rest of their lives behind bars – were in Wakefield. Griffiths was given a cell close to one of them; Mark Hobson, who had stabbed and bludgeoned four innocent people to death, lived a few yards away and was part of the same group left to mingle during association time. In his first week, newcomer Griffiths seemed to have given up trying to cause a stir. Prison staff were impressed by his quiet compliance.

Ten days in Wakefield Prison took its toll on Griffiths. At his next court appearance, on 7 June, he seemed barely able to follow proceedings. Although the hearing lasted only 29 minutes, Judge Goss needed to repeat some of his decisions to him, and at one point the defendant appeared to nod off. The purpose of the hearing was to arrange a timetable for the proceedings, but it was clear that there would be many complications to hold them up. For one thing, Mr Howard said, there were 'issues of concern' about the defendant's 'mental state', which urgently needed to be assessed.

With that in mind, Griffiths' lawyers were trying to arrange a consultation with psychiatric experts from Rampton, the top-security hospital in Nottinghamshire. The defence thought it might even be more appropriate for Griffiths to be kept there before the trial, rather than at Wakefield. Both Mr Howard and prosecuting counsel Heather Gilmore suggested that it might be some time before the case could be dealt with. Judge Goss set a provisional trial date for 16 November, but admitted: 'There may be difficulties in listing the case this year.'

As his case was discussed, Stephen Griffiths, dressed in a grey sweatshirt and tracksuit trousers, sat with his arms folded and his head bowed. The victims' families were once again seated in the jury box, with Christine Thompson breaking down in tears at the sight of her daughter's alleged killer. Judge Goss ruled that the next hearing would be on 16 July before Mr Justice Openshaw, a High Court judge. He concluded the hearing by warning the media to take care in reporting the case. They should avoid poisoning the mind of a potential juror against the defendant by reporting anything not said in court. Without saying as much, he was referring to any mention of crossbows, cannibalism, or any of the other damning material unearthed at the time of Griffiths' arrest. They were told in no uncertain terms to stick within the guidelines of the Contempt of Court Act 1981, which sets out what journalists can and cannot report about a defendant once the prosecution has started.

Two days later, the careful preparation for Griffiths' passage to trial almost became irrelevant. On the Wednesday after his Monday court date, a warder happened to glance at a CCTV screen showing the camera's view into his room. To his horror, Griffiths was collapsed on the floor with a plastic bag around his head and a sock tied around his neck. He had tried to commit suicide. Officers ran into his cell and resuscitated him and, to their relief, he did not require external hospital treatment. One of the prison's doctors checked his condition and said that he had not been too badly injured. Prison staff believed the bag was one issued by catering staff for inmates to take chocolate and other treats back to their cells. Despite the concerns about his mental state, Griffiths had not been put on round-the-clock suicide watch. He was monitored closely but not constantly, and had tried to take his own life when an opportunity seemed to arise. He was subsequently moved to a cell in the prison's hospital wing, again with CCTV coverage, but with the pictures watched constantly from a monitoring station that was staffed round the clock.

Detectives were 'incandescent with rage' when they heard what had happened. The last thing they – or anyone – wanted was a suspected serial killer to be given the freedom to commit suicide. It would have represented justice thwarted. The full story of what he did may not have come out without a court case; the judgment of the legal system would not have been passed; and, worst of all, the families of the victims would have been denied a significant part of their closure.

There was also astonishment that Griffiths had not been regarded as a high suicide risk. Although the number of prison suicides had stabilised in the new millennium, in 2008 an estimated 1,500 inmates were estimated to be vulnerable out of a jail population of 83,240. A hefty proportion of those who harm themselves are convicts serving long sentences for serious offences such as murder and manslaughter. In 2007, of 92 prison suicide cases, four were serving indeterminate sentences and 19 life sentences. Although Griffiths was only on remand, his charges were of the gravest imaginable.

Wakefield Prison's authorities had been embarrassed several times before by high-profile suicides. In January 2004, Harold Shipman, the most prolific serial killer of all time, hanged himself in his cell at Wakefield with a noose made from sheets. In his two previous prisons, he had been on round-the-clock suicide watch. This was thought unnecessary by the time he got to Wakefield. Ian Huntley, the Soham school caretaker serving two life sentences for the murders of 10-year-old friends Holly Wells and Jessica Chapman, has made three attempts on his own life. The second, in September 2006, was made in Wakefield Prison; he gobbled down an overdose of antidepressant tablets collected by bartering tobacco and other luxuries with fellow inmates. Just in time, he was found unconscious, and had his stomach pumped. Exactly 12 months later, in September 2007, Huntley tried again, this time taking prescription drugs. He told prison staff what he had done and was revived in the hospital wing.

Griffiths' suicide bid was regarded by prison staff as a half-hearted attempt. One plausible theory was that he had suffered a fit of pique because his story had been knocked off the front pages after a matter of days by Derrick Bird, the taxi driver who killed 12 people during a shooting spree in Cumbria on 2 June 2010. By now, Griffiths had been rumbled as a chronic attention seeker. He had never been happy unless everything and everyone was focused on him. Now he had had a taste of the limelight, he was not willing to give it up without a fight. A prison source said: 'The general feeling is he would have wanted to be saved.' Following the incident, however, security was tightened around him. He was given one of three cells in the prison's hospital wing and constantly monitored at a cost to the taxpayer of an estimated £160,000.

Griffiths' state of mind was one of the key issues to be considered before his trial. Psychiatrists had to ascertain whether he was legally 'fit to plead'. In other words, they needed to find out if he was sane enough to understand the court proceedings and the evidence against him, instruct his defence, and mount an objection to any unsuitable jurors. The trial judge would decide after considering a psychiatrists' assessment of him. If he were unfit to plead, then it would be wrong to try him normally. A jury would be asked to consider whether he committed the acts he was accused of, but he would not be held criminally responsible. Instead, he would be dealt with under the Mental Health Act or the Criminal Procedure (Insanity and Fitness to Plead) Act. Felicity Gerry, a criminal barrister and legal commentator, said:

'State of mind is down to the psychiatrists. You always start on the basis that someone is fit to plead unless someone tells you they are not. It is more of a question for the defence. At the moment, the test is whether he can give instructions, can he understand what's going on, when he talks will he communicate? A defendant who is unfit cannot participate in the trial.'

Even if he were fit to plead, Griffiths would have available to him the defence of 'diminished responsibility'. This is the common route by which defendants blame their actions on a temporary mental incapacity. Under the Homicide Act 1957, a person will not be convicted of murder if they are 'suffering from such abnormality of mind… as substantially impaired his mental responsibility'. Griffiths would deny murder, but admit killing Susan, Shelley and Suzanne through such 'abnormality of mind'. Such a defence would offer a calculating psychopath the means of securing a more lenient sentence by faking the mental condition needed for a plea of 'diminished responsibility'.

With Griffiths' 2:1 degree in psychology and extensive studies of homicide cases, he would find it easy to feign madness. Peter Sutcliffe claimed that he had been told to murder women by the 'Voice of God' speaking to him through the gravestone of a dead Polish man. He failed to mention this vital piece of evidence until his eighth interview with a psychiatrist, carried out 73 days after his arrest. His credibility was further shot by an overheard boast, uttered while on remand, that he would convince the doctors he was mad and be sent to a 'loony bin' instead of a prison. His defence was thrown out and he was convicted of 13 counts of murder and seven of attempted murder.

But Griffiths surprised everyone at his next court appearance by blurting out that he wanted to plead guilty. Behind the scenes, a wealth of evidence had supported his boasts of being a serial killer, so he was not in a position to deny the act. However, it had been assumed that he would deny murder, claiming that his responsibility had indeed been diminished. Criminal barrister and legal commentator Felicity Gerry believed that such a strategy would have two advantages for someone like Griffiths.

> 'If the defendant is after notoriety, then one way of doing it is to plead not guilty and let it go for trial. Also, if the jury believes you, it makes such a massive difference to the sentence. You are now not a murderer. You are mentally ill and, for sentencing purposes, that is so much better than someone who went out there with an intent to kill. You are looking at hospital orders instead of a minimum 30-year tariff.'

Griffiths also had nothing to lose. With lesser charges, pleading guilty can earn a defendant a reduced sentence. But for a triple murder, there is no credit to be had. It would be life.

Nevertheless, for his next appearance – before Sheffield Crown Court via a video link on 16 July – he was adamant. He sat slumped over a wooden desk in a prison room, but, when asked if he could hear the proceedings, he looked up and said: 'Yes. I want to plead guilty. I want to be re-arraigned and plead guilty.'

Mr Justice Openshaw had taken over the case in his role as a presiding judge on the north-eastern court circuit. He was more senior than Judge Goss and the immediate choice to try Class 1 offences such as murder. On hearing the outburst, he asked the defence if Griffiths' fitness to plea had been tested. He was told that although Griffiths had been interviewed in the weeks after his arrest, the psychiatrists had not yet tackled that issue. Mr Justice Openshaw said it was inappropriate to take a plea before a proper psychiatric assessment had been completed. It did not bode well for the chances of hearing the case on the 16 November date set by Judge Goss. Griffiths, now bearded and wearing a grey prison jumper, slumped down again after his interjection, and spent most of the 26-minute hearing sitting listlessly, arms folded or head in hands.

Mr Justice Openshaw came to the case with vast experience. Educated at Harrow School and St Catharine's College, Cambridge, he was called to the bar in 1970, appointed recorder in 1988 and a senior circuit judge in 1999. In 2005, he was sworn in as a High Court judge on the same day as his wife, Caroline Swift QC. The couple made history as the first couple to serve as High Court judges. His headline cases included that of Mustafa Jama, the Somali warlord's son who played a part in the Sharon Beshenivsky shooting before fleeing to his native country. At Newcastle Crown Court in July 2009, he jailed Jama for life with a minimum tariff of 35 years. Mr Justice Openshaw also handed out a life sentence, with a 30-year tariff, to Ronald Castree, a child killer who escaped justice for 32 years. In 1975, Castree had stabbed 11-year-old Lesley Molseed to death after abducting her near her home in Rochdale, Lancashire. An innocent man, Stefan Kiszko, was wrongly convicted of killing her and had spent 16 years in jail before the mistake was identified. Castree was brought to justice in November 2007 after modern DNA analysis techniques exposed his secret.

For the Crown, Robert Smith QC made his first appearance. He had prosecuted the Mustafa Jama case presided over by Mr Justice Openshaw, and, five years earlier, the case of David Bieber – now serving life in Wakefield – for the fatal shooting of Leeds policeman Ian Broadhurst. Robert Smith also prosecuted Colin Norris, a nurse dubbed the 'Angel of Death' after killing four elderly patients at two hospitals in Leeds, simply because of their age. Norris was jailed for life with a minimum tariff of 30 years. Robert Smith's credentials were considerable: Chambers UK legal website described him as 'the best and most impressive silk on the circuit'.

All sides could see that the case was becoming bogged down in procedural necessities and the 16 July hearing concluded with Mr Justice Openshaw ruling that they would not be ready in time for the provisional trial date of 16 November. He ordered that the case be brought back on 15 October for assessment, but there seemed little chance that it would be over by Christmas.

CHAPTER 14

Sisters, Daughters, Mothers

Craig Preston cut a forlorn figure coming out of St Francis of Assisi Catholic church. His eyes were dark and puffy from three months of tears and sleeplessness. The sky was a doleful grey, and a steady drizzle fell on the mourners as they filed out through the double glass doors. But the most woeful image at Shelley's funeral was the coffin: it was just two feet six inches in length, and built to carry a baby's corpse. It was a stark reminder of how little of Shelley had been left after Stephen Griffiths had finished with her. The tiny casket, with a wreath of white lilies on top, was small enough for one man to bear. Craig, immaculately suited in black for the occasion, carried it alone to the Victorian horse-drawn hearse waiting outside.

The ceremony took place on Wednesday 4 August, 14 weeks after Craig had reported Shelley missing and 10 weeks after her fate was discovered. It was the first chance any of the murdered women's families had to grieve formally. Not surprisingly, it was a massive occasion, with more than 300 mourners, a mixture of family, friends and well-wishers, many of them wearing a single white rose, crammed into the little new-build church in Allerton, not far from where Shelley and Craig had lived. The coffin arrived in a black 19th-century carriage, drawn by two magnificent black horses with purple plumes set in their headpieces. Alongside the coffin were floral tributes that spelled out Shelley's name and the word 'sister' in white carnations.

Among the notes and cards left with the wreaths was one from Shelley's Aunt Anne, to a 'beautiful niece'. She added: 'Your memory lives on in my heart.' Another, from Aunt Pam, read: 'You are so sadly missed. You're with your family now who will take care of you. Good night, God bless. Auntie Pam, Dean and Scott.' From her extended family, Stephen, Darren, Adele and Yvette, wrote: 'To a dear cousin. Deep in our hearts you'll always stay. Loved and missed every day. Love Stephen, Darren, Adele, Yvette and families.'

Carl, Shelley's younger brother, carried the coffin inside during the entrance hymn, 'Walk with Me, O My Lord'. Father Pat Wall's requiem mass lasted all of an hour. Other hymns included 'The Lord is My Shepherd', and one of Shelley's school friends broke down in tears as she read a eulogy. Other readings included Joanna Fuchs' poem, 'A Better Place', which includes the following lines:

> She's in a better place right now,
> Than she's ever been before;
> All the pain is gone she's now at rest;
> Nothing troubles her anymore.

Another was an excerpt from Wisdom 3, 1-9: 'The souls of the virtuous are in the hands of God, no torment shall ever touch them [...] if they experienced punishment as people see it, their hope was rich with immortality.'

In the order of service, it was noted that Shelley had been

'reunited with her beloved grandparents, the late John and Nora Moore and Catherine and Edward Armitage'.

Afterwards, Craig laid the casket gently in the carriage, and it made its way slowly to Rawdon crematorium in Leeds, where, after the last part of the ceremony, her family released some white doves to signify peace.

In the days following Stephen Griffiths' arrest, Bradford woke up to the outrage on its doorstep. Three of its citizens had met with the most barbaric of deaths. Although the general public did not know the gruesome details, it was clear that Susan, Shelley and Suzanne had suffered a terrifying and degrading end. The city responded with an outpouring of personal and public grief. Flowers and messages of sympathy were laid outside the victims' homes, near the River Aire, where the remains were found, and outside Griffiths' apartment block. The Holmfield Court tributes included a set of rosary beads in memory of Shelley and Suzanne, who were brought up as Catholics. There was also a moving poem penned by some of the working girls. Entitled 'Foot Steps', addressed to 'Sue, Shelley and Amba' and signed 'Jae, Anne, Marie (all street girls)', the poem's sad, simple message touched many who read it:

> We'll often lie awake at night when others are asleep
> We'll take a walk down memory lane with tears upon our cheek
> No one will know the heartache we'll try so much to hide
> No one will know how many times we've broken down and cried
> We shared happy times sad ones too, the saddest day of all our lives was the day we lost you
> Night, good bless angels xxx

The Armitage family left two bouquets nearby. One, of pink and white flowers, came with a card which read: 'For our special daughter Shelley-Marie, goodnight, God bless, your ever loving mum and dad.' The other, to her friend and neighbour, read: 'Suzanne, in loving memory, the Armitage family.' They also released a photograph to the media of Shelley in happier times. The snap showed her as a bright-eyed youngster, aged 21, bare-shouldered, pretty and full of confidence. It was taken before she became a drug addict, and helped remind the world that she was somebody's daughter, sister, cousin and aunt. It balanced the image of a hardened street prostitute left by the circumstances of her death. Her parents drove this home in a statement issued with the photograph. 'She was loving and kind even when her life changed,' they said. 'She cared and helped everyone – especially the girls on the streets.'

Suzanne's mother, Nicky Blamires, made the same point:

'Unfortunately, my daughter went down the wrong path and she did not have the life she was meant to have. She was a much-loved daughter, sister and niece and what has happened to her will haunt me to the day I die. Suzanne was a bright, articulate girl who went to college and was training to be a nurse. Even though she ended up on the wrong path, she tried to protect her family and kept herself to herself so people knew very little about her. She always knew she could come home and that the door was always open. We also saw her all the time and were always there for her. At the end of the day, nobody deserves this. All these girls were human beings and people's daughters.'

For Susan Rushworth's family, it had been a devastating climax to a year spent in limbo. Her mother, Christine Thompson, hung on to the faintest of hopes that she would be found alive.

Not only that, but she had to care for her husband Barrie, whose health was failing by the day. He had suffered a number of strokes over the previous few years and, in those months before the fate of their daughter became clear, was suffering from dementia. The other related nightmare was Kirsty. She too was trying to stay clean and off the streets, but as her mother's experience showed, this was no easy task.

At the time of Griffiths' arrest, Christine Thompson was on holiday with Barrie and their grandson James in Haldikiki, a resort in Greece. Had things turned out more happily, Susan would have been with them. As it happened, they received the news they were dreading at the end of the two-week break when James called home. Christine Thompson said:

> 'I don't know how I will cope without her. She was my best friend and like a sister to me. She was my world and it has been agony waiting to hear the news we all feared. I always hoped I might see Susan again alive and well but it was not to be. I'm just devastated. I feel that my world has collapsed. We were enjoying our holiday when James rang home and found out what had happened. He broke into pieces and I started screaming.'

Anna Kennedy, a former prostitute who knew all three victims, summed up the feeling on the street of 'there but for the grace of God go I'. Now working on a programme to rescue women from the sex trade, she had seen Susan, Shelley and Suzanne shortly before they disappeared and had been pleased to hear they were trying to sort out their lives. 'All those girls who died were my friends and I could have been next,' she said. She continued:

> 'This terrifies me and I feel sick when I think how close I came. It could have been me. Susan loved her children

to bits. She had really cleaned up and turned her life around just for them. Shelley had a heart of gold and a beautiful smile. She would do anything for anyone. I saw Amber, that's her street name, at the mission on the Wednesday before she vanished. I could not believe it when I heard that another of my friends had disappeared. I used to stay at her flat: we were good friends. I said: "This can't be happening."'

Lynsey Baron, Shelley's old school friend, also paid tribute:

'All I keep thinking is what her last moments were like. I am just praying that she didn't go in a painful way but now it has made me think the worst. She will always be in my thoughts each day. She will be forever missed and I will always think of her until we find out the truth. I would just like people to remember the good side of her. She was caring, friendly and compassionate.'

In the wider community, the dead women were remembered in a candlelit vigil held in Bradford's Centenary Square, a fortnight after Griffiths' arrest. One of the organisers, an ex-vice girl called Fiona, said the event gave other women their chance to recognise the worth of Susan, Shelley and Suzanne and 'celebrate their lives'. Fiona added: 'We do separate different parts of our society, our community, into deserving and non-deserving for various reasons. We have to recognise these women are somebody's daughter, somebody's mum, somebody's sister – they are part of our community.'

Meanwhile, Bradford Council's newly-elected leader Ian Greenwood said: 'Everybody has their own hopes and dreams for their lives and their families' lives, regardless of what they have to do for a living.'

Every public condolence came with a reminder that the three women had been just like the rest of us: ordinary people with families, friends and lives to lead. Locals might remember them from down their street, from their school days or the pub, or they could know their mothers, fathers, sisters or brothers. Either way, it would be clear that they had not chosen that particular lifestyle and did not enjoy it. They had simply made a bad decision somewhere along the line and found themselves on a steep downward slide. In the end, it was virtually impossible to extricate themselves from the quagmire of heroin, crack and vice. Those from similar neighbourhoods might think the same thing could easily have happened to them, or their sisters or girlfriends. The campaign to 're-humanise' the women by seeing the tragedy from their families' viewpoint was a powerful one. It had also been very much in the air since before the Bradford story began to unfold.

Coincidentally, during the final week of April, just as Shelley was making her final appearance in that CCTV clip, the BBC broadcast a three-part drama–documentary about the Ipswich prostitute murders, which had taken place three-and-a-half years earlier. Entitled *Five Daughters*, it was widely acclaimed for its account of how Tania Nicol, Gemma Adams, Anneli Alderton, Annette Nicholls and Paula Clennell had their lives taken by forklift truck driver Steve Wright. Wright, dubbed the Suffolk Strangler, picked each of the girls up in the town's red light area for sex, throttled them to death, then dumped their naked bodies in isolated countryside. The murders were carried out at an astonishing rate and the girls' corpses were discovered in a 10-day period shortly before Christmas 2006. All five were heroin addicts and, like Susan Rushworth, Shelley Armitage and Suzanne Blamires, sold themselves to fund their habit. The point of the drama was to tell the tragedy through the eyes of 'five daughters' as opposed to five prostitutes. It was made with the co-operation of four of the girls' close relatives, Suffolk Police and charities working to help tackle drug abuse and prostitution. Wright, who was given five life sentences for their murders in February 2008, became almost a marginal figure in the drama.

Philippa Lowthorpe, who directed the three-part film, said she wanted to 'open people's eyes' to the real lives behind the horror: 'People think prostitutes are somehow different from us. I didn't realise how hard it is for them to get off drugs. Anneli Alderton, for instance, was trying hard to get off drugs and had been successful. That was what was so heartbreaking about it.' Stephen Butchard, the writer, had spent weeks listening to each family describe their daughter in the kind of ordinary, everyday detail that fleshes out a character. 'I began with each family by simply asking them: "Tell me about your daughter",' he said. 'It was wonderful to hear about the stories from their childhood. As I heard them I began to build up a picture of who they were. It was a privilege.'

The result was a programme that delivered the families' message and deeply moved the relatives and professionals who were intimately involved in its making. Rosemary Nicholls, Annette Nicholls' mother, said after watching a special preview:

> 'I wanted to put across what kind of loving, caring person Annette was to all around her, and that she was close to myself, her father and her siblings, and we loved her dearly. We as a family want people to know that women who work on the streets do not choose this, but are forced to do so due to crippling drug habits.'

Isabella Clennell, mother of Paula, was similarly moved by *Five Daughters*:

'Straight from my heart I would like to get it across to everyone that this drama was helped by myself in order to help other families have an insight into the terrible effects of drug addiction. If any other parent sees their child going through this, don't push them away. Guide them to someone who can help them.'

Detective Superintendent Roy Lambert, who investigated Anneli's death and who supervised Wright's arrest, said of the drama: 'There was a definite decision to personalise it – it's quite easy to dismiss women who work in prostitution.'

The sympathetic approach began when the murders happened. At the time when the bodies were found dotted around Ipswich's outskirts, the killer was still at large and unidentified. Public interest in the case was so much greater because the killer was on the loose, fear was in the air, and detectives, desperate for information, helped keep the publicity machine running. Since the Yorkshire Ripper was caught in the early 1980s, Wright has been the only high-profile serial killer to be at large after the discovery of his victims. He was the target of the biggest police manhunt since Sutcliffe. However, in the 1970s, women like Patricia Atkinson and Yvonne Pearson were not accorded the same respect and public sympathy as the Ipswich victims. Then, the killer's persona and modus operandi gripped the public imagination more than the plight of the prostitutes he murdered. It was only when Sutcliffe attacked a 'respectable' woman, like Bradford student Barbara Leach, that the victims generated much sympathy. In those days, 'tarts' and 'good-time girls' were 'on the game'. In the new millennium, 'sex workers' earn a living in the 'sex industry'. They even have a strong, representative pressure group, the English Collective of Prostitutes, which campaigns on issues relevant to the trade.

When the Ipswich story broke, the town's local paper, the

Evening Star, together with Ipswich Borough Council, launched a charity – the Somebody's Daughter appeal fund – to raise money for people caught up in drugs and prostitution. The *Star* used the Somebody's Daughter logo to promote and set the tone for its coverage of the tragedy, and afterwards the charity created a legacy for Tania, Gemma, Anneli, Paula and Annette. To date, it has raised tens of thousands of pounds for locals who are in danger of being sucked into the sex trade. In the months following Stephen Griffiths' arrest, for instance, the fund amassed £20,000, which was used to help build a refuge and rehabilitation centre on the outskirts of the town. Perhaps more importantly, it changed the way prostitutes were portrayed and helped persuade people to see them as fellow citizens rather than outcasts. In the late spring and early summer of 2010, this wave of sympathy towards the victims might have provided at least some comfort for the families of Susan Rushmore, Shelley Armitage and Suzanne Blamires.

By the third week of June, West Yorkshire Police had completed their search of the yards and alleys behind Holmfield Court. A few days later, the underwater search team withdrew from the River Aire. The unit had recovered almost all of Suzanne's remains, but could find only a tiny piece of tissue from Shelley's spine. Of Susan, there was no trace, and Griffiths would not tell them anything.

In the cases of Shelley and Suzanne, disparities in what was left reflected how much time had passed since Griffiths had dumped them in the river. The Aire is a major river, and after a certain amount of time had passed, even the most painstaking search would be fruitless. There would be further inquiries, leads, searches, but to all intents and purposes, the search for bodies was over. For the Armitage and Blamires families, it meant that the remains of Suzanne and Shelley could now be released to them for burial. This is done in keeping with strict legal procedure by the opening of an inquest into the death. The coroner formally identifies the victim, notes formalities such as the date, place and cause of death, then adjourns the hearing so that the funeral can go ahead, and, if there is a prosecution pending, to allow the criminal inquiry to proceed.

For Susan Rushworth's family, however, it meant even more heartbreak. They had to live with the likelihood of Susan's body never being found. After the agony of her poor health, addiction, prostitution and disappearance, then the horror of discovering how she died, they would be denied the closure of a burial. Her mother, Christine Thompson, said: 'We can't even have a funeral. Perhaps if we laid her to rest, then I could grieve and move on.'

To add to the family's pain, on 18 July, Susan's father Barrie died. Barrie Thompson had been ill for some time, but since Susan had vanished, his wife had depended on him all the more for company. Aged 72, he passed away in hospital and was cremated on 28 July at Scholemoor crematorium in Great Horton. The family's notice in the *Bradford Telegraph & Argus* remembered the 'dearly loved husband of Christine, much loved dad of Jane, Paul and the late Susan'. Christine Thompson thought Sue's trusting nature was more like her father's. 'They were the two people I loved most in the world,' she said. 'Now they are gone, one after the other. I don't know how I am going to get by. He used to look at me and ask me what I was crying for. I used to say: "It's Susan – she's not coming back."' I think when he saw her on telly then he realised. He never had time to get over it.'

In the early summer of 2010, Griffiths offered the waiting families a shred of hope by writing to Bridget Farrell, promising to tell her where he had left the bodies if she would only visit him in Wakefield Prison. The prison authorities intercepted the letter and contacted the police, who showed parts of it to her. Although Bridget had known Griffiths longest, she was too distraught by the request to go along with it. Instead, a friend and fellow working girl, Joanne Delaney, went in her place. Griffiths sat at his desk, ignoring her. She recalled her visit:

'When I walked in, he was sitting at a desk by himself looking down. He just looked up and said: "You're not Bridget." That's all he said. Then he put his head down again and said nothing. I said: "She asked me to come. I'm her friend. She wants to know where Shelley is." He didn't talk to me – not another word. I kept talking. Then we just sat in silence for about 10 minutes. I gave up. He wasn't going to tell me anything.'

The inquest for Shelley and Suzanne was held at Bradford Coroner's Court on 29 July, the day after Barrie Thompson's funeral. None of the relatives attended, but a police family liaison officer was there on their behalf. Roger Whittaker, the West Yorkshire coroner, read reports by Home Office pathologist Peter Vanezis and listened intently while Detective Superintendent Sukhbir Singh updated him. While the gruesome details of Suzanne's death were known about from reports of the CCTV footage, those present still felt a shudder when Mr Whittaker confirmed the cause out loud in public for the first time. 'The cause is effectively severe injuries caused by a crossbow,' he said. DS Singh explained that, in Shelley's case, it was not possible to determine a cause of death. However, he pointed out: 'She would not have been alive with this piece of spine missing from her body.' He explained that nothing had yet been found of Susan Rushworth. Mr Whittaker said he was anxious to be kept informed if the situation changed because her family were desperate to be able to bury her. He said that if no remains were found, he would exercise the option of writing to the Home Office for permission to carry out an inquest without a body. In conclusion, he said of Shelley and Suzanne: 'Today we are able to release back to the families for funeral purposes their loved ones who have for so long been held back.'

Suzanne's funeral was held six days after Shelley's, on Tuesday 10 August. This time, the ceremony was in St Columba's Catholic church in Tong, south-west Bradford, the very place where, all those years before, the priest had read out her anti-drugs essay. This time, her mother Nicky read a poem to 200 mourners, capturing the pain of her loss and the comfort of believing that Suzanne would be reunited with Norman, her father:

We thought we understood heartache. It has landed on our door before.
But the pain and loss at losing you, Suzanne, will live with us forever more.
We are not gathered in a gloom-filled room, there are no heads bowed low.
We are thinking about how much we love you, and how hard it is to let you go.
You have taken the journey we all must take.
But we take comfort as we know you are reunited with your much-loved dad and it is time to let you go.

As at Shelley Armitage's funeral, a Victorian carriage transported Suzanne's coffin to the church, pulled by two towering black horses, but this time led by two white horses sporting red plumes. Through the glass display case, Suzanne's white casket was visible. Her name was written in red and white flowers on top, together with the word 'sister' in yellow and white blooms.

CYRIL DIXON

Delivering a one-hour requiem mass, Father Frank Smith, the vicar of St Columba's, said:

> 'Today is a day for Nicky and her family to find some peace and be allowed to grieve in private. As a parish we offer them our condolences, our prayers and our support in whatever way we can. To lose a child is one of the most difficult things anyone will have to deal with in their lives, but through faith and the support of friends and family, this will hopefully be made a little easier for Suzanne's family.'

He went on to describe her as 'cheeky, full of confidence and outgoing'. She had, he said, kept her father Norman 'wrapped around her little finger'. At the end of the service, Suzanne's coffin was carried from the 1950s-built church to the accompaniment of Robbie Williams' ballad 'Angels'.

The family also released a set of pictures showing the happiest times of Suzanne's life. At the time she was confirmed missing, police released an arrest mug shot, showing her puffy-faced in her Nike anorak. Now, she was remembered for how she looked on her wedding day, on a horse-riding trip as a little girl, and on a holiday boat trip. In the wedding snap, she was happy but a little nervous, in a white lacy dress and with a circlet of white fabric roses on her neatly-cropped hair. On holiday, she was in T-shirt and shorts with big sunglasses, sitting on the open-top cruiser's bench with a sunny coastline in the background. Three snaps came from the riding trip, showing Suzanne aged about 10 with fair hair. One showed her sitting on a dappled grey pony, another on a chestnut pony, and in the third she stood next to the chestnut pony, holding the reins. There could be no better reminder that this woman would be missed.

CHAPTER 15

End of Term

D-day in the case of Regina v Stephen Griffiths was set for Tuesday 21 December 2010. It was the last day the court was sitting before Christmas, or, to its legal and clerical staff, the 'last day of term'. Oxford Row, the pedestrianised zone in front of Leeds Crown Court, was scattered with hazardous patches of ice. That month had been the coldest December since 1890, and night-time temperatures in Yorkshire had plummeted to around minus 15°C. Although proceedings were not due to start until 10.30am, a queue of about 150 people had extended out of the front door and down the street by 9am. Lawyers, defendants, office workers and journalists all stood, stamping their feet against the Siberian weather. The extended wait was due to the high turnout for the big case, and heightened security to stop anyone who had come armed to hand Griffiths their own justice.

The atmosphere was electric. Big court hearings always are, but the case of the self-proclaimed Crossbow Cannibal had made headlines globally. Outside the court, television satellite vans were parked in Oxford Row. Inside, officials set aside an extra court to house journalists covering the case. They designated 25 seats in court 5, where the case would be heard, and another 45 in the special annex, court 4. The annex was fitted with a television link to the proceedings, with four different cameras broadcasting to four different screens. One gave a side view of the dock. Both annex and court were packed. All the victims' families were, again, present, but once more there was no sign of the defendant's family. Also in court was West Yorkshire's HMET, including Detective Superintendent Sukhbir Singh, the lead officer in the case.

The trial was ready to start. Griffiths had been assessed mentally, was fit to plead, and was prepared to admit to all three murders. Griffiths was to be represented by David Waters QC, a top criminal barrister noted for prosecution as well as defence. It was Mr Waters who successfully prosecuted shamed peer Jeffrey Archer for perjury over a 1980s libel battle with the *Daily Star* newspaper. But Stephen Griffiths' conduct throughout the summer and autumn meant that nothing could be taken for granted.

Griffiths' erratic behaviour had intensified in early June with the breaking news that Derrick Bird, a debt-ridden, depressive cabbie, had gone berserk in Cumbria, killing 12 people and injuring 11 others. Bird, 52, who then turned the gun on himself, had stolen the limelight from Griffiths, five days after he announced himself to the world as the Crossbow Cannibal. To compound the humiliation, fellow prisoners at Wakefield chanted 'You're not famous any more' at him. It was that incident which sparked the first of numerous suicide attempts, when he tried to hang and suffocate himself simultaneously.

A week later, he was moved from the health unit to a segregation cell on F wing. Staff nicknamed his new home 'Hannibal's cell', because of its resemblance to the maximum security unit used to house Hannibal Lecter in the movie version of *The Silence of the Lambs*. It featured a full-length screen made of heavy-duty perspex, so the prisoner could be kept under observation at all times. Rows of bars provided added security for the guard, watching from just a few feet away. As well as being a suicide risk, Griffiths had his security status upgraded after verbally threatening a guard. He had no television in the cell and took to spending most of his time sleeping. 'He doesn't communicate with staff,' said a prison source. 'The guard looks directly at the inmate who has nowhere to hide.' Griffiths' temperament was not helped by the fact that he was trying to give up smoking. He was prescribed a 12-week course of Champix after telling doctors he wanted to quit the habit for health reasons, but he did not have the willpower. Then, a few weeks after the move to isolation, he threw a tantrum because he was not allowed to watch television. Griffiths told his guards that he was missing his favourite programme, *The One Show*, the early-evening magazine show whose presenters have included Adrian Chiles and Christine Bleakley. He wanted a set moved into his cell. They refused.

In August, Griffiths sparked a security alert when warders found out he had been de-boning chicken at meal times and failing to leave the scraps on his plate. Some of the more resourceful prisoners use bones as makeshift blades because they are not detected by security scanners and are difficult to find in a pat-down search. Given his history, members of staff were paranoid about giving him another chance to commit suicide, or a weapon to attack anyone else. It transpired that Griffiths had a phobia about choking on small bones and spent time before each chicken meal meticulously pulling them out. 'There was a major scare,' said the prison source. 'The problem is, chicken bones are used by lags to self-harm and as homemade daggers.'

Because his behaviour had stabilised, the prison authorities moved him to a more private cell. There was no perspex screen and they allowed him a television set in his room. But on 10 September, their generosity backfired. Griffiths flew into a rage, throwing objects around the room and smashing furniture against the walls. He then seized a jagged piece of the broken television screen and began dragging it across his neck. The guards burst into his cell, overpowered him, and took the shard of glass from his hand. He was taken back to the health unit but the wound was not life-threatening. A source reported:

> 'In the early hours of this morning he suddenly got out of his bed and started smashing things up, including his TV set. He then slashed his throat with a piece of glass from the broken TV screen. Whatever people think of Griffiths and his alleged crimes, it is the duty of the Prison Service to care for prisoners and ensure that they appear in court and live to serve their full sentences if convicted.'

This incident sparked another psychiatric assessment, with the prospect that Griffiths would be moved to Rampton. However, the doctors there decided 'he did not meet their criteria'. On 22 September, just a few days after Griffiths was told of their decision, he attempted suicide for the third time. On this occasion, he smuggled a polythene bag into his cell and attempted to choke himself by swallowing it. Again, the prison officers spotted it, this time on a CCTV monitor, and intervened, one sticking his fingers down Griffiths' throat to yank it out. It was reported: 'He was choking and was only a few seconds from slumping unconscious. The plastic bag was quite a long way down his throat. It was clear that this was a serious attempt to commit suicide.'

THE CROSSBOW CANNIBAL

Although Griffiths suffered bouts of depression and failed to cope with the lack of privacy at Wakefield, his self-harm may have had different origins. Given time to contemplate the enormity of their crime, murderers can become overwhelmed with guilt. The suicide attempt could be spurred on by what conscience remained within the psychopathic disorder. But also, psychopaths are the ultimate control freaks, and suicide can be their own self-determined exit strategy. They can avoid being put on trial, being judged, being imprisoned and being under the control of the Prison Service for the rest of their days. Harold Shipman, the killer GP, committed suicide shortly before his 60th birthday. By doing so, he guaranteed his wife Primrose the benefit of his NHS pension. It was worth a £100,000 lump sum and £18,000 annual payout. Fred West, the Gloucester sex torturer, committed suicide on New Year's Day 1995. He was awaiting trial for the murder of 12 young women, including his daughter Charmaine.

So, a few days after his third suicide attempt, Stephen Griffiths was moved back into one of Wakefield's super-secure cells with the screen and goldfish bowl monitoring.

Griffiths' mood swings ensured that his next court appearance was an edge-of-the-seat occasion. The date of 15 October had been listed as a hearing for the court to take stock of the case's progress. At most, Griffiths would offer a plea, and virtually everybody expected that plea to be not guilty to murder. However, three days before the hearing, the police were informed by the defence that he was likely to admit to all three murders. He wanted to get it all over and done with. The news sent everyone connected with the case into a tailspin. If it went ahead as the rumour mill suggested it would, a complex murder investigation could be done and dusted within five months. The police had to put some hasty final touches to their preparation for the case, as did the prosecution and the court, and the media who were covering the case.

Once again, Bradford Crown Court was the venue, and there was a massive turnout. About 20 members of the victims' families attended, including Christine Thompson, her son Paul and grandchildren Kirsty and James Rushworth; Daryl and Gemma Armitage; and Nicky Blamires. Griffiths was required to be there in person this time. His appearance had changed dramatically. He had shorn his hair down to a 'number 3' crop and had lost an enormous amount of weight. He sat looking gaunt in a black military-style shirt and trousers, with his head slumped on his chest.

Mr Justice Openshaw began by warning the press not to write or broadcast anything that might prejudice the outcome of a trial, should Griffiths, after all, enter a plea of 'not guilty'. Since his headline-grabbing appearance at Bradford Magistrates' Court, most media had described him as the 'self-proclaimed Crossbow Cannibal' or the 'man who called himself the Crossbow Cannibal'. Because Griffiths actually offered it as his real name, journalists could just about use it without breaching court reporting laws. Nevertheless, the judge warned that no liberties should be taken. The Attorney General would 'personally monitor these proceedings'.

The defence asked for a six-week adjournment because psychiatrists had not yet established whether Griffiths was fit to plead. Mr Justice Openshaw was annoyed. He said it was 'quite incredible to me' that Griffiths had been in custody for five months without being assessed. 'There must be some degree of urgency in this,' he warned. 'These proceedings can't just meander on.' Robert Smith QC, for the prosecution, said: 'It would appear there is unlikely to be any issue about the facts of the case.' The defence assured the judge that Griffiths would co-operate, and so the next hearing was set for Leeds Crown Court on the last day of term – 21 December.

Griffiths spent the next nine weeks in a running battle with the prison authorities. A week after the Bradford hearing, he applied to be taken out of the prison's segregation ward. He claimed that the sense of isolation brought on his depression, which increased the chances of him trying to harm himself. A few days later, he was seen by a forensic psychiatrist who declared that there was nothing wrong with him. Three weeks later, Griffiths swallowed four radio batteries in protest at being kept under constant observation. He told the authorities later that he was trying to prove the point that they were not really watching him properly; they were just breaching his privacy. He refused medical attention and went on hunger strike. Griffiths went on to complain when his radio was confiscated and was unhappy when the prison guards began turning him over in his sleep to stop the batteries in his stomach injuring him. His antics were nothing more than a campaign to be moved to the relatively cushy environment of Rampton, a campaign that failed. On 30 November, a defence psychiatrist examined him and found him fit to plead, as did a prosecution doctor on 10 December.

On 15 December, in an administration hearing at Leeds Crown Court, Griffiths' lawyers formally challenged the prison authorities' decision to keep him isolated. They claimed that he should be allowed 'association' because his mental health had deteriorated during his time at Wakefield. Matthew Stanbury said on his behalf that, although he may be considered a risk to others, there had been no trouble when he was allowed in the health wing common room. He had stopped suffering from stress and weight loss. On the other hand, when he was kept in solitary confinement, he was observed 24 hours a day, 'like a goldfish', and he became ill to the point of being a suicide risk. Mr Justice Simon told Mr Stanbury: 'Your client is deemed to be a dangerous man and there is nothing in the psychological report that shies away from that.' Mr Stanbury replied that he did not 'shy away' from it, but said that Wakefield Prison is full of dangerous men. The judge turned down the application, and what promised to be Stephen Griffiths' last six days on remand were spent in isolation.

It was shortly after 10.30am on the last Tuesday before Christmas that Stephen Griffiths admitted his guilt before the court, the public and the families of Susan Rushworth, Shelley Armitage and Suzanne Blamires. He could not resist showing his contempt for them – as he was led into the dock, flanked by five prison officers, he mouthed the words: 'Who are you looking at?'

In response, Shelley's father Daryl lunged forward, pointed at him and shouted: 'You're a d**khead.'

With silence restored, Griffiths, wearing grey jogging top and bottoms, was asked to confirm his name as Stephen Shaun Griffiths. He replied 'Yes' in a barely audible voice. He was then asked how he pleaded to the same charges that were put to him seven months earlier. Griffiths replied 'guilty' to all three. There was another outburst from the public gallery, to which the judge said: 'You are entitled to be present in court, but it is better if you are just quiet.' Hush duly descended. There was a final hold-up while the judge made a legal ruling that journalists were allowed to send text messages from court. Robert Smith QC introduced himself as the prosecutor and David Waters QC as the defence, and then began to lay bare the horror of Flat 33 Holmfield Court.

CHAPTER 16

Regina v Stephen Griffiths

The delivery was precise and to the point. Robert Smith QC detailed all the outlandish brutality of Griffiths' murderous regime, but did not linger on the minutiae. To do so would risk gratifying the killer one last time and cause more distress to his victims' families, watching from a specially designated area of the court. He began his opening with Peter Gee, the caretaker at Holmfield Court, reviewing the CCTV footage from Friday 21 May to Monday 24 May. He explained the Monday-morning routine and the positioning of camera 14, on the third floor, pointing towards Flat 33, where the defendant, Stephen Griffiths, lived. Peter Gee knew the defendant only as 'Stephen'. Robert Smith went on:

> 'Mr Gee had noted that the defendant appeared to be what he described as a loner and that he did not generally have visitors. Because of the defendant's unstable behaviour at the property which had been demonstrated in the past, Mr Gee had been instructed not to visit the defendant when he was alone and he had

been warned that he was potentially violent. The defendant had also been noted for his strange behaviour and demeanour by a number of the residents at the flats… He was unapproachable, and he appeared to have no friends. One of the tenants had occasionally seen him bring prostitutes back to his flat, where they stayed for only a brief time.'

The prosecutor explained that Suzanne Blamires was a prostitute who used the alias Amber. She had been working in the early hours of Saturday 22 May on Sunbridge Road. Another women, whom he named only as 'R', saw her there some time after 2am. But, he said, at 2.23am, the camera at the front of Holmfield Court caught the defendant walking along the front of the building with Suzanne. He then described the appalling events captured on camera 14, as discovered by the caretaker on Monday morning:

'At half past two that morning, the defendant was recorded walking towards the entrance to the flats with Suzanne Blamires, and both entered the building and then entered the defendant's flat. It was at 02.34 that Suzanne Blamires ran out of the flat pursued by the defendant, whereupon, as the closed circuit television showed, a struggle then ensued. The limp figure of Suzanne Blamires was then dragged back towards the entrance to the flat by the defendant and left lying in the corridor. The defendant entered his flat and returned to the corridor with a crossbow and fired a crossbow bolt into the inert body of Suzanne Blamires. He then dragged her body into his flat. A few minutes later, he emerged from the flat and displayed the crossbow to the closed circuit television camera and displayed one finger to the lens. He then left the building, holding a bottle up for display to the camera, and walked towards the city centre.'

Mr Smith said that the footage matched the verbal evidence given by Griffiths' neighbours. One had described the walls in the building as 'paper thin'.

'They had gone to bed on the morning of the 22nd May at about 2 o'clock in the morning, and shortly afterwards had heard the sound of banging noises and of raised voices from the defendant's flat. They believed that the noise had continued for about half an hour, until the sound of a woman's scream of pain was heard, followed by the words: "Get off, you ignorant bastard." This was in turn followed by a heavy thump and then silence.'

Mr Smith now related Griffiths' next actions during the small hours of that Saturday morning. It seemed that his appetite for bloodshed had not been satisfied. After walking out of Holmfield Court, he approached the woman he called R. She asked if he wanted 'business'. He said he did, flattering her by telling her she was 'good looking'. Griffiths asked if she could get him some crack cocaine. Mr Smith continued:

'He told her that he wanted her to go to his flat for business and took her on an indirect route to Holmfield Court. It is likely, suggest the prosecution, that he did that in order to limit the scope for the two of them to be recorded on closed circuit television cameras in the city. Outside Holmfield Court, he told her that he wanted to take photographs of her bum, and he said that he was fascinated with bums, and the prosecution say that these thought processes are entirely consistent with the evidence of another woman who had known him and with whom he had had a relationship, and with the evidence which the police were later to recover in the form of digital images from his camera and computer.'

The prosecutor said that Griffiths offered this second woman £80 to spend an hour with him, but added that he would be prepared to hire her for the whole night. He wanted her to get drugs but did not want her to invite dealers back to his flat, and he warned her that he sometimes did 'daft' things like taking all his clothes off when he was high on crack. They walked off into the night to find a supplier. Mr Smith went on:

> 'He then repeated several times that he hated prostitutes. He said he had been ripped off by them in the past. He said he had been ripped off by a girl called Blondie, but that she had got what he called her comeuppance. He also said he had been ripped off by a girl called Catherine, who had jumped into his car and taken his money. He said that he knew where she lived because he had followed her home one night, and he said he was going to get Catherine.'

They bought some crack and went to the woman's flat so she could get a pipe to smoke it. She made excuses to stop him going in with her, and once inside, watched him through the CCTV screen which showed the outside of the building. Griffiths was crouched down between two cars and, when she went out again, he was gone.

> 'What R was unaware of was that the defendant had murdered Suzanne Blamires approximately an hour before the point at which he had asked R to return to his flat with him, and at a time when the body of Suzanne

Blamires was still lying in his flat. Had she entered his flat, it is likely, submit the prosecution, that she would have become his next victim. At 03.35 that morning, the defendant was recorded walking towards Holmfield Court again, but this time with R. He could be seen apparently trying to persuade R to enter the building with him, which she did not do. On the recording, there appeared to be a disagreement between them. R could be seen speaking into a mobile telephone and the two of them then walked away towards the city.'

Mr Smith then set down a timeline for the defendant's movements during the next 48 hours, as they were captured on surveillance cameras in his neighbourhood and further afield:

Saturday 22nd May
04.28: Griffiths returns to Holmfield Court after the failed bid to lure R, takes the lift up to the third floor and goes into his flat.
07.57: goes out carrying a black bag.
08.25: returns with the bag, but it appears to be empty.
22.45: departs again with a rucksack on his back and two heavy drawstring bags.

Sunday 23rd May
00.00: comes back without the rucksack but has the drawstring bags. Both are empty. He leaves immediately with a small bin, which appears to be full, then returns with it empty.
00.23: leaves with a large holdall which appears heavy.
00.27: returns with the holdall, this time light.
12.20: goes out with the same holdall which still seems light.

12.27: returns dragging the bag, now heavy.

14.30: departs Flat 33 with a weighty rucksack on his back and dragging the same holdall as earlier, which now appears heavy. He heads towards the city centre.

14.48: gets to Bradford's Forster Square railway station carrying the rucksack and bag.

14.56: reaches Shipley railway station, still with the bags, and walks towards the River Aire.

16.27: returns to Shipley station with a light rucksack.

17.00: makes it back to Forster Square station.

17.18: gets back to Holmfield Court, via a stop-off to buy shopping at Tesco Express.

22.18: leaves the flat but returns a minute later, carrying a Tesco bag with its handles tied up.

22.21: goes out carrying two drawstring bags and walks towards the city.

22.39: returns with just one of the bags.

Mr Smith told the court:

'It is clear from the closed circuit television recordings which we have just summarised, and given that the police had searched the defendant's flat upon his arrest, that Suzanne Blamires never left the defendant's flat alive, and that within about an hour after the attack upon her, the defendant had attempted to persuade the witness R to enter his flat. Given the results of the investigation, it is for this reason that the prosecution contend that he must have intended that R should be his next victim, and that at the time when he sought to persuade her to enter his flat, Suzanne Blamires was lying dead in the property. The ensuing investigation demonstrates that he went on to remove the body of Suzanne Blamires in sections from his flat, and therefore must have dismembered and cut up her body in the premises in the course of the remainder of the 22nd May and during the following day, the 23rd.'

But that was not all, he said. An almost identical sequence of events was captured on CCTV starting on the day Shelley Armitage went missing.

'Research of other images from locations in Bradford and at Shipley at later stages of the investigation, showed images of Shelley Armitage in Bradford on the evening of the 26th April 2010, in the company of a man corresponding with the description of the defendant. Images recovered from Bradford and from the railway stations at Forster Square and at Shipley also showed that on the 28th April of this year, he had conducted a similar journey. Those images showed that he had carried a rucksack over his shoulder while walking through Bradford and via Forster Square station to Shipley railway station, and the inevitable conclusion is that he had carried the remains of Shelley Armitage to the River Aire, and had deposited them there by a means which he was to repeat when he dismembered the body of Suzanne Blamires.'

The chronology was determined after Peter Gee reported the film's contents to his manager. Mr Smith described how Suzanne was identified by Sergeant Metcalfe with the help of a PC Vincent on the same team. He added that Bradford South vice squad had also recognised Griffiths: 'He had been brought to their attention in the course of a briefing in the latter part of 2009.'

Next came the two nights of confessions at Halifax. The

court heard how, even before being questioned, Griffiths told the officers it was the 'end of the line for him', that he had 'killed loads', and that he called himself Ven Pariah. Mr Smith also quoted Griffiths' cryptic reference to the Ripper: 'Peter Sutcliffe came a cropper in Sheffield. So did I, but at least I got out of the city.'

The interview with Griffiths, conducted without a solicitor and convened to find out if Suzanne was still alive, produced more of the same, reported Mr Smith:

> 'The defendant told the police in the course of this short interview that if she was the one who was known as Amber, she was, to use his word, gone. He said that he had eaten some of her, and she was the third one he had cannibalised and that the remains were gone, and he said: "That's part of the magic, I don't know." He said that there was only so much he was going to disclose, but that Suzie, as he named her, was beyond any medical help. He said that he knew how to get rid of a body. He said that he had told the police he had done it, but that there were no remains to be found, and as the police officers were sealing the tapes, he informed them that he was only going to talk about five Bradford cases, and said: "Suzanne Blamires: I knew I was giving myself up on that one..." While being observed in detention by a police officer, he uttered further comments, including the fact that the first time he did it, he had eaten the thighs, a reference to one of his victims, and that he had disposed of the body.'

On the night of his arrest, Griffiths was examined by Lesley Lord, a forensic physician. She could find no signs of psychosis or any other mental illness. On the contrary, she found him 'highly intelligent' and capable of understanding and answering questions. Griffiths told her he was taking diazepam, an antidepressant called fluoxetine and dihydrocodeine, for the treatment of neck pain. He also detailed his psychiatric history, from treatment at Waddiloves in 1987, after slashing the supermarket manager, to Newton Lodge, Wakefield, just two years before, where he was treated as an outpatient. Dr Lord noticed that Griffiths' hair was singed and there were some cuts on the palm of one hand and on the backs of both. Asked how he got them, he replied: 'Slicing and dicing.'

Mr Smith said that by the time a solicitor had been arranged for him, the following evening, Suzanne's head had been found in the River Aire. Griffiths confirmed everything he had said in off-the-cuff remarks and the informal interview 24 hours earlier. The prosecutor read out Griffiths' flippant account of how he had disposed of his victims' bodies:

'"The murders, they were horrific; butchered, dismemberments, eating parts of all three of them. In the first case with Susan Rushworth, in the aftermath, I got the cooker, was taken apart, and gotten rid of. So it's six months without a cooker or something before somebody moving out of the flat gave me the present one, which you will find traces of Shelley Armitage in. But with the third one, I actually went for it, just tried eating bits of her raw. All three killed and dismembered. The creature that I was, it was just meat in the bath that was chopped and churned, some of it eaten raw and I don't know after that. I don't know where she is." He later said: "It was just a slaughterhouse in the bath tub, just like the other two."'

Griffiths, the court heard, admitted killing all three women.

Suzanne was shot with a crossbow in the flat, before being dismembered with hand tools. Shelley was shot with a crossbow and cut up with power tools. Susan was killed with a hammer in the bedroom and dismembered with machine tools.

'... As far as Susan Rushworth was concerned, he had cleaned the flat up after her murder, and that the police had been to his flat and arrested him in relation to what he described as a jumped-up charge from a bitter ex-friend, and he said that the flat had passed the superficial inspection of a trained officer's eye. He said that he had put part of her flesh onto an old sofa outside which he had set on fire, and that the fire brigade had come, and that he had also lit fires in his flat in order to destroy DNA.'

The detectives had asked Griffiths to help them find Suzanne's body, Mr Smith said. Although the defendant admitted to removing the dismembered parts with bin liners, he 'did not know' where he had put them. He confirmed, however, that the CCTV pictures showed him leaving the building with bags containing her remains.

Court 5 was filled with a low sobbing sound as the victims' families took in the horror of their final hours alive. Griffiths' flippant manner and the relish with which he described his abominations became too much for Kirsty Rushworth. At a reference to her mother's remains being burned on a sofa, she stood up and screamed: 'F**king c*nt.' She was led out.

'He said that he had removed the bodies from the flat because he did not want them rotting and smelling the flat out. He said that he had accumulated a massive amount of bags for the purpose... The defendant was asked why he had felt the need to kill Suzanne Blamires. He said that he did not know, that: "Sometimes you kill someone to kill yourself." He said: "It was like deep issues inside me." He was asked why he had felt the need to kill any of the girls. He said he did not know. He also said that he did not know whether there were other people he had killed, that he was misanthropic and did not have much time for the human race. He said he had no issue against working girls and had not been, as he put it, "street cleaning like Peter Sutcliffe.'"

Mr Smith now turned to what the forensic teams had found in the River Aire and at Griffiths' flat. He said Suzanne was 'reconstructed' from the parts found in the water. A broken knife blade and a crossbow bolt were found embedded in her skull. Griffiths had cut off her nose and ears, removed her hair, scalp and skin, and part of her jaw. She had also been stabbed in the back and left breast, and her right foot had been sawn off. The police divers had found lots of other body parts in a holdall and other bags he had dumped in the river. They also discovered human tissue with a DNA match to Suzanne on knives and tools that had been left in one of the holdalls.

'It was apparent that the exercise of cutting up the remains had been directed towards reducing them to many small parts. A total of 81 separate body parts were identified from the remains of Suzanne Blamires alone.'

Meanwhile, all that was recovered of Shelley Armitage, explained Mr Smith, was found in the river:

'Within the River Aire were found two parts which could be established to have been from the remains of Shelley Armitage. These included part of her thoracic spine and a section of flesh which revealed fine cuts typical of marks caused by a knife. No other remains from her body were discovered.'

Mr Smith said Peter Vanezis, the Home Office pathologist, was able to work out the timetable of the attack on Suzanne. Mercifully, she had died quickly from the knife and crossbow bolt. Griffiths had hit her with a blunt instrument, causing bruising to her body, then stabbed her through the back and into her chest, then stabbed her in the head and shot her through the head with the crossbow.

'The infliction of a stab wound to the head and the crossbow bolt injury would correspond with the events recorded on the closed circuit television images from the hallway of Holmfield Court.'

He added that in the cases of Shelley and Susan, it was impossible to determine much of what had happened to them:

'Professor Vanezis was unable to conclude how Shelley Armitage had died. The remains revealed that she had been subjected to a similar process as that which had been carried out with Suzanne Blamires. The condition of the remains was consistent with her death having occurred at around the time of her disappearance towards the end of April 2010... The remains of Susan Rushworth have never been found, nor has the defendant provided any assistance with a view to their recovery or location, and this feature has had an enormous additional impact on her family. The scientific investigation has, however, confirmed that his confession to her murder stands corroborated as a result of DNA analysis.'

The Crown then went through the evidence gathered at the flat by senior forensic scientist Michelle Walton and her team, from 25 May, the day after Griffiths was arrested. They looked for blood, tissue or bodily matter left over from an attack or body disposal, weapons or cutting tools, damage to the flat or furniture caused during violence, the victims' possessions and clothing that Griffiths wore during the attack or dismemberment. They also had to search for evidence that the killer had, as he had claimed, eaten part of his victims.

'The examination of the property revealed that there were many bookcases full of books, journals and documents in the hallway, sitting room, and in the kitchen area. All of the literature appeared to be related to homicide. In the living room, two crossbows were found on the armchair. Bloodstaining was present on both of them. One of the crossbows had a solid handle similar to that seen being wielded by Stephen Griffiths in the closed circuit television images. Most of the furniture within the sitting room had a small amount of bloodstaining on it, and this included a computer desk, computer chair, a small table, a small bookcase, a sofa, and a bookcase to the left of the sitting room door… Other bloodstains were present on the curtains in a position consistent with deposited blood from bloodstained hands when trying to draw or open the curtains, on the sitting room door handle, and on the wall immediately to the right of the sitting room door. Thirteen small circular holes were found in the wall in this area which appeared to be consistent with practice with a crossbow.'

The prosecutor said forensic officers found a bloodstained toiletry bag in the desk drawer in Griffiths' living room. DNA samples taken from the bag matched Susan's DNA.

In the bathroom, bloodstains or spots were found on all four walls, on the sides of the bath and on the floor underneath. At some point, the bath panel and some wall tiles had been taken off. Samples taken from the wall around the bath and near the toilet, under the hand basin and on the floor beneath the bath matched the DNA of Suzanne. The analysts believed that most of the blood was hers. However, two stains, from under the bathroom sink and on the wall near the bath, matched Shelley and Susan.

> 'In consequence, the scientists were able to confirm that cellular material in the form of blood from each of the victims was present in the property. It follows that each of them is likely to have been dismembered in the bath in that property.'

Mr Smith said that the bedroom walls also had blood on them, as did the chest of drawers, a bedside table and a metal clothing rail. Because the furniture was black, it was not easy to see the splashes, and Griffiths had washed the room, leaving some of the samples diluted. Three stains from the wall produced a profile that matched Susan, as did a sample from the bottom drawer in the chest and the shelf for the top drawer in the bedside table. Her blood was also found on the table's second and lower shelves. Traces of Suzanne's blood were found on the inside of a camouflage holdall found in the bedroom with power tools inside, and on the back of a rug. Tissue recovered from sections of carpet and rug found in the river gave a DNA sample that matched Suzanne.

> 'These findings suggest that there had been significant blood loss from her on the floor in this area and that attempts had been made to clean the blood from the

floor… sections had been cut from the bedroom carpet and rug presumably because they were too heavily bloodstained to be capable of being effectively cleaned after her death.'

Griffiths had tried to clean up the flat using a green liquid cleaning agent. He had squirted it onto the hall carpet and the bloodstained bedroom floor, and on the walls above the bath.

'A fire had been lit, burning part of a duvet which had been found in the bath. The hallway carpet had been removed after the fire by cutting round the furniture present. Carpet had been found in carrier bags in the sitting room and in a bucket on the edge of the bath. The carrier bag on the edge of the bath smelled strongly of accelerant. Pieces of carpet had been removed in the remaining section of the patterned bedroom carpet at the foot of the bed and from the corner of a rug in the bedroom.'

Police search teams recovered Suzanne's clothes from a bin in Baptist Place, not far from Holmfield Court. Her upper clothing had cuts in the back consistent with the crossbow and stabbing injuries. Griffiths had also shredded them to ease their removal.

Mr Smith said that detectives seized a digital camera from the living room table and a laptop:

'Both of these were examined. The police were able to recover a number of disturbing video recordings and images. The video recording showed one of his victims, Shelley Armitage, lying obviously dead in the bath in the premises, and others displayed one of his victims bound with green twine by her wrists and feet, lying on the rug in the living room of the premises. Remnants of the green twine which he had used were to be found in the property by the forensic scientists. And the images were concentrated upon the feet and bottom of the victim, and in some of the films, the defendant's hands could be seen fondling the bottom of the victim in question.'

With that, the prosecutor brought his account of the actual offences to an end. He paused before telling the court about the defendant.

CHAPTER 17

Judgment

Stephen Griffiths barely moved a muscle. In the best part of two hours, as Robert Smith dismantled his web of evil, he sat slumped in the dock. His chin was glued to his chest throughout, and he showed no sign of listening to a word the prosecutor said. There was no sign of the swaggering brute from the surveillance pictures: just a nasty nobody who had been found out. Griffiths' confessions were more like boasts. He clammed up afterwards, telling the police little of use in finding his victims' remains or piecing together what he had done. Consequently, the account given to the court began at the end of the story rather than the beginning.

However, it was clear from the evidence that Griffiths had picked each of the girls up near Thornton Road, Sunbridge Road or City Road, and lured them back to the flat with an extravagant offer for their services. He steered them back to his flat via the labyrinthine network of alleys and side streets between the old mill buildings. Griffiths killed all three women shortly after they disappeared, with a hammer, knife or crossbow, and dismembered them in the bath. Then, true to

219

eccentric form, Griffiths chose to make countless journeys by train to dispose of their remains in the River Aire at Shipley. It was also obvious that Griffiths was content that this was, in his words, 'the end of the line for me'. But he was going out in a blaze of glory. Firstly, there were the sick gestures to the camera after killing Suzanne, then – within the space of an hour – there was his attempt to lure a second victim to her death.

Although Robert Smith did not identify the girl known as R, her identity was revealed later as Rosalyn Edmondson, aged 28 at the time of the trial. His opening statement also omitted some disturbing details of the footage recovered by the police. Some of the film showed Shelley bound and gagged, lying on cushions; the bathroom film revealed that he had sprayed the words 'My Sex Slave' on her back. He also recorded a ghastly voiceover: 'I'm Ven Pariah. I'm the Bloodbath Artist. Here is a model who is assisting me.' The prosecution had not read out any evidence relating to Griffiths' alleged cannibalism other than his 'confessions'. But it was in the final section of the hearing that any doubt about Griffiths' ultimate defilement of his victims vanished.

Mr Smith said the defendant was 40 years old, a PhD student researching serial homicide, had never worked and had a string of convictions relating to psychiatric problems. He detailed the convictions, from the attack on the store manager in his teens to his harassment charge before Wakefield magistrates in January 2009:

'He disclosed to the Probation Service the existence of fantasies and he disclosed his preoccupation with murder, particularly multiple murder, and his apparent idolisation of individuals such as Peter Sutcliffe. He told one probation officer that he saw himself as a murderer, but not until he reached his early 30s. He displayed a morbid interest in knives, terrorism, Satanism and weaponry. The police discovered more than 30 knives in his flat in the course of the investigation.'

The defendant's 'brief relationships' with women revealed an 'unstable and violent personality'. One recalled that 'the defendant was then apparently obsessed with the study of serial killers and murderers'. Another stated that he 'manifested part of a sexual obsession which he displayed towards the victims'. Mr Smith said:

'Over the years, the defendant has been seen by a number of psychiatrists, all of whom have identified the elements of a severe personality disorder and at times have assessed him as a dangerous individual.'

In October 1991, when Griffiths was charged with threatening students with a knife, a psychiatrist reported that he was 'strongly attracted to the idea of killing others'. The following month, he was sent to Rampton to see if medical treatment would alleviate his symptoms. All of the psychiatrists' reports had been reviewed by the defence and prosecution medical experts. Professor Nigel Eastman, who examined him for the Crown, said he did not appear to have a depressive or other mental illness, and he had a clear understanding of the legal process. His condition was 'consistent with previous diagnosis of him as exhibiting a severe personality disorder'. The professor said that, under the Homicide Act of 1957, Griffiths' condition could amount to an 'abnormality of mind', which would justify a plea of not guilty due to diminished responsibility. However, Mr Smith said:

'He was satisfied that the defendant was not a person who could not resist the impulses which he experienced, but rather, as Professor Eastman put it, that he did not resist them. This was, therefore, in his view, a case in which the defendant was responsible for the determined exercise of power over his victims with the object of personal gratification. There were no circumstances in which Professor Eastman would recommend a hospital order for reasons which were implicit in his report. He concluded that the defendant represented a continuing serious danger to others.'

Mr Smith said the defence psychiatrist believed that Griffiths was showing signs of depression but could not detect evidence of 'serious psychotic mental illness'. He also believed that there were no grounds for thinking the diminished responsibility plea was appropriate. Griffiths was, he thought, a 'highly abnormal personality which made him a highly dangerous man'.

Before the defence's mitigation speech, Mr Smith addressed the judge on the question of sentencing. He said the law dictated that for Griffiths, life should mean life, on the grounds that:

* The 'seriousness of the offences' was 'exceptionally high'.
* Three people had been murdered and, in the cases of Shelley and Suzanne, there had been 'a substantial degree of planning and premeditation'.
  His crimes involved 'sadistic conduct' such as Shelley's
       d binding.
              es had been hidden, destroyed and dismembered
                    cases.
                          'eating the remains' of his victims.

David Waters QC began Griffiths' defence by revealing that his client had not actually given him instructions to mitigate the circumstances. He added:

> 'What submissions I make will be restricted to matters which emerge from the reports which your Lordship has, and the history of these proceedings. And the first matter I would draw to the court's attention, which has been very kindly foreshadowed by Mr Smith, is that the defendant has always wanted to plead guilty, and that is so from the outset. The court will perhaps recall a degree of persistence on his behalf in his wish to plead guilty.'

Next, he said that, as a psychology graduate, the defendant would have found it easy to feign madness or temporary madness:

> 'Against the background of fitness to plead, it would have been very easy for him to latch on to the knowledge he acquired during those studies and put up a false but seemingly plausible pretence that he was not so fit to plead. The reaction of the defendant has been in fact entirely the opposite.'

Mr Waters said that Griffiths had told his solicitor that he 'did not want the stress of a long trial', so opted to admit guilt at the earliest opportunity. The defence concluded:

> 'May I just finally bring together the situation with regard to his mental state as it is to be gleaned from the reports which the court has? They recite a condition, this severe personality disorder, which deteriorated during the relevant period. It was then exacerbated by an intimate connection between the subject of his study and his

mental pathology. I quote there, my Lord, from Professor Eastman's report at page 20. The doctorate which he was studying, the actual title of it was *Homicide in an Industrial City: Lethal Violence in Bradford*…His condition then was exacerbated by his isolation.'

As Mr Justice Openshaw prepared to pass sentence, there was at last movement from the dock. Griffiths looked up and was set to rise, but the judge intervened, telling him there was no need.

The sentence for murder, the judge said, was laid down in law: life. In this case, there were three life sentences to be handed down, but, he added, he also needed to consider whether life did mean life:

'I must, however, consider all of the relevant aggravating and mitigating factors, if there be any, including but not limited to those set out in the schedule. Before I do so, I make clear that I am acutely aware of the anguish which these murders have caused to their families. It is obvious, it seems to me, that the defendant lured these women to his flat and then killed them. Quite why he did so is, to some extent, obscure, since the defendant has not spoken about the reasons for his attacks either to the police or to the psychiatrists, but he has set out his attitude in writings which were examined by Professor Eastman. It is his opinion that he needed and indeed derived enjoyment from exerting power over others. It is to my mind plainly established by direct evidence that the murders of Shelley Armitage and Suzanne Blamires involved a substantial degree of planning and premeditation, and it seems to me that in all the circumstances the inference must inevitably be drawn that the murder of Susan Rushworth did so also, and that he planned and intended the murder of the other woman, R. The defendant himself took images on a digital camera which he downloaded onto his computer from which they were recovered. Mr Smith has already described these images. Furthermore, at least one of the killings involved tying up the body, the naked body, by cord. It is possible that the victim may have been dead at the time. As to his claim that he ate parts of their bodies, there is no reason to doubt what he says about that, for why should he tell such a terrible lie?'

The judge quoted Professor Eastman's comments on cannibalism, saying that, although there is little research into it, it is believed that 'cannibalising a victim amounts to exerting ultimate power and control over them'. The psychiatrist thought: 'It was one thing to terrorise and kill a victim, but to terrorise, kill, dismember and then eat parts of the victim is to take the exercise of power to yet another level.' He had gone on to say in his report that it is likely 'that his alleged cannibalism of his victim amounted not only to the exertion of power *per se*, but also sexual gratification'. He then continued:

'There is no doubt, in my judgment, that these murders have a sexual element. In any event, the destruction, dismemberment of the bodies and the concealment of the body of the third victim is plainly a most aggravating feature which has caused and still causes untold distress to her family. Taken together, the circumstances of these murders are so wicked and monstrous as to leave me in no doubt that the defendant should be kept in prison for the rest of his life.'

Before concluding, Mr Justice Openshaw considered what credit could be given for the defendant's guilty pleas:

'It is true, as Mr Waters points out, that his pleas of guilty have prevented a trial. It is also true that his pleas have spared the families of the victims some further anguish. But it seems to me that his pleas of guilty have been entered without any remorse at all. He has never said that he regrets his actions or said even in the most perfunctory way that he is sorry, for he is not. Lack of remorse is a characteristic of his condition… This defendant did not plead guilty in order to achieve a reduction in his sentence. He did so, as he repeatedly told Professor Eastman, because he did not wish to go through a pointless trial. He just wanted it, as he said, over and done with.'

With that, he ordered Griffiths to be taken to the cells.

It was a great irony. The man born just a week after hanging was abolished in 1969 had grown up to be the most brutal and unrepentant murderer imaginable. The change in the law was not meant to benefit the likes of him, but benefit he did. Griffiths left court and was driven back to Wakefield. It was three days before his 41st birthday and his long-held wish of being a famous serial killer had come true.

CHAPTER 18

Coward

Detective Superintendent Sukhbir Singh stood blinking in the bright sunshine. In the two hours it had taken to send Stephen Griffiths to prison for the rest of his life, the sky had cleared and the temperature risen. The ice patches were melting, and the pedestrianised zone outside the court was basking now in a warm sun. Mobbed by journalists, the officer who led the inquiry expressed the collective relief in seeing Griffiths jailed for 'a series of horrifying crimes'. He added:

'He is a heartless and controlling man, who took advantage of vulnerable women. What he did can never be forgotten by the families of his victims. Suzanne, Susan and Shelley all came from families who cared for and supported their daughters. I hope the knowledge that Griffiths is now behind bars will bring some comfort to all those lives he has affected.'

The families chose to mark the end of the case privately. However, they were only too happy to make public their thoughts about the psychopath who ruined so many lives. Nicky Blamires, who had scrimped and saved after her husband died to get Suzanne into rehab, said:

> 'Stephen Griffiths is a coward. We are shocked he pleaded guilty as it is not something I thought he would have the courage to do. This will be the first Christmas we have spent without Suzanne in 36 years and I know I will never get over her loss. I wake up and think about my bright, articulate and much-loved daughter every day.'

Nicky pointed out that, in some ways, her future held as little for her as it did for the maniac now on his way to Wakefield Prison. 'I am serving a life sentence as a result of what that man has done. Quite simply, no family deserves what we have gone through. All of these girls were people's daughters and much-loved human beings.'

Christine Thompson, who lost her husband Barrie soon after her daughter Susan, and still did not have her daughter's body or any part of it, begged Griffiths to tell them where he put her:

> 'Susan went missing more than 12 months ago, and as a family we still don't know where she is. We know that Griffiths has admitted to killing our daughter and there is evidence to confirm that. As a family, we have not been able to put our daughter to rest because she has not been found. So we want to appeal to this man to tell us what he had done with Susan. She was a loving mother, daughter and sister, and our family have been affected at every level by her murder. Our lives will never be the same without her and we are sure the stress and strain of the last 12 months contributed to the death of Susan's father, Barrie. His final words were to ask for Susan, and

what grieves the family most of all is that Griffiths took away the opportunity to speak to her before he died.'

Christine, who had spent £3,000 of her own money trying to put Susan through rehab, warned women everywhere to steer clear of drugs and vice: 'We never want to see another family go through the horror we have and still are enduring.' Susan's daughter Kirsty, 21, who was sucked into the same destructive spiral as her mother, commented: 'He's ruined our lives. All my family want is for him to tell us where my mother is. We don't know what he's done with her and we want to put her to rest. The other families have been able to do that, but we don't have a body and with no body there's no death certificate.'

Susan's brother Paul Thompson revealed that, despite being kept up to speed with the prosecution by their family liaison officers, they were still stunned by Griffiths' depravity. 'We can't even say his name. We just call him "The Monster". I feel nothing for him. He's inhuman. I just want him to tell us where she is. It's horrendous not knowing. If there is any humanity in his body he would let us know.' However, he accepted that 'The Monster' may never tell them what he has done: 'We will probably never really know what happened to her. Everyone is so shocked and traumatised.' Describing their idyllic childhood and Susan's entrapment by heroin, he added:

'There was only 16 months between us and we were so close. We would go everywhere together and people used to think we were twins. I still keep her picture in my wallet… It was horrible to see her ravaged by heroin. Her looks went, her lovely long blonde hair went grey and her face became sunken. She used to have savings and was proud of them but that all went too. She was always asking my mum and I for money. She would tell me: "I'll be all right. I can look after myself." But it turned into an absolute nightmare.'

Shelley's father Daryl Armitage spoke of his torment at having to identify his daughter's body from the sick 'snuff' photographs Griffiths took of her. He told the police officers he wanted to know and see absolutely everything. But the experience almost destroyed him:

'After the police found the pictures they wanted someone to identify Shelley. No one else in the family could do it. It was too traumatic. They showed me a photo which just showed her head. They wouldn't show me it all and I wouldn't have wanted to see. What he did was unspeakable. I just went numb with the horror of it. She didn't look dead; she looked as though she was asleep. She looked like my Shelley. I don't know why but I asked the officers: "Is she all right?" They said: "No, Daryl – we're sorry, she's dead." I still struggle to take it in. I just can't take in the evil of Griffiths. To kill, photograph a victim and cut up bodies is just beyond evil. In my mind he is worse than the Yorkshire Ripper. I think it got to the stage where he couldn't study any more without killing.'

Daryl Armitage also watched the CCTV footage that showed Griffiths taking his daughter's body parts, packed in bags and a rucksack, to throw them in the River Aire. 'As I watched I was thinking: "My Shelley's probably in that rucksack." It just sent me numb. It was like I was in a living nightmare.'

Shelley's mother, Gill, said: 'Our daughter Shelley was very much loved and will be very sadly missed by us all. Unfortunately, she took the wrong path at the young age of 16 years old when she became a victim of heroin. Her death will haunt us for the rest of our lives.'

On behalf of Bradford, the *Telegraph & Argus*, the city's evening paper, welcomed the incarceration of a man whose crimes were 'so vile and depraved that they almost defy belief'. It added: 'He killed without mercy because he wanted to and because he could – then turned his bathroom into a vision of hell as he dismembered his victims before coldly disposing of their remains.' The leader continued: 'If a desire to go down in history was his ultimate aim – and at least one expert claims that is so – then he has achieved it. The sheer horror of his deeds has assured him of that. But it is an empty form of immortality – engendering only contempt and revulsion. He has nothing to offer us.' The newspaper also emphasised the following:

'... The women he murdered so brutally and so callously will be remembered with love and tenderness. Suzanne Blamires, Shelley Armitage and Susan Rushworth did not have the easiest of lives and they chose to walk some troubled pathways, but they were still cherished. And if lives can be measured at all, it is in such things.'

At the University of Bradford, staff were horrified that one of their criminology students had turned out to be a multiple murderer. Mark Cleary, the vice-chancellor, said: 'Our thoughts go out to the friends and families of the three women so tragically killed. We hope the conviction today will bring them some comfort at this difficult time.'

The women in Griffiths' life who had survived their time with him were overwhelmed with emotion. Many had suffered appalling harassment and abuse at his hands and were relieved to be finally free of his menace. The luckier ones, those who never saw his worst side, were stunned at what he had become; they had parted company with him many years before, believing he was just a harmless maverick. Zeta Pinder, who left him after seeing his murder library for the first time, said: 'It was just jaw-dropping. I just couldn't believe it. I cried for quite a bit. It was just such a shock, actually going out with somebody that could actually do that to them poor women.' Zeta, who met him through a dating ad but is now married to someone else, added: 'I said to my husband: "I hope to God that's not the crossbow I touched that he killed them poor girls with." And then thinking back about what he did... I think: "Did I have a lucky escape?", you know, and I think I did.'

Kathy Hancock, the prison officer who spent nine years trying to escape his clutches, attended court to see justice done.

'I sat there in court hoping he'd look me or the victims' families in the eye. But he couldn't do it. He's a coward. I just sat there and thought how pathetic he was. I felt angry at myself for being intimidated by him. He's a weak man who targeted very vulnerable people. He'll suffer in prison because he hates any kind of confrontation with strong people. I'm convinced Stephen's taste for killing began with animals. He even boasted how he'd slaughtered two of the cats I cared for at my flat. And my two dogs were never found.'

Amanda Judson, who had an 18-month relationship with Griffiths in the late 1990s, said he deserved to be hanged. 'I feel lucky it wasn't me he butchered. I'm positive he's killed other women – he's got the taste for it. He's sick in the head to have done what he did. But he said he would do it one day. He shouldn't be alive – hang the bastard.' Pauline Bond had complained about Griffiths when he stalked her after their entirely platonic friendship came to an end. She reported him to the police a week before he killed Susan, and officers visited his flat weeks after. They inspected the property looking for stolen DVDs, but did not see the tiny bloodstains after Griffiths had scrubbed the surfaces. The killer even made reference to the police visit in his admission. Pauline said: 'Poor Susan was probably already dead before the police came knocking.'

Rosalyn Edmondson, the 28-year-old brunette who Griffiths tried to pick up after murdering Suzanne, was beside herself with relief. She described how she escaped becoming his second victim in an hour. Griffiths, she said, had approached her as she came away from an all-night chemist with a methadone prescription.

'At first he was okay when he approached me and asked if I could get him some drugs. He wanted some crack cocaine and I got him some. But as soon as I gave him it, he changed. He asked if I was a working girl and when I told him no, he said: "You are too fit to be working on the streets. I can't stand prostitutes. I hate them." That is what he said to me. Then he invited me up to his flat. I didn't like his smile and I didn't like the way he suddenly changed. It was as soon as he did the crack cocaine. It was all about what he didn't like about working girls. Some instinct inside made me say no. He was arrested the next day. The police have taken away my jacket and the CID officers told me I am a survivor of his. I know I am so very lucky. I can't believe I got that close to him. I took a decision and somehow it was the right one. It is the lottery of life and death – and I won.'

The case left Bridget Farrell in turmoil; she had been a friend of all three victims and of Griffiths. She had been working with Susan, Shelley and Suzanne near the time they disappeared. Also, she had spoken to Griffiths about them a few days later, receiving a smug dismissal of her worries. Her final meeting with him was on the Saturday he murdered Suzanne, when there were almost certainly parts of her body hidden in the flat. She said that Flat 33 Holmfield Court was unusually messy and Griffiths was acting strange. Police had questioned her as a possible accessory when they found out about her visit to the killer's home by viewing the CCTV footage. Forensic officers had searched her flat while she was at a police station. However, she was released without charge but told that she was lucky to be alive herself.

Bridget, 35, said she was traumatised by the flirtation with death, and guilty about surviving when her friends had died:

'It haunts me every night. Why did he let me in? Why didn't he kill me too? Why am I still here now? I can't answer any of it. It's driving me mad. Shelley was like a sister to me and he'd been like a brother. I'd introduced him to both Shelley and Suzanne. I still can't believe he's done it. I blame all that studying on murder he was doing. It must have driven him insane.'

Lisa Thompson, a friend of Susan Rushworth who slept with Griffiths every week for four years, at £40 a time, told of how he had once strangled her and showed her web images of women being attacked. 'I pray to God every day,' she said. 'I'm thankful that was not me, I really am. The police say I'm the only one who got out of there alive in the last 12 months. It could have been different. I found it a bit strange when Shelley vanished. He said she deserved what she got because she robbed everybody.' Lisa, 37, added:

'The only thing he could do now is let the families know where the bodies are. But he likes the upper hand; he'll take that to the grave with him. I feel physically sick about what he's done. Jail's too good for him. He's very intelligent, he knows right from wrong, so he knew what he was doing. He deserves everything he gets and everything that's coming to him.'

Everybody had a story to tell about Griffiths, usually connected with the vice trade. Christina Mullinario, a former prostitute, claimed Griffiths kidnapped her and refused to let her get out of his car. Christina, 45, said he picked her up on Lumb Lane in its red light days. He took her on a two-hour ride, with the car doors locked and windows blacked out with bin bags. He refused to let her out and drove her to a deserted quarry. She only escaped by telling him her boyfriend was watching her. Christine said she recognised Griffiths when he was arrested for the triple murder. 'I knew it was him,' she said. 'I knew it was that man who picked me up and scared me to death.' Describing the ordeal, she said:

'A car drew up and a voice asked: "Do you want business?" I said yes and he said "get in". I told him to drive out on the Keighley road to a pitch we girls all used. We watched out for each other there. I suddenly had a very bad feeling about him. I said: "Let me out now", but he closed the central locking. I was scared to look at him. His eyes were cold and dark like ink. They were like a shark's with no emotion. I knew he was going to kill me.'

Christina escaped when a car appeared and she told him it was her boyfriend. 'He let the catch off and I just jumped out, stumbling down the track to the road. I stood and waved the first car down.'

Peter Gee, the caretaker whose routine Monday morning security check uncovered the nightmare, spoke movingly about how his life had changed 'forever'. Mr Gee, a burly 53-year-old, said the images of Suzanne being murdered will stay with him for the rest of his days. A father of seven, he had been given compassionate leave from the job he had enjoyed for the last three years. He read a short but powerful statement at his local working men's club, in Buttershaw, south-west Bradford:

'On the morning of May 24, 2010, a day unknown to me at the time as one that would change my life forever, I came into work at Holmfield Court as usual. What I saw on that tape horrified and distressed me and I called the police straight away. As I am sure you will understand, I have no wish to re-live my feelings at that moment and go into the details of what was on the tape. The sight of its horrific content has deeply affected me and my family and those images will stay with me for the rest of my life.'

Mr Gee was receiving counselling himself, but sent a message of sympathy to the victims' families: 'Although I can never forget what I have seen or imagine their suffering, I take some small comfort that it was my actions that helped to bring the killer to justice.'

Joe Dewhirst, the killer's uncle, was the only member of his family to speak publicly. He said he barely recognised the man whose face was now well known for the wrong reasons. For Joe Dewhirst, Griffiths was the 'last person in the world' to commit such awful crimes:

'I was actually amazed when I saw it in the press – this huge young man. The last time I remember him being very slim, and quiet. To me he had just totally changed in appearance – I was shocked at the size of him. And even more shocked at what he was accused of. I can only imagine what it must be like to lose a child in those circumstances. It must be horrific. I know how I would feel and how most people would – just shock and horror.'

After Griffiths' conviction for murdering Susan, Shelley and Suzanne, the police were asked about those unsolved cases he had been linked to at the time of his arrest. There was that of Rebecca Hall, the working girl found dead in Thornton Street in 2001, and Yvonne Fitt, whose body was left in Otley in 1992. In addition, at Halifax police station Griffiths had boasted: 'Peter Sutcliffe came a cropper in Sheffield. So did I, but at least I got out of the city'; was he responsible for the deaths of Dawn Shields and Michaela Hague, who both died in Sheffield? After the hearing, a senior detective dismissed such a possibility:

'He was just using it to justify the quote and the comparison with Sutcliffe. He made suggestions that he did something in Sheffield. We worked with our colleagues in Sheffield and managed to disprove that he had done something in the city. After a few days we interviewed him again and he admitted it didn't happen. We are very, very confident he didn't do anything there. We dealt with it and there was nothing.'

But officers planned to keep talking to Griffiths. Detective Superintendent Singh said they were not currently linking him with any specific person. He added that Griffiths 'likes to control the situation', so officers could not rely on his help. Operation Pinstripe had, he said, been in three phases. The first was to gather enough evidence for him to be charged. Then, they had to secure a conviction. Now the third phase would involve 'reviewing a comprehensive timeline looking at his movements with colleagues both nationally and locally to see if there are any links between him and other disappearances'. DS Singh added: 'We have no evidence to do so at the moment so it would not be right to speculate, but that is why we will be working with colleagues around the country.'

Nevertheless, after the emotion of Griffiths' court hearing subsided, there were tough questions too about why he had managed to stay at large for so long. He had been diagnosed a 'sadistic schizoid psychopath' 19 years previously, and had been constantly in trouble with the law ever since. He had spoken to girlfriends, psychiatrists and probation officers of his fantasies of becoming a serial killer. The explanation was that his condition is classed as a 'personality disorder', which is not a mental illness under the terms of the Mental Health Act. Both psychiatrists who examined him for the court case agreed that he did not suffer from any condition that could be treated medically. Therefore the law says he is a free man until he commits an offence. But Philip Davies, Tory MP for Shipley, where Griffiths dumped his victims' remains, called for a review of the way in which people with personality disorders are dealt with.

'We have to look at this issue again. Everyone is shocked by what he did and what has happened. It seems extraordinary that someone with his profile was considered to be allowed in the community. It is a perverse situation in that we are waiting for people to commit a crime before we are prepared to do something with them. What this case does show is the status quo is not working.'

Griffiths' conduct had been flagged up to the police on at least two occasions. Pauline Bond reported him for harassment the week before he killed Susan, and officers visited Flat 33 Holmfield Court two weeks after she was killed there. If he had been detected then, Shelley and Suzanne would still be alive. Robert Smith QC told the court that Bradford South's vice team had also been made aware of Griffiths during a briefing in the latter part of 2009. The controversy was fuelled two days after Griffiths' conviction, when a former senior employee of Accent, the housing association that owns Holmfield Court, claimed that the police had been sent a dossier of complaints about him from tenants two years before. He claimed that officers were so concerned that they visited him and confiscated one of his crossbows. The neighbours' worries were that he had repeatedly threatened women living there, and a previous caretaker had had the office fitted with a panic alarm. The former Accent employee claimed that, although there was a whole file of complaints, the police did not have a strong enough case to get an Asbo issued against him. After the housing manager left in 2008, the case was left on file. 'The housing company worked with the police,' the source said. 'We believed he would kill. We all thought he was a serial killer in the making.' He said an officer told him that, during a previous visit to the flat, Griffiths had hunting-style knives, other weapons and a crossbow, which was confiscated.

However, Detective Superintendent Sukhbir Singh said after the case that it would be 'inappropriate' to comment on any 'missed opportunities' in the years leading up to his killing campaign. Detective Chief Superintendent Andy Brennan, who was acting head of HMET following the retirement of Max McLean the previous autumn, said that Griffiths was not an immediate suspect because he had not been linked to prostitute attacks. 'I think we would see if any local residents had convictions for attacks against sex workers and then we would see if any had any dealings with sex workers. There was no intelligence linking Griffiths to sex workers, but eventually I think we would have found him a long way into our inquiry because of his previous convictions.' He also spoke of the search strategy when Susan and Shelley were missing:

> 'Working girls don't just disappear, as a rule, unless they have come to some harm. The incident rooms were linked, but we kept the two inquiry teams going because we didn't want to miss anything. We wanted separate teams on it so that every piece of evidence was referenced in its own right.'

HMET began by compiling a list of known offenders who lived near the district and had convictions for attacking sex workers or kerb crawlers. After eliminating those, they planned to widen their search to include criminals convicted of violence against women. Officers had also set up a 'trigger plan' to commit more officers to the inquiry if more women vanished. The plan was mobilised when Suzanne disappeared.

In the days following the case, police in Bradford's red light area insisted that there was no 'tolerance zone' for prostitutes or their punters. To prove the point, Superintendent Angela Williams announced that, in just the last month, 40 kerb crawlers had been arrested on the Bradford South patch. She commented:

> 'In Bradford we do not have a tolerance zone for prostitution. Our focus continues to be around reducing the harm associated with this behaviour. For many years the police in Bradford have worked closely with partner agencies and local groups to tackle the root causes of the

sex trade, such as drink and drug dependency. The women involved are able to sign up to a wide range of specialist services to help them address these issues. Those who refuse to engage willingly with the specialist services available are tackled by the vice team who utilise the laws available to their full extent to ensure their engagement. This is about tough choices and we are making a difference. Not only do we enforce the law regarding the women involved in prostitution, but also the men who solicit them. If there is no demand, there is no service. In the last month alone, our operations have seen 40 men arrested for kerb crawling offences in the city centre and we will continue to target those who purchase the services of women.'

But, nationally, senior officers suggested that perhaps there should be a softer line. Simon Byrne, the Association of Chief Police Officers' spokesman on prostitution, spoke up for decriminalising part of the trade. In the wake of the Griffiths case, he said the whole law on prostitution was 'complicated' and needed an overhaul. Critics pointed out that, at present, the law allows the selling of sex, but not brothels and street prostitution. The effect is to drive women onto the streets and away from where they can easily be caught, leaving them in the darkest, least-protected alleys. The result was a postcode lottery where Britain's 80,000 sex workers are treated differently depending on where they work. In Liverpool, attacks against sex workers were prioritised as hate crimes, while in Blackpool, just 55 miles away, the council was still cracking down on brothels. Asked about fundamental reforms such as legalising brothels, Simon Byrne replied: 'Perhaps the law does need changing – some of it is frankly complicated. We would be keen for a dialogue to see if there is a better way of managing the problem, be it ideas around criminalising some parts of it and not others.'

CYRIL DIXON

A Deputy Chief Constable of Greater Manchester Police, Mr Byrne went on to suggest a national database of men suspected of attacking sex workers. Women in some parts of the country were already benefiting from a gallery of 'ugly mugs' with a history of violence towards prostitutes, but it was not co-ordinated. The Home Office was planning a national scheme and a new set of guidelines on how to police prostitution. Mr Byrne said it would be worth investing the money to save lives and avoid the cost of large-scale murder investigations. 'Any murder is one too many,' he believed:

> 'If we can do something simple and effective to stop that, then we should do so. There is a significant cost to investigating a murder. When times are tough and you have all the austerity and revolution going on in the public service, there is some hard-edged maths to be done here. If you can invest a small amount of money in rolling the scheme out, you can prevent an awful lot of crime.'

Just a few hundred yards from Holmfield Court, a newsagent sparked anger by selling imitation crossbows and samurai swords. The fake weapons were spotted by the Reverend Chris Howson, a mission priest for Bradford city centre. 'There is something wrong in this culture which glorifies violence and murderers,' he said, and expanded on his point:

> 'There is the constant drip, drip, drip of violence and this is one example. We, as a society, need to be on our guard against things which lead to violence. The people of Bradford have been shocked by these horrific murders. We are trying to put the rightful image of Bradford across as it is a safe and decent city full of good people, and to have shops selling imitation weapons like this is

totally unacceptable. They are selling paraphernalia looking just like the weapons which this guy used and the imitation weapons are on sale barely 500 metres from where he lived.'

At Wakefield Prison, the man who called himself the Crossbow Cannibal reverted to his old trick of seeking attention. On Christmas Eve 2010, Griffiths' 41st birthday, it emerged that he had stepped up the hunger strike he had launched when the prison authorities refused to take him out of segregation. In court, he had appeared gaunt, and doctors – who examined him to see if he was well enough to go ahead – had described him as 'weak'. Now, some people at the notorious prison feared he might die within weeks, taking the secret of what he had done with his victims with him. In his latest protest, the triple killer had given up fluids.

'If nothing is done and he keeps refusing fluids, he could be dead by the end of the Christmas period. If a prisoner chooses to refuse food, the Prison Service works with healthcare staff to monitor their health. Prisoners considered mentally capable are entitled to refuse health interventions like force-feeding, provided they fully understand the consequences of their decision.'

Griffiths maintained his protest until just before New Year's Eve, when he agreed to resume taking fluids.

However, by the first week of January 2011, Griffiths' condition had worsened. According to one source:

'Griffiths is skin and bone. He doesn't look anywhere near as big as he did in the photo where he is bare-chested and showing off his muscles. One or two people have tried talking to Griffiths, but he doesn't want to know. He is a difficult prisoner, in that he has no interest in interacting. He's in his own little world. He spends most of his time just lying on his bed. He does go to the association room on the healthcare wing, but he just sits in a chair and doesn't talk to anybody. If anyone approaches him, he tells them to go away. He has had no visitors. Even his legal team had consultations with him via a video link.'

CHAPTER 19

Killing for Fame

In the summer of 1993, Scotland Yard was faced with a perplexing series of unsolved murders. Five gay men had been killed in their own homes, dotted around London, in the most sadistic and inventive fashions. Their killer had been allowed into the property, bound them up on the pretext of preparing them for kinky sex, then strangled or suffocated them. He had then stayed with the bodies for some time, posing them in sick, ritualistic ways, before cleansing the flat of forensic evidence and leaving. After several of the murders, the killer made a telephone call to draw attention to his 'work': the Samaritans heard from him, the *Sun* newspaper, and even the police.

Colin Ireland eventually walked into a police station of his own accord. But it was not to give himself up. He had been caught on surveillance television with his final victim and, under the pretext of establishing his innocence, he spent days in interviews, playing a cat-and-mouse game with detectives. On 20 December 1993, Ireland was given five whole-life sentences after admitting all five murders.

Ireland's first victim was Peter Walker, a 45-year-old choreographer. After killing him, he carefully placed two teddy bears on Walker's body in a '69' position, simulating oral sex. The second, Christopher Dunn, 37 and a librarian, had been left on the bed with four mirrors standing on each side, creating an infinite room effect. Third was Perry Bradley III, an American businessman. Here, Ireland placed a child's doll on top of the dead man's body. Andrew Collier, 33, was next. Ireland killed his cat in front of his eyes as he was restrained on the bed. He then posed the body, placing a condom on Collier's penis with the cat's mouth over it, while the pet's tail was pushed into the victim's mouth. His fifth and final victim – Emanuel Spiteri, 41 – was left in a burnt-out flat with the chairs neatly stacked up around his corpse.

Ireland had met all five men at a pub used by gay men and robbed them by taking their cash machine cards and personal identification numbers. After confessing to the crimes, the 39-year-old drifter, told the police: 'I just wanted to be a serial killer. I read the books, and thought: "I could do that."' Ireland had studied books on crime and serial killers. He had immersed himself in the evil world of Peter Sutcliffe and Dennis Nilsen and rented the then-recent movie *The Silence of the Lambs*. He had also read an FBI handbook on serial killers written by Robert K. Ressler, the former FBI agent who helped to create offender profiling. He classified a serial killer as 'one over four', meaning five victims.

Consequently, in one of his taunting calls to the police, Ireland said: 'I've got the book. I know how many more I have to do.' When he reached five, Ireland rang again and said: 'I've done another.' On remand, awaiting his case to come up at the Old Bailey, he sent cards to his friends, urging them to watch the news on 20 December. Ireland – dubbed the Gay Slayer – was told by Mr Justice Sachs: 'You expressed a desire to be regarded as a serial killer – that must be matched by your detention for life.'

Colin Ireland had decided to become a serial killer after failing in everything else he had done. His education and career had come to nothing, all his relationships were disasters. He claimed to be heterosexual, but the ease with which he fitted in at the pub where he chose his victims suggested an ambiguity. Ireland had tried everything and failed. He turned to murder as a last resort. He did not want an ordinary, everyday kind of success, like having a steady job and a stable relationship. Ireland wanted to be a name. He told the police that he had nothing against gays, but he wanted to be a serial killer and they were the easiest targets.

Two hundred miles north, the same ambition was growing in the mind of Stephen Griffiths. Life was not treating him well, but he had a masterplan for achieving success. Griffiths, like Ireland, was a 'wannabe' serial killer. The place, the date, the methods and the victims are different, but the motive remains the same.

After Griffiths' conviction, David Wilson, Professor of Criminology and Criminal Justice at Birmingham City University, said:

'He was like a nightmarish version of a wannabe *X-Factor* contestant, desperate to grab the attention of the British public. He was the very opposite of the stereotyped dangerous loner who keeps himself to himself. That is why he styled himself in court the Crossbow Cannibal, precisely because he knew that the horrifying nickname would be picked up by the media. It is also why he so relished boasting about his cannibalism and the extent of his killing spree. He was so desperate for infamy. He was so desperate for any kind of attention, even though that attention would bring him notoriety rather than conventional admiration.'

David Canter, professor of investigative psychology at Huddersfield University and the man who compiled the first criminal profile used in British crime investigation, said in an article for *The Times*: 'Every now and then an applicant emerges who seems besotted with the darker side of human nature... They can confuse the horror and notoriety that leads to murderers' names being remembered, but not their victims', with some sort of fame and significance.'

But Stephen Griffiths was not just any wannabe. Otherwise he would have found another vehicle for his vanity. He was a 'sadistic schizoid psychopath'. He had a personality disorder that disposed him to carrying out certain violent acts. The monster he became was shaped by his background and the times we live in. 'We want to see serial killers as real aberrations, as different from dominant beings in our culture,' said Professor Wilson, 'but often they are just extreme versions of other beings of their time.' He elaborated:

'It's like *X-Factor* kids are told that, these days, you are famous for being famous: not because you have any underlying talent. It's instantaneous. You don't have to pay your dues by doing thousands of gigs and knowing how to sing and how to craft a song, or work an audience. You can simply go on a talent show and that brings fame for you. It's the same with Griffiths. He wants to be famous instantaneously because it's fame in our culture that everybody aspires to. It's that kind of exaggerated example of the cultural forces which are dominant in late modernity.'

Griffiths' foibles and failures were poured into his evil 'alter ego' Ven Pariah, so that the serial killer's behaviour paralleled that of the supposedly everyday Griffiths. Firstly, there was the narcissism. Griffiths was obsessed with the way he looked. Whether it was putting baby oil on his hair, dressing up in his long black leather coat and boots, or strutting around Bradford's student quarter with a pop star's pout, he was a shameless peacock. Then there was the huge professionally-shot photograph of himself on his wall, and the snaps that he handed out to women he dated. There were the pictures he put on his Myspace page, whether they were of him as a young man or in full bare-chested Ven Pariah mode. As the serial killer in action, he must have got a massive buzz out of raising his weapon to the camera and giving his one-fingered salute. He would also have enjoyed filming himself next to Shelley Armitage's body and delivering a twisted voiceover.

His vanity also had an intellectual flavour. He was clearly a bright and well-educated man, who could have done many things but for his psychiatric record. As betrayed in his ramblings on the web, where he called a book reviewer an 'imbecile', and at his tutorials, where he threatened people who beat him in an argument, Griffiths thought he was better than everyone else. The trait is central to psychopathic behaviour. Psychopaths, be it Sutcliffe, Shipman, Fred West or Ian Brady, are by definition people with no empathy or feeling for others. They live life by their own rules and only their needs and wishes matter. Stephen Griffiths' delusions of grandeur in everyday life fed into a fantasy world where three innocent women were of so little value that he could kill them with impunity.

His penchant for self-publicity meant that he could not resist telling people about his goal to become a serial killer. When he had actually killed, he dropped hints to people. He told a few of his girlfriends that he would be bigger than the Yorkshire Ripper. After he killed Susan and Shelley, and 24 hours before he killed Suzanne, he went on Myspace to talk about being a 'pseudo-human' and a 'demon'. He actually told prison staff at Wakefield that he could see himself being locked up there. Then there was his performance at Bradford Magistrates' Court when he called himself the Crossbow Cannibal: that was the biggest moment of his life. Professor Wilson agreed:

'The narcissism is manifest in many different ways. The images he placed of himself on the internet, his musings on the internet. He was desperately keen to be noticed, to be seen, to be part of the story. That's not too unusual with serial killers, but he is such a wannabe. He wants his 15 minutes of fame. At the magistrates' court, he stood up and called himself the "Crossbow Cannibal". It's so contrived. He has simply created an image very much as one would create an image for a new company or a car or an inanimate object.'

Criminology played a big part in creating the Crossbow Cannibal. Stephen Griffiths' own barrister said it had influenced the way his unbalanced mind worked. Griffiths had read all of those hundreds of books about homicide as 'how to' manuals. Just like Colin Ireland, years before, he used them both for technical knowledge and to feed his fantasies. As Ireland had read that he needed five victims to be a serial killer, so Griffiths knew he needed three. It was a different measure for a different time. As soon as Griffiths had his third victim, he knew he was there. He could afford to give himself up. Because, like Ireland, he knew there was no point in killing to be famous if you do not get caught. The tenant of Flat 33 Holmfield Court also used forensic knowledge gleaned from the homicide books to cleanse the crime scene. He washed everything down and threw out anything that could not be cleaned properly. When the detectives were questioning Griffiths, he said he had acted like a 'robot' or an 'aberration'. This is all basic criminological language for psychopathic serial killers. Then, of course, there is Griffiths' obsession with Peter Sutcliffe. He can hardly stop himself mentioning the man's name. Whether it is to the police, his girlfriends, or the sex workers he befriended, the Yorkshire Ripper is never out of the conversation for long. Curiously, some of his friends got the impression that Griffiths did not 'rate' the Ripper, thinking him a sloppy amateur rather than a slick professional like himself. Either way, he was obsessed with him, desperately trying to parallel his behaviour with that of Sutcliffe. Hence the reference to Sheffield and how Sutcliffe 'came a cropper'.

Although Griffiths had some normal sexual relationships, he also had the kind of kinky tastes that are common in serial killer cases. In the United States, research found that serial killers are 'intensely interested in voyeurism, fetishism and sadomasochistic pornography' from an early age. Griffiths fits the pattern with his foot and bottom fetishes, and with his taste for violent computer porn. His real relationship with womankind is one of power and control. Women ultimately were Griffiths' victims. Peter Gee, the caretaker, may have been warned about him, but in truth there was a deeply misogynistic strand to the killer's behaviour. He would not have found Peter Gee as repugnant as a woman.

Professor Wilson was asked in his professional capacity to analyse the terrifying voicemail messages Griffiths left for Kathy Hancock. He replied:

'He is disdainful, controlling, misogynistic, and there is a particular tape in which he simply laughs maniacally at her for a good 20 or 30 seconds. He is laughing, cackling like something possessed, and it is very very chilling, and that is the effect he is seeking to create. He is simply trying to scare her and I think what it did for me is reveal the depth of his dislike for her, his misogyny, his dislike of women. He betrayed the feeling that his gender made him superior to her and he could do as he wished. Had I not known who this man was, I would still have been very fearful over what he would be capable of.'

Yet in those same messages, the killer pours out his heart about how he has always been there for her. He has another side that allows him to manipulate the opposite sex. As Kathy Hancock herself said, he is not all about violence. 'It was very slow control,' she said. 'He wants control of everything but he does it in such a passive way. He would make me think how I came across to other people. He would make you doubt the way you are.'

Professor Wilson said that, since the 1960s, serial killers have targeted five groups of people, and women make up four of them. They are prostitutes, the elderly, babies and infants, and what Professor Wilson called 'runaways and throwaways', the kind of troubled young women targeted by Fred and Rose West. The single male group is gay men.

Professor Wilson said the trend reveals an underlying 'misogynistic culture', which Griffiths represents a mutation of. But his desire to control women is at the centre of everything he did: 'He seeks power and control through murder, and it's power and control that's denied to him in virtually every other aspect of his life. He's a no-mark. He's a nobody in every other aspect of his life, but when he's murdering he has got complete power and control over his victims.'

Griffiths demonstrated this control by kidnapping and murdering Susan, Suzanne and Shelley. But psychiatrists such as

THE CROSSBOW CANNIBAL

Professor Wilson believe that defiling the body, posing it, dismembering and eating parts of it are even more potent forms of control.

> 'It is about making the body act to your will. This could be posing it, writing on it or whatever. To despoil the body is an aspect of the need to have complete power and control. So, for example, Dennis Nilsen would put the bodies of the young men he killed in an armchair and have conversations with them. Griffiths similarly would be maintaining contact with the body of his victim, which again is about him totally controlling her. It's almost like she is a doll that he can make move in a way that he would like that body to move.'

Griffiths' appalling treatment of animals is another classic serial killer trait. It is part of what psychiatrists call the 'Macdonald Triad', a set of three behavioural characteristics usually associated with sociopaths. Animal cruelty is one; bed-wetting and fire-starting are the other two. Griffiths began torturing creatures as a child, shooting then dismembering birds. However, he never grew out of it. He loved to play with the lizards and mice, teasing the reptiles by swinging the rodents above their heads and watching them snap. Eventually, he would lower them far enough for the lizards to reach. Occasionally, he would kill the mice himself. He once ate a live one and boasted about how he had skinned another alive. There is no reason at all to doubt his claim. 'Clearly he found live mice and lizards a way of desensitising himself to a life being taken,' said Professor Wilson, who continued:

> 'Often you find that serial killers have a way of desensitising themselves to the pain and suffering of other

people. Nilsen was a butcher in the Army catering corps; Shipman was constantly surrounded by people who were suffering. There's a sense in which they try to desensitise themselves to the pain their victims are going to suffer, and Griffiths' use of the lizards is part of that process for him. It would be a general pattern of how serial killers can do what they can do.'

Chris Gregg, retired Detective Chief Superintendent and founder of West Yorkshire Police's Homicide and Major Enquiry Team, believes serial killers are 'born evil'. He was part of the Ripper manhunt in the 1970s and has investigated any number of psychopaths. The last serial killing case he investigated before retiring was that of Colin Norris, the staff nurse who murdered four elderly patients at the Leeds hospitals he worked at. Norris was jailed for a minimum of 30 years in 2008. Chris Gregg said:

'The actual process of taking someone's life – and I have heard this from killers over the years – gives them such exhilaration that it is overwhelming. They enjoy killing. Using Norris as an example, I don't think there is a lot of scientific stuff going on here. The exhilaration these people get from the act of killing is such a buzz to them that it drives them on and when that buzz reduces, they go out and kill again. That's Shipman, Sutcliffe, whoever. That process of having power and control is overwhelming. There will be occasions when someone's background is influenced by visual things, computers or whatever, but that's only part of the story. People who go out to commit these grotesque crimes have got something they are born with.'

However, Professor Wilson takes a different view to Chris Gregg on whether criminals such as Griffiths are born evil and explains why:

'I think people become evil because of what happens to them and it could be happening to them in a direct way or in an indirect way. They lack attention, they lack love, so it doesn't necessarily mean they have to be bullied or something dynamic happens to them. I don't believe people are born to kill; I believe people eventually learn how to kill. It's neither nature nor nurture. You have to see nature and nurture as being different sides of the same coin that's going to produce the person who is going to kill and, in different circumstances, the person who will become the managing director of a multinational corporation.'

Felicity Gerry, criminal barrister and legal commentator, said: 'Generally you get damaged goods, very occasionally you get people you can't explain.' One client she defended was apprehended after his mother rang the police. He had apparently been chased from a park by a gang of people after he grabbed a 13-year-old girl and pulled her to the floor. He dropped a bag as they chased him. Gerry said:

'On the face of it, it was really only a minor common assault which carries a maximum of six months – neither here nor there. The police recovered the bag in the park, and in it there was a complete rape kit: cable ties, lubricant, condoms, the works. They arrested him and took his computer, and on it was a file containing a fantasy movie about adults abducting a schoolgirl. So he had gone to that park and acted out that fantasy. I met him, his mum and dad. There was nothing, no indications, no criminal convictions, nothing to indicate why on earth he had done this. There is your random person. Every so often you get a defendant that you cannot explain why he's done it.'

Whether born or made wicked, Stephen Griffiths displays evidence of nine out of 14 character traits usually associated with serial killers. They include the fact that he comes from a broken home: his parents split up in the late 1970s and he lived with his mother in Wakefield. Griffiths hated his mother by the time he was an adult. The list of 14 traits also includes torturing animals, which he did from childhood to adulthood, and an involvement in petty crime, which he was linked to from at least the time he was caught stealing from a garage.

But one of his old school friends at Queen Elizabeth Grammar School in Wakefield is probably on the right track in working out where the story of the Crossbow Cannibal began. Griffiths used to bring into school a 'vicious-looking dagger and some throwing stars' and play Dungeons and Dragons. The friend remembered: 'If you look at the boy Griffiths, he was a small, thin, below average-sized pupil. Yet in his books and in his games he was an all-powerful big macho type that was killing and slaying and winning.' It was the beginning of a fantasy in which Griffiths was no longer a lonely, shy boy who did not get on with his mother. He was a champion among men. Admired by the same sex, desired by the opposite.

Paul Britton, a leading criminal psychologist who assisted the police in the case of Colin Ireland, later wrote of his experiences in an autobiographical book, *Picking Up the Pieces*. He said of Ireland:

'Colin Ireland suffered problems with his sexuality. These can be very distressing, but most ordinary men find acceptable ways of dealing with them – by seeing a doctor, perhaps, or a sex therapist. In Ireland's case his problems were coupled with his emerging sadistic feelings and needs. There are numerous theories about where such urges come from but they don't necessarily evolve through choice. At some point Ireland chose to submit to these feelings and develop them. This man had failed in most areas of his life. All his important relationships were disasters. He never knew his father and felt let down by his mother and stepfather. He turned his back on their way of life and took to crime. His two marriages failed. So it seems did other relationships with women. He failed in his education (his intelligence warranted more). He failed in crime (continually getting caught and apparently not learning by his criminal experiences). He failed in his occupation (never managing to hold down a steady job). Some would say he had 'loser' written all over him. He began to develop a militaristic survivalist persona based on macho self-discipline and self-sufficiency. This increased his isolation but at the same time began to compensate for all his failures. Finally, he had found one area of his life where he had total control – or so he believed… This man resented how his life had turned out. He was angry and frustrated. He wanted to show the world it was wrong about him… he wanted respect. So he chose to kill.'

Britton's analysis could have been written for Stephen Griffiths. The only difference is that Griffiths developed his ambition over a period of about 20 years. He accepted failure at an early age and retreated into his bloodstained imaginary world. Young Stephen began to show an unhealthy interest in weapons and violence at school. It might have been a response to being skinny and shy. Whether it was or not, lots of his classmates would have messed about with knives and air guns as well, and they did not become serial killers. The other boys developed more normal interests like girls or sport that rounded off their personalities. Griffiths, meanwhile, retreated further into his own little world. It seems certain that he learned about Haigh, the acid bath murderer who, decades before him, had sat in the very same classrooms. Did that set his mind off in another dangerous direction?

And how much interest did the young grammar school boy show in Peter Sutcliffe? He grew up in the 1970s when stories about the Yorkshire Ripper filled every news bulletin. He would have just turned 11 when the bearded lorry driver from Bradford 'came a cropper in Sheffield', as he would later put it. Sutcliffe's first court appearance was before magistrates in Dewsbury, where both Griffiths' parents hail from and where he spent the first five years of his life.

Griffiths' attack on the store manager in 1987 revealed that even at that youthful age there was a violent fantasy running in his head. More to the point, he was acting it out in real life. Even the most hardened thug would not have felt the need to react with that degree of violence. Once inside the criminal justice system, he does not show remorse. Neither does he become a mundane career criminal. The pseudo-intellectual vanity takes over and he decides he will take his interest in violence to a more sophisticated level. It was a time of great leaps forward in scientific crime investigation and the academic study of criminology. The discipline ticked all his boxes. When he told his probation officers that he wanted to be a serial killer, was he joking? They didn't think so, and the ruthless nature of the store guard slashing proves he meant business. Then came 20 years of collecting books, magazines, films and eventually downloads about rape, torture and slaughter. He mugged up on how to kill people efficiently, how to destroy bodies and how to avoid detection. Like a grotesque magpie, he used his library to borrow ideas from history's most monstrous. His bright shiny baubles were methods of causing pain and humiliation to other people. All the time, the deadly ideas were being played out in his head, in preparation for the day he could make them a reality. And when that day came, he was determined to outdo his predecessors.

It might be a coincidence that he ended up living in Bradford's red light area, but once there, he would know its significance in the story of his hero, Sutcliffe. It was also only a matter of time before he realised what easy targets the working girls were. His friend Kenneth Valentine demonstrated it when he murdered Caroline Cleevy. Like Colin Ireland, Stephen Griffiths turned to murder as a result of failure, ego, sexual kinks and opportunity. Like Ireland, he could not help telling people about his newfound notoriety.

On the day after Griffiths was jailed for life, Professor David Cantor of Huddersfield University wrote in *The Times*: 'Eventually, these images of himself as some deadly movie character burst into the real world.' That catastrophe came in June 2009, but even Griffiths himself probably has no idea what the trigger was. He had been in trouble with the law again for harassing Kathy Hancock and Pauline Bond, but that was another symptom of the brewing storm rather than a cause. According to the working girls who knew him, he was smoking massive amounts of crack cocaine and suffered instant mood swings when it kicked in. He killed Susan Rushworth at the end of June 2009, then Shelley 11 months later, then Suzanne just one month after that. He was bent on killing another girl after Suzanne, and who can say that, after Rosalyn Edmondson escaped his clutches, he did not go out again into Sunbridge Road and City Road looking for another victim?

The sequence of murders follows the killing cycle described

by criminologists. Griffiths killed Susan, and was, for a time, satisfied and nervous about killing again. He was excited about it and weaved the memory into his fantasy for a while. When the buzz came again, he killed Shelley. Once more, he was sated. But this time the feeling of fulfilment lasted no more than a few weeks. Then he killed Suzanne, and would have killed Rosalyn had her instincts not served her right. In keeping with what the experts say, Griffiths was inexperienced the first time he killed and lucky not to get caught when the fire brigade attended the fire at his flat.

Three decades before anyone had heard of Stephen Griffiths, a Bradford detective made a strangely prophetic remark. Detective Chief Superintendent Trevor Lapish was asked about the death of Yvonne Pearson. She had been killed by Peter Sutcliffe, but, at the time, the police thought someone else was responsible. DCS Lapish said: 'Some unhinged person, jealous of the attention given to the Ripper, might be trying to follow in his footsteps. There is no doubt that the publicity could spark off this sort of reaction.' His prediction was spot on. Little did he know that his words would come true in such a roundabout way. Because, in the end, Stephen Griffiths was just that sort of copycat. A deranged nobody who realised that his only way of being noticed was to model himself on a monster and then try to better him. In the end, he was a hopeless failure.